FRAGILE TREATIES

FRAGILE TREATIES

✛ ✛ ✛

A NOVEL

FAYE ROBERTS

WESTERN REFLECTIONS
PUBLISHING COMPANY

MONTROSE, COLORADO

First Edition

Printed in the United States of America

ISBN 1-890437-62-x

Library of Congress Catalog Number 2001088438

Cover and book design
by Paulette Livers Lambert

Western Reflections Publishing Company
P.O. Box 1647
Montrose, CO 81402-1647

www.westernreflectionspub.com

Good words do not last long
until they amount to
something.
—Chief Joseph

April 25, 1876
Nauvoo, Illinois

Self-pity is the lowest state to which a woman can fall," Grandma Donovan had once remarked when Aunt Agnes was having a spell of the melancholy. It was just one of the many childhood memories that raced through Lily's mind as she hastily tried to decide what to take and what to leave behind. How did one pack twenty-two years worth of memories into one small carpetbag?

Grandma had been right, Lily thought. Never had she felt this deep depth of despair, even after Mama had been taken home to live with the Lord. At least during that trying time she'd had her family and the church for support. Now she was utterly alone, scorned and rejected by those she loved and those she had once thought loved her. From the clouds of heavenly love to the hell of bitter betrayal was a long, hard fall.

The mantle clock chimed. Ten, eleven, twelve; it was time to go. Lily took one last look at her childhood, feeling the strong walls of the old house enfold her in its strong arms. Familiar smells embraced her as she quietly walked through the kitchen: clean pine soap, the lingering odor of gingerbread, Grandma's lavender toilet water, Papa's leather coat by the back door. Pepper glanced up from his bed behind the stove. His tail thumped against the wood box as she hugged him one last time.

"Take care, old boy," Lily whispered, wiping her eyes on the hem of her sleeve. She picked up the bag that contained a few clothes and toiletries, her mother's photograph, and Isabel's rag doll. She would not be able to take any more, knowing the burden would be too heavy to bear, both physically and emotionally.

She was careful not to let the screen door slam as she slipped out the door. No one in the family could see her leave so when confronted they could honestly say they did not know when she had left or where she had gone. Lily prayed that just maybe with her hasty departure the church would finally grant her family some peace.

A horse was tied to the bridge on the Bear River. Lily stiffened when she saw the shadowy figure of a man, and then relaxed when she realized it was only old Joshua.

"You shouldn't be here," Lily whispered. "I thought you were just going to leave the horse. I told you not to come. If anyone sees you . . ."

"Now, Lily Belle. You do what you gotta do and I do what I gotta do," he said, patting her cheek with his wrinkled hand. He tied the handle of the carpetbag to the horn of the saddle and then bent down and clasped his black, gnarled hands together, as he had done at least a thousand times before. She put her boot in his hands and he gave her a boost up onto the mare's back.

"She be a good bit o' horseflesh. A bit small, but sturdy."

He handed Lily the reins.

"I be a prayin' for da Good Lawd to watch over you, chile."

Lily reached in the bag and pulled out Isabel's rag doll. "I want you to have this, but be sure to hide it. You'll be in grave danger if they find it. They will know you helped me."

"No. Ain't no need to hide dat what's good." Joshua took the doll as carefully as if it were made of fine porcelain.

"Now don' you go worrin' none 'bout you papa an grandmam. Old Joshua will take care of dem. You a good girl, Lily Belle. "If'n you cain't 'member nuthin' else I teached you, you be shore an 'member dat."

He cradled the doll in his arms and hobbled away into the trees. The last sound Lily heard as she crossed over the bridge was the sound of a low, baritone singing, "coming for to carry me home."

Home. The lilacs in spring, the daisies in summer, the crimson maples of autumn, the warm fire in winter. It had comforted her many times in the past but it was of no comfort now. If only she would have appreciated it growing up as she appreciated it now. She would treasure this place, locking the memory into her heart and vowing that if she ever again would have a home, she would plant lilacs by the back door.

The warm blanket of childhood innocence had been savagely wrenched away. Cold reality now poured in like a harsh Illinois blizzard, freezing her soul and blinding her to what may lay ahead. After taking one final gaze, Lily pulled her papa's stiff felt bowler hat down over her forehead, gave the horse a gentle kick, and never looked back.

✛ ✛ ✛

Lily guided the horse carefully alongside the soft riverbank. The raging spring runoff had the river running high and muddy. Its torrent boiled and tumbled, yanking trees and brush from the bank as if it were an angry gardener pulling out bad weeds from his garden.

The river wanted to pull her under, too. She could feel it. Moonbeams through the trees cast eerie shadows and branches were knobby claws reaching out and grabbing her cloak and hat. Her body shivered uncontrollably in the damp night air as the moon went behind a cloud and the narrow path went dark. Ahead was shadowy and sinister blackness.

She loosened her grip on the reins, knowing she would now have to trust in the horse's instincts. But it was hard to succumb to trust. Lily fought burning tears forming in the back of her eyes and felt only a bit reassured as she felt the horse move forward slowly, step by step.

The hard knots in her neck didn't loosen until the sun finally peeked over the horizon. They made decent time on the rest of the fifty-mile trip to Quincy, arriving at the edge of the town late the next afternoon. Lily was thoroughly exhausted, dirty and hungry but there was no time to think about that. She rode up to the livery. Every bone and muscle in her body screamed as she forced herself to dismount.

"Looks like you've had quite a trip," the proprietor said, giving the horse the once over while filling his cheek with a large wad of tobacco. "Even under all that muck, that's a mighty fine looking mount you've got there. Where you headed?"

Lily declined to give him any information, other than to tell him the mare was for sale, and that she was sure-footed and sturdy.

"She's been rode awful hard," the proprietor said, affirming his statement by wiping away foamy white lather from the mare's breast collar. "I'll do you a favor and take her off your hands for one hundred dollars."

Joshua had said not to take the first price offered. She grabbed the reins and turned to walk away.

"Okay, one twenty-five."

She kept walking.

"One fifty, and that's my final offer." The man spat on the ground, barely missing her boot.

"And twenty-five for the saddle. Be sure to give her a good rub-down and a ration of oats," Lily stated firmly. She stashed the bills deep inside the right front pocket of her pants, bringing the sum total of her traveling money to $287 before train fare.

Lily silently vowed to someday pay Joshua back for all he had done for her but knew that a few dollars would never be enough. She was glad that at least she gave him Isabel's rag doll.

The shrill of a train whistle came from down the street and quickly she walked towards the sound. She purchased a ticket to Kansas City but before boarding the CB&Q railcar, she was careful to look around and see if anyone was watching her. The depot was packed with travelers like herself, hungry with the anticipation of going west and with loved ones begging them to write. She longed for a hug, too, feeling more alone than ever, but knew she would never be able to take a chance on writing home, and could never hope for a letter in return.

Lily found the lavatory in the station and washed away as much of the travel grime as she could. She then took a hard look in the mirror and didn't recognize the reflection that looked back at her. The woman was so unlike the Lily Hastings of yesterday. Long auburn curls now lay inside a hollowed-out tree, replaced by an uneven short bob. The face with the complexion once so envied by other young ladies in Nauvoo, was now sallow, with deep charcoal gray circles under the eyes. And the eyes that once sparkled like polished amber were now as dull and brittle as a wilted cornhusk.

She climbed aboard the train and waited impatiently for the car to start rolling and take her away from the past. What the future held she didn't know, but anything was better than staying in Nauvoo. She breathed a deep sigh of relief when the whistle blew one last mournful time and the train pulled away from the depot.

"Where you headed?"

That question again. Lily looked across the aisle at the man speaking to her. He was dressed in an indigo blue cavalry uniform with bright yellow stripes down the side of his pants.

"Colorado." She tried to keep her voice as low as possible without sounding fraudulent.

"You a miner? Fella told me that silver is pouring out of the mountains just like a stream during the spring." The man took a swig from a silver flask, and then offered it to her. She shook her head.

"Yes, a miner." Lily stated abruptly, turning her head toward the window.

The soldier would not be put off. "Name's Samuel Bodeen." He tapped her on the arm and put his hand out to meet hers.

Having never shaken a hand before, Lily tried to remember how Papa had done it. Did he squeeze it hard, or lightly, like she would do with Pepper?

"Name's um, Lyle. Lyle Donovan."

Samuel's hand was firm, but clean. She touched it lightly and pulled her hand back.

"You ever mined before, Donovan?"

"Oh sure, been mining coal for a couple of years around Springfield. Knew I would never get rich that way and heard about the silver in Colorado, so decided to pack up and head west."

"So you're going west to strike it rich, huh?" Bodeen looked amused.

"Something like that." She turned back towards the window.

But still the soldier continued. "Orders are to meet up with General G.A. Custer's regiment. I'll be boarding a supply train for the Powder River in the Dakota Territory as soon as we reach Kansas City. Seems there's a big summer campaign brewing to keep the Sioux in check. Someone discovered gold up in the Black Hills and the Indians are sure not to like settlers prancing into their territory, eager to pick up the nuggets the newspapers say are laying on the ground just waiting for those eager and willing to bend down and snatch them up."

"You sound skeptical," she said.

The man in the seat next to Bodeen spoke up. "You ever seen a gold rush?"

"No." Lily looked hesitantly at Samuel's companion. He was the largest black man she had ever seen. Unlike Joshua's lighter, chestnut colored skin, this man's was the color of stout boiled coffee. He, too, was dressed in a cavalry uniform, but unlike Mr. Bodeen's coat which was spotless with polished brass buttons gleaming like stars on a dark night, the black man's coat was worn and looked as if had not been washed in over a month. The buttons that weren't missing were dull with dust. A long scar ran the length of the man's left cheek.

"It ain't a pretty sight. Greed can breed big problems, no doubt about it."

"This is Mr. Isaiah Dorman," Samuel said. "Just about the best buffalo soldier in the whole United States Cavalry."

"Buffalo soldier?"

"That's a fact," Dorman said. "Now if you'll excuse me, I think I'll find the dining car." He rose and lumbered down the aisle, barely fitting between the narrow seats.

"Good man, the best. Eats like an army mule and is twice as strong," Samuel stated.

"Just what is a buffalo soldier?" Lily asked. Curiosity got the best of her. It always had.

"After the Civil War, Isaiah, along with all the other slaves, found himself a free man. But he also found himself without food, without a job, without a home, and without a family. Isaiah drifted for a time, looking for work. But in the South there was no money, and in the north no one would hire him. No matter where he went he was an outcast, an outsider."

Samuel paused to pull out a pipe and a packet of tobacco from his shirt pocket. He carefully packed the bowl of the pipe, then tamped down the tobacco with long, well-shaped fingers. He didn't rush the ritual. He then drew out a matchstick, struck it on the bottom of his boot and held the flame to the bowl, puffing until the tobacco glowed.

Lily thought about Joshua, once again thankful that her mother had chosen to offer him a home when they moved north to live with Grandma Donovan after the war. He would often smoke a pipe as well, hiding in the loft of the barn to escape Papa's wrath. Papa had detested tobacco and called it the devil's weed. But Lily had loved the sweet smell.

"Then Isaiah found the cavalry. He and a group of ex-slaves like himself fought off the renegade Mexicans in Texas. In 1867 they were assigned to relocate the Colorado Plains Indians to a reservation in Oklahoma. The black regiment soon developed a reputation as some of the toughest and most cunning Indian fighters in the United States Army. Apache, Paiute, Arapahoe, they all knew and all feared the buffalo soldiers. The name came from the black men's wiry hair, much like the hair of a buffalo. Some tribes said the black skin held some sort of special black magic. Either way, the buffalo soldiers earned the Indians' respect, something hard to come by, and it's something that many white soldiers have yet to achieve."

Samuel took a long draw on the pipe. Smoke encircled his head like a misty halo.

"Isaiah has been a courier for the past year, making a good wage of one hundred dollars a month. While other couriers carry the mail by horseback, Isaiah carries the mail on foot. Riding a horse through the Dakota Territory is much too dangerous."

That explained Isaiah's strong, muscular body, Lily thought. There was not an ounce of fat on his large physique. "And he will go with you to the Powder River?"

"He's on his way now to meet up with General Crook in Fort Lincoln. Together they will try to secure mounts and supplies to take to General Custer. The two regiments will join together in June. Isaiah's saved my skin more than once. Maybe this time I'll be able to return the favor."

Suddenly nervous, Samuel pulled the silver flask once more from his pocket and took a swig. "I wonder if Isaiah left anything to eat. Would you care to join me and grab a bite of whatever he left? May not be much, mind you."

"No, I'm not hungry." Lily was ravenous but knew the price of food in the dining car would not agree with her slim budget. She said she would wait and eat at one of the refreshment stations advertised to be along the railway line.

"You've got a lot to learn, Donovan. With the stops only fifteen minutes in length and the cleanliness of many of the establishments highly questionable, you'll soon learn the term 'refreshment' is shamefully misused. I'd rather eat hardtack and beans than some of the overpriced slop they serve up to you greenhorns," he said with a teasing glint in his eyes. He rose and followed Dorman's route to the dining car.

Exhausted and saddle-sore from the long ride to Quincy, Lily tried to sleep but every time she shut her eyes Bertram's face loomed against hers. She could smell his foul breath and feel his callused hands pawing her. She tried to erase the image of Bertram's hairy, meaty fingers by thinking of the image of Bodeen's strong, clean hands as they had so gracefully lit the pipe. But even though Bertram was now miles away, he was still able to control her thoughts.

The men returned and Lily shut her eyes, pretending to be asleep. She didn't want to have to feel inclined to politely partake in idle travel conversation, and she especially didn't want to answer any questions.

When Lily heard the even breath of sleep and a bit of quiet snoring, she opened her eyes and stared at the pair. Neither of the men were what she would have expected from cavalry soldiers. She had seen plenty of them; they would come down from Fort Madison into Nauvoo and cause a good deal of trouble with their drinking and carousing. But these men were different. They were neither boorish nor crude. They seemed to share a special and smooth camaraderie. And oddly, she felt a strange safeness knowing that they were beside her.

Even though Dorman's body reminded her of a bear, with his large hands like paws, the eyes that had shown through the scarred face were kind. Samuel Bodeen was already developing deep creases around his eyes, with tiny white lines that disappeared into the tan face when he smiled, which was often. His eyes had twinkled with a hint of boyhood mischief and were without the lecherous stares most soldiers had. Then she reminded herself of the workingman's attire she was wearing: a rough muslin shirt, sturdy boots and canvas jeans, and Papa's hat. Of course he would not look at her that way. He thought she was a man.

Bodeen was handsome in a rugged sort of way, with a strong jaw line and unruly dark hair, the sides streaked with gray. He looked harmless enough but when he had touched her hand it had taken all of her willpower not to yank it rudely away. She rubbed her hand, trying to erase the sensation of his touch.

The mere thought of any man's hand sickened her. Time would heal her body, but never her soul. There were no more tears left to cry and home was now a distant memory.

But Bertram's memory was not.

As Lily looked out into the dark night, the wheels underneath the car clanked steadily westward. She could feel her heart beat in rhythm, pounding, growing stronger. Self-pity turned to anger. Anger turned to white-hot rage.

By the time the train slowed down the next morning and the conductor called out that the next stop was Kansas City, Lily's jaw was set. She could not change what had been done to her, but she could make sure it would never happen to anyone else. She felt for a letter hidden deep in the pocket of her cloak. It was addressed to the attorney general of Illinois and contained her sworn statement. The information would take the powerful Mormon elder out of the pulpit and put him behind bars. Bertram Ellis would never hurt anyone again.

The wheels of the train screeched to a halt in front of the Kansas City station.

"Best of luck to you, Donovan," Dorman said as he rose from his seat.

"Be careful out west, greenhorn," Samuel added with a sly wink.

"And you too, Mr. Bodeen," she said. "And best of luck to you as well, Mr. Dorman." He gave her a broad white-toothed grin. "Would you happen to know where I might be able to post a letter?"

"Just a couple blocks north down the street at Ike's General Store." Samuel advised. "I could walk with you."

"No, that won't be at all necessary." She quickly grabbed her satchel and cut in front of him.

He looked oddly disappointed.

Lily stepped off the train and began walking north along the muddy street. She posted the letter and then purchased a slab of cheese from a large wheel and several soda crackers from a barrel. She splurged and bought a bottle of cherry soda and a couple chocolate drops. She then returned to the train depot and purchased a ticket on the Union Pacific. It read: Destination—Denver, Colorado Territory.

Maybe now she could move on.

She found a seat and anxiously waited for the sound of the departure whistle. She took a long, sweet drink of the soda, letting the cool liquid soothe her parched throat, devoured the chocolate before it could melt and then ate a couple of the crackers with cheese. The sustenance calmed the jitters in her stomach but not the gripping anxiety she still felt in her heart.

Lily feared for what the church would do in retaliation when they found out about the letter. She shut her eyes and prayed for justice. She prayed that God would restore the elder's vow of doing what was upright and virtuous. She prayed for heavenly wings to cover Grandma, Papa, and Joshua and shield them from the vengeance that was sure to follow.

But no matter how she tried, she could find no words to pray for herself. The trust was gone, snatched away along with her innocence. God was no longer the Supreme Being, dependable and mighty. The shield of his protection was shattered and she had lain exposed like an open wound the night she had screamed for God to make Bertram stop. Bertram had laughed. God had been silent.

And Jesus was no longer her best friend and confidante. She had prayed for her savior to come down and somehow rescue her from the madness, but he had been nowhere in sight. The only thing she had seen was the yellow, evil eyes of Bertram Ellis. And when he was finished with her, she had been left alone in the barn, battered and broken.

Just as she was alone now in the cold, misty morning, moving steadily into the unknown. The bruises on her face were healing, turning a sickly, jaundice yellow. Lily unconsciously pulled the hat lower to hide them and her humiliation. But inside, she was still raw and bleeding, not just from Bertram's vicious assault but from the reaction of Harold and her church family when she had come forward with the truth.

In the end, it was she the elders had put on trial, not Bertram Ellis. And unanimously they had all found her guilty . . . even her own father.

✠ ✠ ✠

Lily was surprised when once again Samuel Bodeen took the seat across from her.

"So we meet again," he said with a grin.

"I thought you were heading to the Dakota Territory." Lily could not help but smile back.

"My orders were changed in Kansas City. It seems that with the silver strike in western Colorado, miners are swarming like bees to honey in the San Juan Mountains, shattering the Brunot Treaty made in '73 with the Ute Indians. And the Utes are as angry as she bears. Can't say that I blame them. Chief Ouray and me have been friends a long time but it may still prove to be a long summer. I'll be going to Fort Garland to try and keep the peace."

"And Isaiah?"

"He'll just have to fight the Sioux without me. I never much liked G.A. Custer anyway. He's as cocky as a lone rooster in a house full of hens. I guess you'll be the only one blessed with my company. You up for a game of poker?"

"I've never played. But I do know how to play hearts."

Bodeen laughed boisterously. "Hearts?"

"And Old Maid."

"It's a good thing I'm still with you, Donovan. You really do have a lot to learn."

They spent a good part of the afternoon playing cards. Lily skunked him at five card draw, and he beat her at hearts.

"Hey, Bodeen, there's a hot game starting up in the dining car," a fellow soldier said as he passed them.

"How about it? You ready to play for more than matchsticks?" Samuel asked as he put the cards back in the box.

"No, I think I've played enough for one day," Lily answered.

After Bodeen left, Lily snacked on a few more crackers and the rest of the cheese. The sky grew black as evening closed in, along with the dark clouds that had threatened all afternoon on the horizon. Lightning flashed across the vast, rolling prairie and thunder boomed. The heavens opened up and the light mist that had fallen earlier now transformed to a steady rain, baptizing the earth with cleansing, precious water. Lily prayed for goodness to be restored to her as well. To feel clean inside again, warm and whole, pure and safe.

Lily watched as the father of a young girl covered the child's body with his coat, protecting her against the damp night air. Even in the stormy night, the little one was warm and safe.

Lily shivered with an icy emptiness. She pulled the canvas cloak around her and concentrated on the water dripping down the glass, wishing that the glass, or the child, were her.

She didn't remember falling asleep. Nor did she remember Samuel Bodeen covering her with his blue woolen coat.

✚ ✚ ✚

"How about some breakfast?" Samuel asked when she returned the coat to him the next morning in the dining car.

"No, thank you anyway. And thank you for the use of your coat," she said and then turned to walk away.

The soldier caught her arm. She flinched and pulled back.

"Now, Donovan, I know you must be hungry. I don't recall you eating last evening, am I right? Come on, my treat." He pointed to the chair beside him.

The bacon was crisp, the biscuits flaky, and the coffee strong and steaming.

"Hey there, David!" Samuel motioned to a small, wiry-looking man entering the dining car. The man walked over to the table and took a seat opposite Lily.

"This is Mr. David Wood," Samuel said. "Surely you have noticed his fine horseflesh in the back two cars of the train?"

Lily nodded that she had. At every stop, Mr. Wood had gone to check on the horses, unloading several at a time and walking them to ease their travel-worn muscles. She had gotten off the train at the last stop to walk away some of her own traveling knots. Noticing that Wood was having trouble loading a young filly, she had offered him some assistance.

"And this is Donovan. What did you say your first name was?"

"Lucas." Lily said.

Samuel looked at her queerly. "Yes, well. Donovan's a miner," he stated.

"Actually, we've met." Wood explained. "I've got an ornery filly who doesn't like anybody. But when Donovan took the reins, she calmed right down. You have a good touch with horses, Lucas."

"I could have got you a good price for those horses back in Kansas City and saved you a whole lot of trouble," Bodeen said.

"Now, Samuel, you know the army offered less than a third for what I can sell them for in western Colorado, even with the price of hauling them to Pueblo. And they will carry a pretty profit over the mountains for me on the way."

Mr. Wood extended his hand. Lily shook it, trying to emulate the same firmness she had felt in Samuel's handshake.

David looked at her skeptically, then at her hand.

"You ever mined before, Lucas?" he asked.

Lily became uneasy. "Yes."

"Donovan has mined coal. Going to strike it rich in the silver mines."

"I see," David replied cordially. "It's been done. But I am choosing to make my fortune by hauling supplies to the mines. The David Wood Transportation Line will be the biggest and finest freight business in all of Colorado." He did not sound like a puffed-up braggart but spoke simply, with an air of confidence of someone who believes in his dream. Self-assured. Committed. Lily knew that with that kind of determination, it was sure to be true.

David went on to explain that indeed there was an abundance of ore in western Colorado, especially in the San Juan Mountains. But he added that getting silver out from under a fourteen thousand foot mountain was not as easy as most seemed to think. He spoke of the dangers: the cold, dank darkness, invisible poison gasses, and the constant threat of cave-ins.

"Not to mention that they are mining on Ute land, which, I might add, Ouray and his braves are not too happy about right now. If it were me, Donovan, I would seriously ask myself whether gold or silver is worth the price of my life."

Samuel and David then began discussing a plan for providing

cattle to the mines. Wood stated that the mining towns of Ouray, Silverton, Pandora, and Lake City, would pay top dollar for good beef.

Bodeen pulled a tattered piece of paper from his coat pocket. "This is my own dream I've had for when I finally call it quits in the cavalry. Last time I was at Fort Garland I got into quite a heated game of five card stud with a down-and-out miner. He had three queens, I had four deuces. I won a deed to several hundred acres in the valley north of the town of Ouray. I've never actually seen the place, but a couple of trappers said the valley is lush and green, just the ticket for growing prize beef cattle."

Wood said he knew the area well and that the valley was at the base of the San Juans, just a day's ride from the mines. He looked at the deed and hesitated for a long moment.

"Your section is right in the middle of the land that was allotted to the Utes in the Brunot Treaty. It could easily be null and void."

Both Lily and David could read the deep disappointment on Bodeen's face.

"But of course with the government once again attempting to change the borders to accommodate the silver miners, this deed could actually be worth something. I know of a good lawyer in Denver who is very adept at land transactions and might be able to help. And once I get my delivery business established, there would be no need for trailing the beef up to the mines. You could butcher and I could deliver in the same day. It could be a very profitable proposition for both of us."

Lily believed in Wood even more. And from the look on Samuel's face, it was obvious that he did, too.

"I guess I'll just have to work that much harder at keeping my scalp intact this summer," Bodeen said.

"You just do that," David said with a wink. The train began to slow down and he rose to feed and water his future. "I don't know who will be more thankful to be on solid ground, the horses or me."

Wood placed his chair under the table and turned to go, then stopped.

"Oh, and Donovan, when you get your fill of the underground mines, look me up. I'm always looking for a good hand like you."

✛ ✛ ✛

Samuel offered Lily the last biscuit on the platter. She took it without hesitation.

"Well, at least you eat like a man," Samuel said, as he wiped his mustache with a napkin.

"Excuse me?" Lily set down her coffee cup, sloshing dark liquid into the saucer.

"Now look, I don't know what your story is and frankly, I really don't care. Everyone headed west has a story of one kind or another. See that woman over there? That's Ann Eliza Young. Proclaims herself to be the nineteenth wife of old Brigham Young himself."

Lily gasped, almost choking on a bite of biscuit. What if. . .?

"She finally left the old guy, and is set on doing away with polygamy once and for all. Says she will take her cause all the way to Congress with the hopes it will be banned by a federal law. She's going to Denver to deliver a lecture on the many trials she endured."

Lily let out the breath she had been holding.

"And see those women over there?" Samuel pointed to a table of four young ladies, none looking over sixteen. A beautiful woman accompanied them with blond curls piled on top of her head and dressed in tailored clothes of the latest fashion. Lily had noticed them before. They had been on the train when she boarded in Quincy. Along with the women was a skinny, dandy looking gentleman they called Cort. The ladies spent most of their time in the Wagner sleeping car.

"That's Miss Mattie Silks, and those young ladies with her are soiled doves."

"I beg your pardon? "

"Donovan, just how old are you?"

"Twenty-two." At least that is true, Lily thought. It was becoming hard to keep her stories straight.

"Mattie has a tiny pocket made into all her frocks, just the size for a small derringer. You see, Donovan, we are all running from something. But you should know, you're not fooling anyone."

"I don't know what you are talking about." Lily put down her napkin.

"If you want to continue your pretending, I suggest you get a bag that is not covered with cabbage roses. And stick with one name. You told me it was Lyle. You told David it was Lucas. Frankly, neither one fits."

"Well, he didn't seem to question me. But maybe that is because he is a gentleman and you're a scoundrel!"

"He was just being polite, though you're right about one thing. He is a gentleman. But only ladies use a word like scoundrel, and proper ones at that."

He stared at her and winked. She wanted to slap him.

"Oh, yes, I've seen that look many times from other ladies who were contemplating what you just were."

"Are you quite finished?" Lily asked, her amber eyes snapping in anger.

The woman is even more beautiful when she's angry, Samuel thought. The red color in her cheeks made him think of a juicy, ripe peach. Though her hair had obviously been cut with a pair of kitchen shears, the auburn curls sticking out from the ridiculous bowler hat shone like beams of sunlight.

"Not quite. Don't dab your napkin daintily against your lips. Don't sip your coffee as if you're at a Ladies Aid Society tea. The men's room is opposite of the one you have been using. Get some baggier pants, ones that don't show off what's underneath. Buy a pair of good leather gloves and don't take them off. It's your hands that first gave you away clear back in Quincy. You have very beautiful hands. The hands of an elegant, refined lady."

Her eyes shot him a white-hot glare, but all she could see in his was brutal but sincere honesty.

"I've been around men all my life, even those who wished they weren't men. They can't be a lady, no matter how hard they try. Just like you can't be what you're not. God made men and women different, and frankly, I'm awfully glad he did. I know the difference, just like every other hot-blooded male on this train."

Lily nearly knocked over her chair as she rose to leave.

"Your secret is safe with me, Donovan. Lord knows I have a few of my own. Just be careful. Trying to be something that you're not can only lead to trouble. Especially out west."

✢ ✢ ✢

Lily returned to her seat, stunned and angry. Bodeen had been blunt, but deep down, Lily knew he had also been right, a fact which angered her even more. She had spent her life being forthright and honest with people. She was not good at deception, a fact that even a stranger like Samuel Bodeen was able to realize.

Was she really so transparent? Lily began to seriously wonder how many others would see through her charade. But she also knew the severe consequences of what would happen if the church were to find her, especially when they found out about the letter.

There had been many stories about the "Danites," a group of masked avengers who sought out and punished those who spoke out against the Mormon Church. They burned houses and barns, killed livestock and poisoned wells. There had even been a rumor that the buggy accident that had happened to a non-Mormon shopkeeper in Nauvoo had not been "accidental" at all. The Mormon sheriff said the accident had been caused by a large snake in the road, but Joshua had trained the man's horses and said there was no way they would have spooked, especially on the flat road where Joshua swore there were no snakes within five miles. Those who chose to leave the church usually did it under cover of darkness and were never heard from again.

Lily knew two things for sure. First, she would stay as far away from Bodeen as possible. And second, she would heed his advice. She turned and looked down the aisle of the train. There were only a few seats not taken. One was beside a straggly looking buffalo hunter dressed in filthy buckskin. The whole traveling car had been disgustingly aware of his presence because of the odor he emitted; it was clear why no one had chosen the seat next to him. Another vacant seat was next to one of the "soiled doves" who had returned to a seat near the back and was now devouring a *Godey's Lady's Book.* Lily grabbed her satchel and moved down the aisle.

"Is this seat taken?"

"No, I guess not," the young woman replied, looking back nervously to the Wagner sleeping car. Seeing no one, she relaxed and became thoroughly engrossed in a picture of a chic lady dressed in a luxurious crinoline gown.

"I am sorry to see that fashion houses have still not come to the realization that a woman's comfort is of substantial importance in design," Lily said. "Though I do admire that split skirt for riding."

The girl looked at her in astonishment and Lily realized her indiscretion. Men were not to know of such things.

"Or so my sister says," she quickly added. "Where are you from?"

"Springfield."

Lily felt a firm tap on her shoulder. It was the man she had heard called Cort.

"This seat is taken." His voice was firm.

"Oh, excuse me. I didn't think anyone was sitting here."

"There is now." He picked up Lily's bag and placed it firmly in her lap. She could feel the girl cower next to her.

Lily quickly looked around for another empty seat. There was one at the very back next to a middle-aged woman.

"Mind if I sit here?"

The lady smiled a near toothless grin. "No, please, have a seat." She patted the seat next to her.

"I'm Louisa Eleanor Simpson, but I'm not a bit fancy so Lu suits me just fine. And yours?"

"Donovan." Lily remembered Samuel's words and decided just to leave it at that.

"Well, Donovan, I can see by your store-bought duds that you're new to the West. My husband Franklin says you can always tell a greenhorn by the starch in their new britches. Those who have been around these parts don't have a pair of pants that isn't patched. Where you headed?"

That seemed to be the question that everyone used to start up a conversation. "Colorado. I'm going to try my hand at the silver mines," Lily said.

"So the fever got to you, huh?"

"Yes, I guess so."

"It got to my husband Franklin once, too. He said none of the rocks he picked out of the field was worth a dime, just a bad back. So if he was going to have a bad back anyways, he just as well try his hand at picking up rocks that was worth something. Franklin was back in six months and said he would rather lose his life above the ground, rather than below it. Well, I says to him, that's where we're all going to end up anyways!" She laughed heartily and her weathered face broke into a myriad of creases.

"So you and your husband have a farm?" Lily asked.

The woman nodded.

Lily looked out the window at the vast emptiness of the prairie. "It looks like such a lonely land."

"Ah, don't just look at the surface. There's much more to the prairie than meets the eye. See there, the bluebells are just coming into bloom."

Lu pointed out a white-tailed deer hidden in some underbrush and a lone coyote watching the train from the distant horizon. Then she directed Lily's eyes to a thin band of smoke that looked to come out of the ground itself. She said the smoke came from a "soddie," not much more than a hole dug into the side of a small hill, the opening covered over with blocks of dense buffalo grass sod.

"I was to abide in such a dwelling when Franklin and I came to the prairie in 1862 after the Homestead Act was enacted. Just married and without much more than a poke full of dreams, we moved from Pennsylvania to escape the war and claim our 'free' 160 acres. All we had to do was live on the land for five years and it was ours. Well, the next time the United States government offers anything for 'free', I'll turn and high tail it in the other direction. Only those who have been stubborn enough to endure what Franklin and I have all these years can truly know the final cost of the price we paid per acre."

Lu went on to explain that on the first morning in her soddie she found a snake curled up beside her newborn baby, both sleeping quite soundly. She spoke of summers hot enough to fry an egg on a rock, and winters so cold that the milk froze in the bucket on the way back from the barn. But she added that the soddie was surprisingly warm in winter and cool in summer, "if the supply of buffalo chips and twisted grass didn't run too short."

"In 18 and 68, a prairie fire consumed everything we had worked for six years to build, including a frame house Franklin had finished just two weeks earlier. And two years ago we could only stand by and watch an entire year's crop vanish under a horde of locusts so thick that they drowned out the sun. After munching down every living thing in sight, they ate the cloth and leather harnesses for dessert."

Lu paused for a long moment.

"Of the five children I bore on the land without the aid of a doctor, and twins without even the aid of another woman, only two have reached their twelfth birthday. The twins were taken by the cholera within just two days of each other, and Indians carried off my first-born, Emily, when she was five years old. To this day I don't know if she's living or dead."

Lily could not decide which alternative the woman preferred.

"I'm not complaining, mind you. This past year God rewarded Franklin and me. We got a fine price for our corn, and I'm on my way to Denver for a new set of teeth. Seem to have lost at least one, sometimes two, with each baby. Course, Franklin sulked all the way to the train station, fussing about how I could even think about throwing our hard-earned greenbacks after such a luxury as a new set of choppers. Pure vanity, he said. Well, I says to him, I'm not quite forty yet and am still a long way from the end of the row, but before I die I want to enjoy a good beef steak from one of those steers I've been feeding all these years. And better sooner than later. After all, a body never knows now, does it?"

She picked at the sleeve of her worn dress. "Course there just may be a bit of vanity, but I sure wouldn't admit that to him. I was quite a looker back in Pennsylvania." The woman giggled like a schoolgirl and the wrinkles around her eyes deepened.

Lily was surprised at Lu's age. She would have guessed her to be much older.

"But little does my Franklin know that I set aside my butter and egg money this past year and before I left, I ordered him that new plow out of the Sears and Roebuck that he's been drooling over."

Lu added that even with the rough times she would not sell the homestead for all the gold in Colorado.

"The secret of the land is not to give into it. Lord knows it's tested my faith more than once. But when I feel it pulling me under I reach for the Good Lord's hand and he keeps me in his firm grasp. Farm life is a good life, an honest life. Deep inside my soul I feel a kinship with the land and it gives me a kinship with its Creator. It's home."

Lu sighed. "Goodness, pardon me. How I've gone on so. Haven't talked this much in a coon's age. Course, I don't have anyone to listen to me anyways."

Lu patted Lily's hand, then stared at it, and at Lily. She frowned and once again, turned to look out the window. She sat in silence for several minutes before turning back to Lily and giving her a knowing but kind smile.

"One thing is for sure, the West is no place for the vain or the faint at heart. Just wished I would have worn a hat more. It's not like my Mama didn't warn me. If I was you, the first thing I would do in Denver is purchase a good straw hat with a wide brim.

"Donovan, every good farmer knows that you won't reap a good crop if you never get any rain. It's not an easy life out here. Sometimes it's even cruel. But what may look like a black cloud later becomes an answered prayer, a godsend. And just like he did Franklin and me, he is sending you west for a reason."

Lu laid her head on the back of the seat and shut her eyes.

"Best get some sleep. We'll be in Denver before you know it. I heard it said that this train can go up to thirty miles in just an hour. Who would have thought a body could have dreamed up such a thing. I thought I'd seen it all but life has a way of still surprising me".

Denver, Colorado Territory

Lily stepped off the train, confused and bewildered. The anticipation of finally arriving had been replaced with sheer terror. Never in her life had she been someplace where there had been no one waiting for her—someplace where she didn't know a soul. She stood in front of the station, clutching her satchel.

Denver was much bigger than she had imagined. The town was alive, bulging with fortune seekers. There were miners who looked to be without so much as two bits to buy a meal, and those in fancy carriages who seemed to have already found their fortune. Bible-waving zealots stood outside Soapy Sam's Saloon next to the depot, proclaiming that the end was near and fervently admonishing those who dared enter the establishment. A carnival barker added his loud voice to the noisy din.

Lily got her first glimpse of the savages she had read about in dime novels. They sat on the wooden sidewalk in front of a mercantile store across the street. The group consisted of an old man and woman, their shoulders draped with colorful blankets, a young woman with a baby in a strange carrier made of slatted boards, and two boys kicking a leather ball. They were well-clothed and did not have the look of degenerate savages as had been depicted in the books.

Several braves, who didn't look very brave to Lily at all, were of medium height with broad chests and bowed legs. Their faces were square with wide noses. The men were playing some sort of game which involved betting and pitching sticks. The obvious winner of the game entered the store and returned with peppermint sticks for the children and a sack of tobacco for the old man.

Barefooted street urchins begged to carry travelers' belongings for a dime. One of the children bumped into Lily, fell down and began crying hideously. Lily set down her bag to help the child up. Two other children came up behind Lily, grabbed the carpetbag, and ran down the street.

"Stop! Stop, I say!" Lily cried out, running after them. But it was too late. The small thieves disappeared down a narrow side street and vanished. The child who had been crying ran the other way.

"Well, my dear, it seems you have just been taken by the oldest scam in the book."

Lily looked around to see who was talking to her.

It was Mattie Silks. "Except mine, of course. Is anyone meeting you here?"

"No."

"Now don't tell me that you had all your funds in that bag?"

Lily's heart sunk. She had taken over half the money from her trousers pocket and put it in the bottom of the bag.

"Not all of it."

"But a good portion, am I right?"

Lily did not answer.

"I'm not a woman to beat around the bush. I watched you on the train all the way from Quincy. Even under that ridiculous hat you have a very pretty face. It is my business to notice such things. If you ever decide to come out from under it, look me up. I don't have an address yet but just ask around. Within a month everyone in town will know Mattie Silk's place."

Mattie opened her heavily beaded silk purse and drew out a calling card. "But anyone who enters will need one of these. Specialized clientele, so to speak."

Lily handed the card back. "I won't be needing this, but thank you anyway."

Mattie tucked the card into Lily's shirt pocket. "Don't be so quick to decide. You never know what's around the corner, now do you?"

Lily sat down on a bench in front of the train station clutching her canvas cloak, the only belonging she had left. Now even Mama's picture was gone. Mattie's words played over in her mind. Never, Lily vowed, never. She took the calling card out of her pocket, tore it in two, and threw it on the ground.

"That's littering you know." Lily looked up and saw Bodeen's boyish grin.

"What do you want?"

"Well, I can see you still think I'm a scoundrel. Actually I just wanted to say good-bye. You were good company on the trip. Almost made me wish we were still on that train. Though I do have to say I'm offended that you chose that woman's company over mine." Samuel winked.

Lily rose and started walking. Where, she had no idea, but anywhere was preferable to where Bodeen was. Samuel stepped in front of her. "Where's your bag? Or did you take my advice and get rid of it?"

"Look, Mr. Bodeen, the only person you are amusing is yourself. Now if you will excuse me. . ."

"Donovan, wait. I'm sorry. I saw what happened. Have you got any money?"

"Some." Lily bit her lip. He sounded sincere.

"But not much. There's a boarding house two blocks north of here. It's cheap but clean. Run by a woman named Myrtle Gilliam. Tell her I sent you. I'd take you there myself but duty calls. I just received word that Chief Ouray and a couple of Indian agents are waiting for me. Will you at least let me buy you dinner?"

"I don't think so."

"You'll change your mind after you've had a good hot bath. I'll pick you up at seven o'clock."

Once again, Bodeen had been right. Myrtle Gilliam was a kind, matronly woman who kept a respectable boarding house. The room was small but neat and tidy.

"Ten dollars a week for the room, paid in advance. I don't allow spirits of any kind and the doors are locked after ten at night. Meals are extra, a dollar a day for both, but they are good and there's plenty of it. Breakfast is at seven and supper is at six."

She looked at Lily firmly. "And the washroom is down the hall to the left."

Lily shut the door, took off her hat and looked in the small mirror over the bureau. It was as she had guessed; she looked as dingy and rumpled as she felt. The bowler hat had left a distinctive circle of dirty, sweat soaked curls plastered down on her forehead. Her face looked as though it had not been washed in over a week. The once peaches and cream complexion was now waxy and wan, and the dark gray circles under her eyes had deepened. The bruise on her cheek had turned a sickly yellow. Her only shirt was grimy, with white circles of stain under the arms. Given her ragged appearance, she was surprised that Mrs. Gilliam had opened the door to her.

Lily reached down into the pocket of her pants and pulled out several bills and some change. Seventy-eight dollars and fifty-two cents. With room and board at seventeen dollars a week, she had enough for about a month. But she needed clothes, a hairbrush, and she definitely needed a good pair of leather gloves.

It took over half an hour of scrubbing in the washroom before Lily felt even somewhat relieved of the grit on her skin. She longed for a bar of Grandma's homemade lavender soap and a large cast iron tub but made do with the tin washtub and bar of castile soap that served the same purpose. But her clothes, the only ones she owned, were still filthy. Lily thought about washing them out but her body did not want to cooperate. They would just have to wait a while. Lily put the soiled clothes back on, went to her room and lay down on the bed. Her last thought was of how could a body be so tired when all it had done was sit on a train. Like her life, it made no sense.

+ + +

"Donovan? Donovan?" Lily woke to loud rapping on her door. She shook herself awake. "Donovan, are you there?"

Lily jumped up and opened the door.

"Goodness, I thought you'd died in there." Myrtle looked concerned.

"I didn't realize how tired I was."

"I shall take that as a compliment that the room is indeed comfortable. Samuel Bodeen is downstairs. Says he's here to take you to supper."

"Tell him to go away."

"Now you and I both know that if I tell him that, he will just come up those stairs and get you. He's a good man but as stubborn as an army mule, been around them so long he picked up all their bad habits. I suggest you tell him yourself. He won't go away otherwise."

"Myrtle, I can't. You see, my satchel was stolen after I got off the train and I don't have anything, not even a hairbrush."

"I was wondering why you didn't have a bag, but I've learned my place is not to question my boarders, just feed them. I'm a far sight bigger than you but I may have a shirt somewhere that might fit. I can help you with the rest."

Myrtle returned with a variety of toiletries: toothpowder, a hairbrush, and a small jar of talc that smelled like lemon verbena. The rough, gray muslin shirt was several sizes too large, but it would have to do. At least it was clean. "I'll tell Samuel you'll be down in just a few minutes."

Lily did what she could to make herself presentable but the oversized shirt made her look like a stuffed mushroom. Her hair was a mass of short, unruly curls. It saddened her to think of the long auburn hair buried in a rotted out stump behind her grandmother's house in Nauvoo. She put on the hat, took it off, and then put it back on again.

Bodeen was waiting at the bottom of the stairs.

"I see you dressed for the evening." He laughed heartily. "Just remember, Donovan, a gentleman always removes his hat at the table."

"I just came down to tell you that I'm not going."

"And disappoint Chief Ouray? Let me tell you a little about Indians. More than one greenhorn has lost his scalp disregarding Indian etiquette. You don't turn down an invitation from a big chief like Ouray unless you want to lose what little is left of your hair, isn't that right, Myrtle?"

"Oh, go on now, both of you. I'd say that if this tight old coot is offering you a free meal, take it." Bodeen gave the woman a wink and one of his infamous smiles.

✚ ✚ ✚

Samuel led Lily into a fine restaurant located in the elaborate Markham Hotel.

"As you can see, Ouray likes to take advantage of all the good things the whites have to offer."

"Samuel, I'm not dressed for this. Really, I would be terribly out of place." Lily turned to leave, but Bodeen stopped her.

"Don't worry, in Denver you see all kinds. Just don't let on that you are thinking of becoming a miner. Ouray's a might touchy about them right now. Now just relax and remember to remove your hat."

He guided Lily over to a table occupied by a handsome Indian couple. "Ouray and Chipeta, good to see you again. May I introduce

Donovan, my traveling companion on the train." Ouray rose and offered his hand, an unexpected gesture that Lily found engaging. Even Indians, Lily thought. Samuel pulled out a chair and gestured for Lily to be seated, then took the seat across from her. He removed his hat and his eyes told Lily to follow suit. She meekly removed hers, slid it under the table and fluffed her rumpled curls.

"Your hair is quite lovely, " Chipeta said. "Mine is as straight as a porcupine quill."

"Thank you," Lily managed to say. She was taken by Chipeta's beauty. The woman's hair was indeed straight, parted down the middle, and it shined like ebony. Her eyes were as black as onyx, but with the softness of fine velvet. She wore a soft, white doeskin dress decorated with ornate beadwork, every seam thick with fringe.

Ouray was also dressed in buckskin, his shirt a deep caramel color. The sash around his waist was colorfully beaded. His hair was plaited into long braids and wrapped at the ends with silky brown fur.

The meal was delicious: a hearty vegetable soup, thick steaks, au gratin potatoes, fresh asparagus swimming in butter, fluffy rolls and a light chocolate mousse. Samuel noticed that Chief Ouray had only eaten the bowl of soup, leaving much of the rest of his meal untouched.

"Is the meal not to your liking?" Bodeen asked.

"I have found that white man's rich food is very disagreeable," he said. "But my wife finds it quite delectable, as you can see."

Chipeta laughed. She had not only taken a chocolate mousse from the dessert tray, but strawberries swimming in cream as well. She laced her coffee heavily with sugar.

Lily soon realized how wrong her perception of Indians had been. She was surprised at how quickly she felt at ease with them. She found the couple to be gentle, caring and even quite funny. Ouray and Chipeta were extremely intelligent, witty and polite. They did not ask her any pointed questions but Lily found herself opening up to them, especially when the conversation turned to horses.

Ouray explained that Utes did not believe in breaking a horse's spirit, but in gently leading them into trust. Lily heartily agreed. He further explained the Utes love of horse racing. "The faster a man's horse, the more he is respected." He went on to add that he had just completed a straight horse track behind their home at the farm.

"You have a farm?" Lily was intrigued.

Chipeta explained that Major James Thompson, brother-in-law to Edward McCook who was the prime candidate to become the first governor of Colorado, had convinced the government to allot the couple 160 acres and build them a home near the Los Piños Indian Agency for farming. They, in turn, were to be an example to others in their tribe.

Chipeta never openly criticized this change in her life, though she hinted that she was not terribly impressed with the possessions given to her by the whites. "I don't find the crystal stemware very functional," she said. "I'm always worried that I will break the fragile goblets."

"It has been a hard change for us," Ouray said somberly. "But I realize the destiny of my people. We shall fall as the leaves of the trees when winter comes . . . my part is to protect my people and yours, as far as I can, from violence and bloodshed. But I don't know how much longer I can keep my people from fighting back for what they feel is rightfully theirs."

"What can I do to help?" Bodeen asked, his demeanor turning serious and businesslike.

"The Brunot Treaty took away much of our prime hunting ground. The government promised beef and rations in return for the portion of the San Juan Mountains they desired. President Grant also gave me his solemn word that settlers would be banned from what is left of our land. It has been over three years and neither promise has been kept. Otto Mears has tried to help push for the payment, but he has not been able to get anywhere either."

Ouray put down his spoon and looked at the feast before him as if he was almost revolted by the abundance.

"My people are hungry," he said with a deep grief in his voice.

Bodeen's eyes narrowed into angry slits. "I give you my word, Ouray, I will do what I can. Maybe with Colorado being granted statehood in August, I will have more leverage in making the federal government keep their promises. I will bring your concerns before Edward McCook tomorrow morning. Will Mears be there?"

"He will."

Bodeen pulled a gold pocket watch from his coat. "If memory serves me right, Myrtle locks the door at ten o'clock. If you want a bed tonight, Donovan, we had better call it a night."

"It was very nice to meet you, Donovan," Chipeta said kindly. "I wonder if I could ask your assistance in something? Ouray will be in a meeting with Bodeen and McCook most of tomorrow. I am to purchase goods for our home and would sincerely appreciate any advice you could give me. I am still a stranger to many of the white ways but would like the visitors to our home to feel comfortable."

"I would be happy to go with you. As a matter of fact, I have some shopping of my own to do," Lily said.

"I'm not much in the way of shopping, especially for things such as household goods. But if I were you I would stay away from Tucker's Mercantile by the train station. Houlihan's General Store over on Larimer Street has just about anything a person could want or need, with the lowest prices in town," Samuel advised.

Lily agreed to meet Chipeta in the front of the hotel the following morning.

On the way back to the boarding house Bodeen was quiet and subdued. The pale gaslights lining the street added to his somber mood.

"Do you really think you can help them?"

"I don't know. I honestly don't know. My heart says I hope so, but gut instinct says no, especially if Mears is involved."

"Who is this Mears?" Lily asked.

"We both served under Kit Carson back in 1868. The man is very smart; I will give him credit for that. But he is as cunning and wily as a fox and would sell his mother if he thought he could make a dime. The man never sleeps. While the rest of us would drop into our bedrolls at night, he would stay up and shine some top dog's boots or dream up schemes to swindle the soldiers out of their pay. I'm afraid that with Mears involved, greed will soon destroy the life the Ute people have known for hundreds of years, and God help the man who tries to stop him. He's determined to amass a dynasty, and knowing Mears, he will stop at nothing to get it. And he's got the Utes thinking that he's their best friend."

✛ ✛ ✛

"Why is it that white women take such stock is what is so easily broken?" Chipeta asked, as she looked at the china and crystal at the May Company department store that specialized in household goods. The sheets were soft and the blankets fluffy, but Chipeta could not decide on anything.

They stopped in at a millinery shop. Chipeta had a wonderful time trying on hats but again, purchased nothing. Lily could sense that Chipeta was becoming frustrated with their shopping expedition.

They went to the Daniel Fisher Co., which specialized in fine clothing for women. Lily noticed the suspicious stare from a sales clerk as Chipeta fingered the fine material and intricate lace.

"Wouldn't my goats think I was something in this?" she said with a coy smile. She picked up a corset and looked puzzled. "Do women actually wear these?"

Lily smiled. "Well, yes they do."

"Do you?" Chipeta looked at Lily's gray muslin shirt.

"No, not anymore." Lily grew uncomfortable.

Chipeta instantly felt Lily's uneasiness. "I'm truly sorry, it is really none of my business. Please, excuse me for asking. There seems to be nothing in here for either of us." She put the corset back. "I am suddenly very thirsty."

They stopped in at a small eatery next to the May Company. The lemonade was cool, but the lighthearted camaraderie the women had shared earlier had turned tense. The Indian sipped her drink quietly.

"I'm sorry Chipeta. I feel I owe you some sort of explanation," Lily said.

"No, please, I am the one who should be sorry. I am entirely too curious at times. I should have been more discreet."

"No, you had every right to ask. Please, I want you to know my name. It is Lily."

"Does Bodeen know this?"

"My name? No. That I am a woman? He guessed it right off."

"Then I will call you Donovan as well. I guess we have both been trying to be something that we are not, for whatever our reasons are. But thankfully, we no longer have to pretend with each other. This is good." Chipeta seemed relieved.

They took Bodeen's advice and sought out Houlihan's store. Lily found everything she was needing: a pair of coarse denim pants, a sturdy muslin shirt, a pair of leather gloves, undergarments, an extra pair of socks, a fine boar bristled hairbrush and some tooth powder. Chipeta purchased several spools of thread, a wide variety of colorful beads, a packet of needles and a cast-iron dutch oven.

When they returned to the hotel, Chipeta asked Lily if she was hungry.

Knowing she had already spent too much of her meager funds, Lily politely declined.

"No, I really had better be going."

"Going where? What are you going to do Lily?"

"Find employment, though where or what I am not quite sure yet."

"Ouray and I will be leaving on the stage in the morning. You are welcome to come with us." Lily could see that Chipeta's invitation was sincere. As tempting as the offer was, Lily knew she would never be able to afford the fare.

"I can't Chipeta. But thank you for the offer."

"I understand. Our home will always be open to you, my friend. I will remember you with smiles and good thoughts and will ask the Great Spirit to protect you."

Chipeta reached out her arms and Lily took and held them for a long moment.

The warm touch of human kindness felt wonderful.

✤ ✤ ✤

Lily went back to the boarding house and changed into the new clothes. She then went back out and began inquiring about employment, spending the afternoon going in and out of the many businesses in town: banks, hotels, restaurants, and shops. Most of the business people never even looked up at her but said, "Nope, nothing."

Lily went into the newspaper office and was given some very discouraging words from a gruff-looking editor.

"How's a body supposed to get any work done with all this interruption? You're the seventh person that's been in here today looking for a job. Good luck in finding anything around here, even with the boom. Horace Greeley and the eastern papers convince people that Colorado is some kind of 'Promised Land'. They advertise jobs, profits and riches. And the Denver Board of Trade offers perpetual youth, saying the climate is exceedingly favorable to those suffering from the consumption. They boast that the sick are sure to find instantaneous relief and a rapid and permanent cure."

He paused and took a swig of muddy-looking coffee.

"Then there are the mines. People set out to make their fortunes and come away with empty pockets. Sure, there's those few who have found the mother lode. They build their mansions and sip their sherry from France, while paying their workers $1.50 a day to lose their lungs in filthy smelters. The wages are low and conditions appalling.

"And surely you have noticed the number of abandoned children in the streets. They get by on the new twenty-five cent bounty offered by the City of Denver for dogs, dead or alive. Six months ago the streets were filled with mongrels. Today, citizens are afraid to let pets out of their houses."

He took off his spectacles and rubbed his eyes.

"Then there are the Chinese. Now that the transcontinental railroad is complete, the Coolies are coming to Denver in droves. They beg for every menial job out there: laundry workers, servants, and janitors. They are even exploited by their own people. Opium dens have sprung up all over town."

The newspaperman withdrew a handkerchief from his back pocket, wiped his glasses, put them back on, and looked seriously at Lily.

"Do yourself a favor, go back home. I'm certainly considering it. If you're still not convinced, take a walk down by the Platte River and look at the destitute living in tents and shanties. Many suffer from malnutrition. Then there's scarlet fever, pneumonia, and typhoid. Pick your poison."

The man dismissed her by turning back to setting type. "Like I said, good luck."

Lily returned to the boardinghouse disappointed and dejected. She sat on the bed and wondered what to do. She had no real skills. Grandma Donovan had tried to teach her how to sew but she had been too fidgety and impatient to listen. She had never been any good in the kitchen. She had received a teaching certificate and had taught school for two years but she was sure any good school would require references. She could not take that chance.

The only person she had ever really listened to was Joshua.

✦ ✦ ✦

Bodeen showed up at the boarding house just as dinner was being laid out on the table. He handed Myrtle two dollars

"Now, Samuel, you know it's only a dollar."

"Then give me two of everything."

Myrtle scooped a ladle full of chicken and dumplings into each boarder's bowl. Everyone ate heartily and talked about the upcoming plans for the celebration of Colorado becoming a state. The tureen was soon empty and the conversation turned to the recent news of an Indian uprising in the Dakota Territory. Bodeen turned uncharacteristically quiet. One of the boarder's boisterously gave his opinion of what should be done with the "red devils."

"So where is the apple pie?" Samuel asked, his demeanor growing lighter when Myrtle set a chocolate layer cake on the table.

"Come back this fall." Myrtle handed him a large slice.

"I guess I'll just have to get by with two pieces of cake," he teased as he held up his plate for more.

"I say just get rid of the red skinned bastards once and for all!" a boarder at the end of the table said angrily.

Samuel slammed down his plate and walked out. Lily rose to go after him.

They sat in silence on the porch while Samuel lit his pipe. After several minutes he said, "He only said what I've been hearing all over town."

"I take it your meeting didn't go well?"

"Yes and no. I finally convinced McCook to get rid of Henry Bond."

"Who is Bond?" Lily asked.

"The Reverend Henry F. Bond has been the acting Indian agent at the Los Piños Agency for the past year. Even though he went to Harvard it seems he had trouble with numbers. The Inspection Bureau of the Indian Department finally figured out that the good reverend was loading cattle twice through the chutes, charging the Utes twice for the number of cattle received. His books said the Utes received twelve hundred head of beef. And of the six hundred actually counted, four hundred of those mysteriously strayed away. So instead of the Indians getting twelve hundred head, they only received two hundred. Not much to feed 5,000 hungry mouths for a year. And to make matters worse, settlers who aren't even supposed to be on the Ute reservation have either slaughtered or run off the deer and elk. It's no wonder Ouray's people are full of fight. That's what happens to a man when he knows his children's bellies are empty."

"Who will take Bond's place?"

"Major W.D. Wheeler will be arriving this fall to assume the position. Being an ex-army paymaster, I have been assured that Wheeler will be more precise and businesslike."

"So what is the problem?" Lily asked.

"The newspapers. They are encouraging people to take the same attitude that the boarder has. I have been a soldier all my life, fought a lot of different enemies. But I don't know how to fight against words. You can't shoot at them with a cannon. And then there's Otto Mears. Sure, he acts mighty concerned, but my gut instinct tells me he should not be trusted."

Samuel looked at Lily, forcing a smile to his solemn face. "But enough of that. What do you say to getting your money back?"

"Bodeen, it's gone. You know that."

"Maybe not. I have a plan. I'm a soldier, an expert in smoking out all kinds of doers of bad deeds. Shouldn't be too hard to rustle out a couple of kids. Meet me at the train station tomorrow morning at nine o'clock."

He stood up to leave but then bent forward as if he were going to kiss her. She tensed and leaned back.

He stopped and pulled himself up short. "Even in that getup, you're as pretty as a moonlit night in autumn. Goodnight, Donovan."

As Lily watched Bodeen walk down the street, she could not help but wonder if she would have had the courage to stop him, or if she would even have wanted to.

✦ ✦ ✦

There was a light rain falling the next morning when Lily met Samuel at the station.

"Now remember, you go up at him from the north. I'll be just around that corner to the south," Bodeen advised.

The children had their usual place in front of the train depot. Lily instantly recognized the child who had been crying the day she got off the train. She walked up quietly to him and grabbed his arm. He pulled away and took off running around the corner, right into Samuel's outstretched arms. This time his tears were real, especially when Bodeen told him how hungry the coyotes were on the edge of town.

"I spent it. Honest I did," the small boy whispered, wiping his nose on his sleeve.

"Maybe we best just tell your mama what you've been up to. Where do you live?"

"Can't tell." The boy tried to wiggle out of Samuel's firm hold.

Bodeen pulled a knife out of his boot. Even Lily gasped.

"Okay, I'll show you," the boy said, his lower lip trembling.

Lily smelled the shantytown by the Platte River before she saw it. The muddy streets were covered with filth and open sewage and shabby tents lined the riverbank. The child led them to a small, hastily constructed tarpaper shack. Rain dripped in where the paper had been torn from the roof. There were no beds, only a couple of soiled blankets lying on top of some old newspapers. A young woman laid on top of the blankets, shivering in the cool dampness but Lily could see beads of perspiration on her brow. Her cheeks were bright red.

"I used my share of your money to get some medicine for my mama," the child said. "But it didn't do no good."

The woman sat up and tried to speak but broke into a deep, raspy cough. Lily felt the woman's forehead, then quickly took off her cloak and put it around the woman's shoulders.

Lily looked at Bodeen. "She is sick, burning up with fever. You've got to get her a doctor. Please hurry. I'll stay with her."

"There's nothing you can do, Donovan."

Lily ignored his comment. "What's your name, child?"

"Jimmy."

"Jimmy, I need some firewood. And bring me a bucket of water."

"There ain't any firewood. And we don't got a bucket; someone stole it last week."

"Samuel, I said go for help, now!" Lily commanded, as she saw him still standing in the doorway.

He leaned down and grabbed her by the shoulders. "Listen to the woman, she's got the consumption for sure, and probably pneumonia."

"So we do nothing? Are you really so heartless?"

"Listen to me Donovan. There's nothing we can do."

Once again the woman tried to speak, her lungs wheezing loudly. "He's right. I'm sorry about the boy. I wished I could give your money back," she said with tears in her eyes.

Lily sat down on the blanket next to the woman and held her, feeling the rumbling inside the frail, thin body.

"The least I can do is bring her a hot meal," Bodeen said. "I'll be back in a few minutes."

He quickly returned with two quart jars of beef soup. Lily found a spoon in a wooden box and wiped it on her shirt.

"Here, eat this," she told the woman.

"No, give it to Jimmy."

"He brought some for your boy, too," Lily said, holding the spoon to the woman's cracked lips but she was only able to take just a couple of bites before breaking into another fit of coughing.

"Here, try some of this." Bodeen took the silver flask from inside his shirt.

The woman took several sips before handing the flask back.

"Keep it. You need it much more than I do," Bodeen said. He turned to Lily. "Come on, Donovan, it's time to go."

"I'm not leaving her."

Bodeen grabbed her arm. "You stick around here and you'll be as sick as she is. Besides, my regiment is due to pull out in about an hour."

Lily shrugged his hand off her arm and glared at him. "You just go then. I'm staying right here."

Bodeen could see that her mind was set and there was no talking her out of it.

"Suit yourself, Donovan. But there's some things a person can't change."

Men, Lily thought as she watched Bodeen turn and walk out the door. And she had thought he just might be different. But he wasn't. Cold, ruthless, heartless. Men were all the same.

✠ ✠ ✠

At dawn the next morning an undertaker's wagon pulled up beside the shack.

"How did you know?" Lily asked, exhausted from the long night's vigil.

"A soldier came by yesterday. Gave me fifty dollars and told me to give the woman a proper burial. Then threw in an extra ten to buy her a new dress and a couple of flowers to put on the grave. He also said to give you this." The undertaker pulled an envelope from his back pocket. Lily opened it and found one hundred dollars in cash. The note attached read: *Be sure the boy is taken care of.* It was simply signed *S.B.*

Lily started to remove the cloak from the dead woman's shoulders.

"Can't do that ma'am." The man looked down at her over his crooked beak of a nose. He reminded Lily of a vulture waiting to pick the bones clean.

"I'm not stealing it, it's mine."

"Never said you was. But the City of Denver says I'm to burn anything that's left on a person. It's the only way to stop the disease down here. They'll be sending someone over later to burn the shanty."

Lily started looking through the wooden box where she had found the spoon.

"And don't be taking that box there, neither."

"Well, at least let me try to find some sort of identity for the woman, a letter or something. I need to know where to send the boy."

The man looked at the small child cowering in the corner. "Sure, no harm in that, I guess."

Lily found a small bundle of letters in the bottom of the box. As the man loaded the body, Lily tucked the bundle inside her shirt.

"Well, Jimmy, it looks like just you and me now," Lily said as the wagon pulled away.

"I wanna go with my mama."

"You can't do that child. She's gone to Heaven to be with God."

"Then I'm going, too!" He started to run after the wagon.

Lily grabbed the boy and gathered him into her arms. "Listen to me. You will see your mama again someday. I promise you that."

"That's what Mama said about Pa."

"So your father is dead?"

"He was buried in a mine cave-in. Mama got us back here and tried to get enough money to get us back home, but then she got sick."

"And where is home?"

"Kansas. We come to Colorado two years ago after the bugs ate up all the wheat."

"How old are you, Jimmy?"

"Six now, but I'll be seven next month. Mama says I'm a big boy, but I'm scared. Everybody's done left me." His bottom lip quivered.

"I know you're scared, but I promise you will not be alone. You will stay with me until someone comes for you." She gave him a gentle hug.

She knew exactly what it was to have no one.

Myrtle gave Lily a hard stare. "I have no more rooms available. And I don't allow children, the other boarders don't like it."

"But I can pay for him and he can sleep in my room. I'll pay you double."

"I'm sorry, Donovan. As much as I would like to help . . ."

"It's okay, ma'am. Me and Mama was used to being where nobody wanted us. I couldn't hope to stay in a place as grand as yours. Thanks anyway." The boy let go of Lily's hand and turned to go.

Myrtle's face softened.

"Wait a minute. What's your name, child?"

"James Andrew McCluskey. But everyone just calls me little Jimmy. Kids tease me cause I'm kinda small for my age, but Mama said that's okay. Says the very best things come in small packages. It's how big the heart is that counts."

"I see your mama was a smart woman. Well, Mr. McCluskey, are you any good at hauling wood?"

"The greatest."

"And can you be quiet?"

"Yes'm. My mama taught me good manners."

"There's an extra bedroll in that closet. You fetch it up to Donovan's room. And you could do with a good scrubbing. I don't allow any dirty feet in my beds, understand?"

"Yes'm." The boy's tear-stained face beamed with relief.

Myrtle checked his head for any signs of lice. "No, vermin, thank goodness, but I'll need to take the scissors to that mop of hair anyway."

While Lily was washing the boy in the tin washtub, Myrtle brought in a change of clothes and took the old ones. "These will need to be incinerated."

"I understand. Where did you get these?" Lily took the clothes.

"Have a boy of my own. He'd be nineteen now. Haven't seen nor heard from him for nearly two years. The last I knew he was driving cattle up from Texas. He never was much on writing."

Myrtle motioned Lily outside the door.

"I couldn't turn the lad away, just losing his mother and all. But he can't stay here, you know. I have a business to run. I can't afford to lose even one boarder."

"Yes, I know. It seems his father's parents are from Emporia, Kansas. I will send a wire to them this afternoon."

After his bath Myrtle took the scissors to Jimmy's hair and soon he looked like a different child. She fed him some bread and cheese but he fell asleep at the table before he finished.

"I'll carry him up to my room," Lily said. She was surprised at how light the child was.

Myrtle tucked the blankets around his small body. "He'll sleep for a good while. Why don't you head over to the telegraph office and get word to his kin? It's down by Hank's livery on the south edge of town. I'll keep an eye on the boy."

Lily posted the telegram. As she came out of the office she glanced over at the livery. A man was standing with a bit in hand. Lily could see that the large sorrel gelding was determined not to take it. The horse pawed the ground furiously and threw his head. Suddenly the words she had thought yesterday hit her like a bright explosion of light. The only person she had ever listened to was Joshua. And he had taught her well. She walked over to the livery.

"Mind if I try?" She looked up at the man who was almost as big as she remembered Isaiah Dorman to be, only this man's hair was a bright orange and his face was covered with tan freckles.

"He's a stubborn one," the man said, sounding frustrated. "Don't want anyone even close to him. The army left him here for me to try to sell but I'm afraid the only thing he's going to be good for is bear bait."

"Name's Donovan, " Lily said, taking the bridle out of his hands.

"Hank O'Rourke."

"Well, Mr. O'Rourke, are you a betting man?" Lily asked.

"Been known to be."

"Tell you what, give me a half an hour. If I can't get him to take the bit by then, I'll clean your stalls for a week for nothing. But if I can, you will give me a job."

The man pondered the proposition. Just yesterday his hired hand had left for the mines. He decided that either way he would come out the winner.

"Deal," he said.

"No matter what happens, don't say or do anything," Lily said, carefully watching the horse. "I'll need quiet and a bucket of oats."

She waited until Hank returned with the oats. She filled the breast pocket of her muslin shirt with oats and opened the gate.

Lily walked inside the corral and set the bridle over a fence post. The horse, seeing a newcomer to his territory, ran wildly in a circle around the corral. When he got near Lily, he turned, shook his head, and ran the other way. Lily walked to the center of the corral and stood silently. The horse retreated to a corner.

Lily pulled her hat lower, bowed her head, and watched the horse's hooves out of the corner of her eye. She could see his stance was defensive, his front legs wide apart, body tilted back, as if ready to strike if she came closer. It took five minutes before she saw his body relax. Good, she thought, now he was becoming nosy.

Lily moved forward slowly with her head still down. When she saw the gelding's muscles tense, she turned back around, walked forward several steps and stopped. She bowed her shoulders and waited. She stood quietly for several minutes, turned back and walked toward the horse until she saw him tense up again. She turned back and, once again, slumped her shoulders. The pair performed the game several times.

Lily took off her hat, laid it on the ground beside her and resumed her slumped position, her back away from the horse.

Finally curiosity overcame the gelding's fear and he took several steps toward the middle of the corral. Lily could hear him sniffing at her hat, and then at her back. She turned slowly to the horse and crooned softly, "Good Boy."

She held out her hand but did not attempt to touch him until he touched her first. She waited until she saw him lick his lips. She then touched his jaw and spoke softly. His muscles quivered as she touched his neck but he did not back away. Still talking to him, she rubbed her hands down his neck and onto his back. When she felt him tense up again, she took several steps away from the horse, turned her back and slumped her shoulders.

The horse moved forward and nudged her arm. She waited until she heard him lick his lips before she turned around and resumed touching him once again. She rubbed him all over for several minutes before she reached in her pocket and offered the horse a handful of oats.

She walked over and got the bridle from the fence post. The horse immediately tensed up when she walked forward with it. She laid it on the ground beside her, then turned her back to the animal and slumped her shoulders.

The horse remembered this game. He walked forward and sniffed at the bridle, then sniffed at her. She picked up the bridle, turned around, held it out to the horse and once again, waited for him to make the first move. He put his nose out and breathed in the scent of the leather, then licked his lips.

Lily rubbed the bridle against the horse's neck, then down his back and under his belly. His muscles quivered but he did not back away.

She brought the bridle back up and rubbed his ears with it, then his forehead, then his mouth. She slipped her thumb into the side of the horse's mouth several times, then rubbed the saliva on the bit. Once again she slid her thumb into the side of the horse's mouth and pried gently. The opening was just big enough to slide in the bit. She did this several times until the horse seemed comfortable with the object in his mouth. She then put the bridle up over his ears and buckled the neck strap.

"Good boy," she crooned softly. "Good boy." She took off the bridle and fed the horse the rest of the oats. He nuzzled at her pocket, searching for more.

"That's all for today, boy. You did well."

"Well I'll be jiggered," Hank said. "Never seen nothing like it. Looks like you got yourself a job, Donovan. Pay is three dollars a day, six days a week. We close up on Sundays. Come on, I'll show you around the place."

The large tack room was a mess. Lily remembered Joshua's tack room and could see that this one had the same potential. It just needed some soap, water and elbow grease.

"Tell you what, if you let me bed down here, I'll clean this place up and the stalls as well. And in addition, I'll throw in an extra hand. You'll get two of us for the price of one."

"Is he as good a hand as you?"

"He's the greatest."

"You've got a deal, Donovan."

Lily walked back to the boarding house so excited that she wanted to skip. Jimmy was at the kitchen table reading out loud from a McGuffey's primer and eating soft molasses cookies. Lily gave the boy a big hug and told Myrtle the good news.

"I will be sorry to see you go," Myrtle said. "Little Jimmy was mighty good company this afternoon. He swept the front steps, hauled in wood, and brought up some canned goods from the cellar."

"She's got a whole room down there just for food," Jimmy said brightly. "Jars full of peaches, and cherries, too."

Myrtle got up and checked the contents in the kettle simmering on the stove. "I've got a good roast cooking, along with some new potatoes and onions. You'll at least stay to supper before you leave?"

"The tack room will need some work before we can move in tomorrow, so we will stay the night. And supper does smell heavenly. To be perfectly honest, Mrs. Gilliam, I'm not much good with pots and pans. Besides, I don't have any utensils anyway. Would it be too much of a bother to stop by for supper every evening? Of course, I would be willing to pay you the going rate."

Myrtle's beaming smile gave Lily her answer. "Seems I should open a restaurant. My cooking is worth more than my beds."

"Good. Now, James McCluskey, we have some shopping to do. You can't be a good hand with horses without a sturdy pair of boots."

"Horses?"

Lily thought the boy would be thrilled, but he looked scared to death.

"Now, Jimmy, horses aren't really much different than people. If you treat them with kindness and respect, they will treat you the same way."

"We had a pair back in Kansas. I just remember they were so big and I was so small."

"Something tells me they will love you. You'll have them eating out of your hand in no time."

"Well, okay. If you say so. I just hope they don't take my arm with the food."

Lily laughed. "Go on now, and put the book back on the shelf before we go," she said.

"He's one smart boy, Donovan." Myrtle said. "Already reading like a fourth grader. Good-hearted, too. If you ever need help with him, I'll be here."

✛ ✛ ✛

Hank O'Rourke looked down at the small child clutching Lily's hand as they walked into the livery early the next morning.

"Now just wait a minute, Donovan, you never said anything about a kid. This is a livery, not a nursery school. You bluffed me," he said angrily.

"Sir, may I speak to you privately for a moment?" She instructed Jimmy to sit down on a bale of hay and wait for her.

"Mr. O'Rourke, I didn't mean to deceive you but it seemed I had no other choice. Do you have a mother?"

"She passed over to the other side a year ago."

"Then you should know how the boy feels. His mother died just yesterday and his father was killed in a mine cave-in. The boy has no one."

Hank's green eyes softened.

"I've sent word to his grandparents and expect them to come for him as soon as possible."

Hank looked back at the boy. Even the dog had instantly taken a liking to the child and was busy licking his face. "This is no place for a child. He could get hurt."

"Do you not agree that he stands more chance of being hurt out on the streets of Denver alone? There is a school nearby and I will enroll him on Monday. I promise you he will not be a bother."

Lily pulled an ace out of her sleeve. "Besides, his name is McCluskey. Surely you could not turn away a fellow Irishman, could you?"

Lily could see that she had won. O'Rourke melted like ice cream in August.

"Okay. But only until his grandparents come for him."

Jimmy was thrilled when Lily and Hank showed him around his new home.

"Thanks, mister. You got a real nice place here. Nice dog, too. What's its name?"

"Mollie. Mollie the collie," Hank replied. "And I can see she has sure taken a shining to you."

The boy giggled. "That's a funny name."

"Come on, Jimmy. I'm sure Mr. O'Rourke has work to do. And so do we." Lily took the boy's hand and headed back toward the barn.

They spent the morning mucking out the stalls. It was a dirty, backbreaking job, but Lily loved it. She had always felt more at peace in the barn at home than in the house. The smells were the same: new hay, leather, horse sweat, and yes, even dung.

Hank was impressed when he entered the barn just as Lily and Jimmy were sitting down on some hay bales to eat lunch. "Hasn't looked this good since it was built. I'm known around town as a pretty decent farrier and with everyone anxious to head up to the mines, I just haven't had time to keep the place up."

"You just wait, we're not through yet." Lily was grateful that Hank proved to be a boss who appreciated hard work. She pulled a sandwich out of the tin pail Myrtle had packed for them that morning and unwrapped it for Jimmy.

"About the gelding," she added, "I would like to continue gentling him, but right now he's got a tender mouth. Whoever used him in the army must have kept a constant tight rein on him. And he's got some pretty rough-looking cinch sores on his belly. I put some lanolin on them earlier, but would like to wait a few days before trying to ride him."

"I'll trust you to do with him what you think is best. You had just better be close by when it's time to put shoes on him. Otherwise, he'd kick me clear to kingdom come."

"The horse doesn't like men. He associates your smell with the soldier that must have abused him."

Hank looked down at his soiled shirt.

Lily could see he was somewhat offended and quickly added, "What I mean is, it will just take some time for him to earn your trust. Would you like a sandwich, Mr. O'Rourke? It seems Myrtle has packed a lunch big enough for a small army."

It did not take Hank long to down the sandwich. "Haven't had roast beef like that since, well, I can't even remember, it's been so long. Don't know how I ever got this big. I'm not much of a cook."

"I take it that you are not married?" Lily asked, handing him another sandwich.

"Nope, never could find anyone who would have me."

"You should ask Miss Gilliam. She's really nice," Jimmy said. "Then you could eat roast beef every day. And peaches and apples and cookies, too."

Hank smiled. "That would make me about the luckiest man in town, wouldn't it?"

Lily spent the afternoon cleaning up the tack room. She

pounded long nails into the north wall and hung up the bridles and halters. She organized the tack into neat piles: leather in one pile, snaps and bits in another, and pieces needing repair in yet another. She found some old boards in the back of the barn and made racks for the saddles. She noted that they needed to be oiled. The leather was so dry on several that it was beginning to crack. Joshua would have never allowed that.

Jimmy swept the floor and scrubbed rust off an old cast iron stove in the corner. He washed the tiny window that faced west toward the rugged Rocky Mountains. The sun streamed in, adding a rosy glow in the room. The warmth and light was comforting.

Lily stepped back and with a satisfied smile declared the room livable.

"Yep," Jimmy said. "Looks mighty fine. But where are we going to sleep?"

"We'll make us each a bed."

Lily took several longer boards and fashioned a box just her size. She nailed it together while Jimmy held the boards. Then she took some shorter boards and nailed them together for his bed. She filled her bed with straw and Jimmy did the same with his. They covered the straw with some old quilts Hank brought them, then took the new wool blankets Lily purchased at Houlihan's and tucked them in neatly.

✛ ✛ ✛

By the time Lily and Jimmy returned from supper at the boarding house, the sun was already setting behind the Rocky Mountains. They were both ready for bed, tired from the long, fruitful day.

Lily handed Jimmy a nightshirt from the bag of clothes Myrtle had given him. Having no proper sleeping attire for herself, she took off her boots and crawled under the blanket.

"Donovan, aren't you going to say your prayers?"

The question surprised her. She had nothing to say to God. "No, Jimmy. But you go ahead."

He knelt beside his straw bed. "God bless Mama. God bless Papa. And Uncle Henry and Aunt Sarah. And Grandpa and Grandma. And Mr. O'Rourke and Mollie and Mrs. Gilliam. Thank you for this new home. And thank you, God, for Donovan."

Satisfied he had blessed everyone, Jimmy crawled into his new bed and was soon sound asleep.

Lily stared out the window into the moonlight. As tired as she was, she could not shut her eyes without seeing Bertram's face looming down at her.

She got up and tucked the blanket around Jimmy. He's lost everything, she thought. Everything but the love in his heart and his childlike faith. Who was the woman who had given her child such a deep, unshakable sense of goodness?

Lily reached for the packet of letters she had hidden beneath her blanket, grabbed the kerosene lamp she had put on a crate beside her bed and went to an empty stall next to the tack room.

She felt like she was intruding on a pair of young, star-crossed lovers as she read of the passion felt between Andrew and Kathleen McCluskey.

My love, my life, I can't bear another day without you. I pray for our Lord to protect and keep you safe. Please come home, wrote Kathleen.

My beloved Kathleen, I'm doing this for you, for us. I promise I will be back in the fall. Until then, your dear sweet face will be with me every moment I am away from you, wrote Andrew.

Dearest Andrew, I miss the way you hold me in the early morning. I miss the softness of your voice whispering to me at night, wrote Kathleen.

My beloved Kathleen, my heart, my soul aches for you. I can't eat, can't sleep without your warm body next to mine. The Good Lord graciously brought us together. You were meant to be beside me always. I am sending you and Jimmy a ticket to join me. Let us not waste another day apart, wrote Andrew.

By the time Lily finished reading the letters, she realized that Kathleen McCluskey had not died from disease, but from a broken heart.

What was this kind of love? Lily wondered. She doubted that Harold had ever loved her with the passion and fervor that Andrew had loved Kathleen and sadly, she knew deep in her soul that she had never felt for him the passion that Kathleen had felt for Andrew.

And she could not help but wonder what Andrew McCluskey would have done if Kathleen had been violated. Would he have thought of Kathleen as "soiled goods" as Harold had thought of her?

Lily tied the faded ribbon back around the letters, just as she had found them, and blew out the light. She went back to the tack room and looked at Jimmy. He looked like a cherub sent down from Heaven.

James Andrew McCluskey had been conceived and raised in a love that had known no boundaries. His faith was a testimony to the sanctity of his parents' passion and commitment to each other and to their God. And even now, even in death, the gift of their faith and love was being passed on through the fruit of that love.

Lily knew that she had to start somewhere. Maybe that place was as a child again. She tried to remember what it felt like back when she never questioned that God was indeed, good. She walked outside and looked into the starlit heaven.

"God bless Mama." she whispered. "And Grandma. And Joshua. And yes, Lord, bless even poor Papa. He needs you most of all."

She stopped and pondered all the new blessings that had been placed into her life since she had stepped onto the train just a few short weeks ago. "And Lu and David Wood. And Ouray and Chipeta. And Myrtle Gilliam and Mr. O'Rourke. And James Andrew McCluskey."

The same moon that had cast eerie shadows back when she was fleeing to a new life now filled Lily with a comforting light. She felt a soothing sense of peace as Samuel's words he had said to her that night on the porch came into her mind like a soft, gentle breeze— "you're as pretty as a moonlit night in autumn".

"And Samuel Bodeen," she said aloud, as she thought how he had given to Kathleen McCluskey the only thing he knew how to give. She smiled as she thought of Kathleen meeting Andrew in Heaven wearing a new dress. She would not be tattered and frail. She would be beautiful.

Lily went back to the tack room and slipped into bed. But this time when she shut her eyes, she saw Bodeen's mischievous grin.

✢ ✢ ✢

Lily was pleased. In one short week, the gelding had become a different horse. He was healing well and would soon be ready for the saddle. She curried his long golden mane and tail and pulled out the burrs. He followed her to the gate of the corral and waited impatiently while she went and got him an extra ration of oats.

"You're starting to trust me, aren't you boy?" Lily said, patting his neck.

"What you going to name him?" Jimmy climbed up on the fence.

"Hey, buddy! How was school?"

"Great! We had a party today. Susie brought cupcakes for her birthday. But kind of sad, too."

"Why?"

"The teacher said we only have one more week until school gets out for the summer."

Lily had already made arrangements with Myrtle to watch the boy during the summer for two dollars a day. If she didn't get a telegram soon, the money Bodeen had left would be half gone. Not only had she bought Jimmy a pair of new boots and slicker, she had splurged and bought him a small set of carpentry tools. The child had an inventive mind and uncanny ability for building things. He had built a boat to sail in the horse trough and most recently had built Mollie a sturdy doghouse with a little help from Hank. She just hoped there would be enough for the fare to get him back to Kansas if his grandparents weren't able to come for him. She had checked every day for a return telegram, but there had been no word from them and Lily was becoming more worried.

"But you will get to spend more time with Mrs. Gilliam," Lily said, trying to reassure him.

"Yes, I suppose so."

"And just think of all the books she's got."

The boy's frown turned to a smile when he thought of the large bookcase in the parlor. "So what you gonna name him?"

"I don't know yet. Any suggestions?"

"How about Goldie. His mane shines just like gold."

"That's a girl's name. He's a boy. What about Jake?"

"No," Jimmy said. "There's a boy at school named Jake. He calls me sissy all the time."

"Let's get some of those cookies Myrtle packed up and think about it."

"Mr. O'Rourke said his real name is Henry," Jimmy said as he took another gingersnap. "Hank is just his nickname. Kind of like my name is James, but everyone calls me Jimmy. I wished I had a brother like my pa did. His name was Henry, too. Maybe I could pretend the horse is my brother. I could call him Henry like Pa called his brother."

Lily questioned the boy. "Does your Uncle Henry live in Kansas, too?"

"Yes, but in a different town. So can we call the horse Henry?"

"That would be a fine name," Lily said. "Tell me, do you remember the town where your Uncle Henry lives?"

The boy thought hard for a moment. "Nope. We visited him once on our way to Colorado. It was a long ride, I sure do remember that. And I remember the word started with a 'P'."

Lily's heart sunk as she wondered how many names of towns in Kansas started with the letter 'P'. Finding Henry McCluskey would be like finding a flower in a snowstorm.

"What are you doing for supper tonight?" Lily asked O'Rourke as he helped her finish stacking the new hay. "Myrtle told me last night that she was going to take yesterday's leftover leg of lamb and made a thick Irish stew. Are you interested?"

Hank's eyes lit up. "Well, if you think it would not be a bother to her."

"No bother at all. She always has enough to feed half of Denver," Lily said. "But she does charge a dollar for those who are not boarding with her."

"Shoot fire, I'd pay double that for real Irish stew. Haven't had a good bowl since I left the old country. My mouth is watering already."

"And there's strawberry shortcake for dessert," Jimmy said.

"I can't turn that down, now can I? Let me go on home and clean up a bit." Lily gave him directions and agreed to meet him at the boarding house.

She was amazed at Hank's appearance when he walked in the door. In 'cleaning up a bit,' he had obviously taken a full-blown bath. His bright red hair was slicked down to his head and he had even shaved. He was dressed in his Sunday best, complete with white shirt and string tie.

Myrtle told him flatly that her boarding house was not a funeral home and there was no need for such finery, but Lily could see Myrtle was obviously impressed that he had taken such effort to make himself presentable. And she grinned from ear to ear when Hank told her the stew had been every bit as tasty as his mother's. She filled his bowl a third time.

✣ ✣ ✣

The days fell into a comfortable routine. After school let out for the summer, Lily rose early and took Jimmy to the boarding house. She then returned to the livery and spent the day exercising horses, oiling saddles, repairing cinches and bridles, and helping Hank by holding the horses he shod.

She spent an hour a day with the gelding. He had taken the saddle well, and Lily was able to ride him around the corral. Loud noises still bothered him a bit, but he was becoming calmer around Hank. The horse still had a keen distrust of him and all men that came to the livery, especially those dressed in a blue cavalry coat.

Cleaning out the stalls proved to be a never-ending job but the work hardened Lily's muscles and she felt healthy and content. Even with the hard physical exercise she noticed her jeans were getting tighter around her waist. Myrtle's cooking was just that good, she thought. Even Hank was complaining about having to loosen his belt a notch. The Irish stew had convinced him that a dollar a day was a small price to pay for Myrtle's good cooking, and he began eating at the boarding house every night as well.

Hank began escorting Myrtle to church on Sundays, and they took Jimmy along. But every Sunday, Lily politely declined.

"How come you don't go, Donovan?" Jimmy asked her several times. It was getting harder to come up with legitimate excuses.

One Sunday evening Lily noticed that Myrtle had cooked up Hank's favorites: Irish soda bread, corned beef and cabbage, and potato dumplings. And she could not help but notice Hank's tenderness when he looked at the cook.

"Myrtle, when you get to Paradise, you'll have to look up my dear sweet mama and tell her what you used to make these dumplings so light. You know, you even look a bit like her, especially in that apron. Her eyes were the same shade of blue. . ."

"That's it!" Jimmy said brightly. "That's where my Uncle Henry lives. Your mama lives there, too?" Jimmy asked Hank.

"Your Uncle Henry lives where, Jimmy?" Lily quizzed.

"Paradise. Yep, Paradise, Kansas. See, I told you it started with a 'P'," he said proudly. "And you know what? He has red hair, too!"

Lily went to the telegraph office the next morning and waited behind the two men in front of her.

"Got a new one for your wall, Cyrus," one of the men said, handing the clerk a poster.

"Pretty lady," the clerk said. "Looks too fine to be wanted for anything."

"Seems she roughed up an old black man back in Nauvoo, Illinois. Then took all his money."

Lily looked over the man's shoulder and saw her own face staring back at her from the poster.

"Next," the clerk said.

But Lily was already gone.

✣ ✣ ✣

"Hank, could you run over to Houlihan's and get some more Neatsfoot Oil?"

"I thought you bought some last week."

"I did, but I left the lid off the bottle and Mollie knocked it over," Lily said.

"Okay, I'm needing some horseshoe nails anyway. Be back in a few minutes."

Lily waited until Hank was out of sight, then ran to the barn and threw her clothes in a saddlebag. She tried to saddle the gelding quickly but the horse sensed her nervousness and became agitated.

"Look, Henry, I don't have time to be gentle. I know you're not quite ready for this, but I don't have a choice." She climbed on his back.

Just as she made her way out the barn doors, Hank returned.

"I forget, Donovan, did you need . . ."

Lily kicked the horse past him.

"Hey, what are you doing?" He grabbed the horse's reins and it bolted.

The last thing Lily remembered was the dull thud of her head hitting a fence post and two hooves crashing down on top of her.

Lily tried hard to swim out of the darkness, but the water was murky and heavy. Her body ached with tiredness as she tried to fight her way out.

"Donovan?"

The water cleared a bit. She struggled to reach the surface.

"Where am I?"

She heard a strange, soft voice. "It's me, Donovan. You're at the boarding house."

Lily tried to sit up but her head pounded and white-hot streaks of pain flashed throughout her skull.

"Who's Donovan?"

"Lay still now. The doc says you need your rest."

"Where's Jimmy?"

"Downstairs with Hank. He's a bit shook up, but he'll be fine. Now just rest."

Lily gratefully shut her eyes and drifted back into the murky blackness.

The sound of voices outside the door pulled her back yet again to the surface.

"She's got several broken ribs and quite a concussion, but Myrtle said she asked about the boy yesterday. That's a good sign. But I'm afraid she miscarried the baby," she heard the stranger's voice say. Must be the doctor, Lily thought.

"Baby?" Hank's voice sounded shocked.

"You didn't know she was with child?"

"Shoot fire, I didn't even know she was a woman."

Hank came into the room and Lily fought to open her eyes.

"No wonder I never could get a woman," he said with a gentle smile.

"What?"

"Well, you sure proved to me how little I know about 'em."

"I'm sorry," Lily whispered.

"Not your fault." His face grew dark with guilt. "I should have never come at that horse like that. How are you feeling?"

"Like I just got clobbered by a train. How long have I been out?"

"Three days. The doc says you're going to be fine, though you won't be bucking bales for a while. You've got several broken ribs. If I would have known you were a lady, I'd have never given you such a hard job in the first place."

"That's why I didn't tell you."

"He also said you lost your baby. I'm sorry, Donovan."

"It's probably for the best. I suspected for the last couple weeks, but deep down hoped it wasn't true."

"You don't have a man?"

"It's not what you think, Hank," Lily said icily.

"And none of my business anyway."

She could see the hurt in his eyes. "Where's Myrtle?"

"Putting Jimmy to bed."

"Would you tell her I would like to speak to her?"

Myrtle came into the room and Hank turned to go.

"No, please stay. You need to hear this, too. My name is Lily."

She told them the whole story, everything from the barn in Nauvoo to the poster in the telegraph office. When she had finished, she felt like a heavy load had just been lifted off her chest.

"So you see, Hank, I couldn't stay but I knew the gelding wasn't ready. The fault is mine, not yours."

"What are you going to do?"

She rubbed her bandaged ribs. "Well, I'm sure in no shape to work for you."

"You're welcome to stay on in the tack room."

"She will do no such thing," Myrtle said firmly. "She will stay right here until she's healed proper."

"Myrtle, I have exactly thirteen dollars in my pocket." She refused to use the money set aside for the boy for her own keep.

"Don't you worry about it. Bodeen wired and said to keep you right here."

"You told Bodeen?" Lily cried.

"Before he left for Fort Garland, Samuel told me to watch over you. Sooner or later, he said, that lady's bound to find herself in a rattlesnake nest. Then told me to wire him if you needed anything. He's on his way. Should be here by the end of the week."

"Lady, huh? So you have known all this time that I was a woman?"

"I would have known even if he hadn't told me. I suspected from the day you graced my doorstep. Remember that I gave you some lemon verbena talc? When you came down the stairs that night, you smelled mighty nice. Besides, anyone who can mother a child like you mother Jimmy has got to be a lady. And a fine one at that."

✢ ✢ ✢

Myrtle wrapped the bandage tightly around Lily's chest.

"I was hoping now that you know the truth I wouldn't have to bind my breasts anymore, what little of them I have." Lily started to laugh but felt sharp spikes of pain course their way throughout her midsection like bolts of lightning.

"Broke a few of my own ribs, once. Fell off my papa's hay wagon. Don't worry, the pain will subside in a couple of weeks," Myrtle said, helping Lily slip on her shirt. "So are you going back to wearing dresses?"

"Not a chance. Not with those posters up all over town," Lily said.

"Samuel says he's got a plan. Seems like that man always has a plan."

"He's here?" Lily asked, nervously fluffing her short curls.

"Waiting downstairs for you. He's got a lady with him. Or would you rather I send him up here?"

"No. I'll come down," Lily said, wondering with a bit of dismay about Samuel's lady friend. She stood up quickly and her head pounded unmercifully. Then everything went dark.

The first face she saw when she woke up was Samuel Bodeen's. He was sitting on the bed beside her.

"Hey, there, sleepyhead," he said kindly.

Then Lily saw the face of the lady standing behind him. She was very beautiful and looked vaguely familiar.

"Feel up to a visitor?" the woman asked.

"I must look quite a fright," Lily said, staring at the lady's fine dress.

"You look wonderful. Let me introduce myself. My name is Ann Eliza Young."

Lily sat up, her head becoming clearer. "You were on the train."

"That's right. Samuel told me your story. I think I may be able to help you. Now Mr. Bodeen, I would like a few minutes alone with Lily."

Ann began by telling Lily the story of how she had been raised in the Mormon faith. Her father had four wives and by the time she was twelve, Ann herself had received ten proposals of marriage by leading saints.

"When I was sixteen, Brigham Young began courting me. He was sixty-one. But I fell in love with someone else, married, and had two children. Unfortunately, my first husband was an abusive man and we were divorced. Brigham was thrilled with our break up and once again asked my parents for my hand. They heartily consented, considering it a great honor to receive such a fine offer from their religious leader, and besides, I was divorced. What other offer would I get? I did not love Brigham but he promised to provide security for my children. When I still refused he told me it was my duty. And so did my parents. I broke down and consented.

"We went to Utah, but instead of the Promised Land, I found

myself and the children in a small, shabby house. I received only the castoffs from the other wives. I was nineteenth, so there was little food and certainly not enough love to go around. Finally, the old wood stove fell apart and my children were freezing. That was the last straw."

She looked down into Lily's pale face. "So you see, I know what it is to be imprisoned by the Mormon way of thinking. Would you like to tell me about it?"

Lily looked deeply into the woman's eyes. They were firm and resolute, but also very understanding. Lily motioned her to sit down on the bed beside her.

She began by telling Ann how her father had promised her hand to Bertram Ellis.

"I was not raised in the Mormon faith like you were. When we moved from the South to Illinois, Papa was in a bad way. He had lost his leg in the war but more importantly, he had lost his pride. Pride in his way of life, pride in being able to provide for his family, pride in his country, and pride in himself. He became intrigued with the Church of Latter Day Saints. They did not like the United States Government any more than he did. He tried to get Mama to move to their promised land in Utah, but Mama would not budge, said she was finally home and planned on staying put."

"Did your father take any more wives?"

"No, without his leg he said he wasn't a man for any woman. Besides, my mama was a strong willed lady and would never have allowed it anyway. She also refused to go to church with Papa and this did not please the elders. He made me go with him though, saying it was my duty as a daughter to help her crippled father. Then when I was sixteen, he tried to get into their good graces by offering my hand in marriage to Bertram, the most influential elder in our church."

Ann Eliza poured a glass of water and handed it to Lily.

"Mama pitched a fit. So did my grandma; she was raised a

Quaker. It caused a terrible split in our house but Mama stood firm, saying that even the slaves were now free. She told my father in no uncertain terms that I would be free to marry any man that I chose, not an old man who already had three wives and was only looking to put another gem in his crown.

"Mama sent me away to Chicago. I went to school, got my teaching certificate and began teaching at a school for the blind. But Mama took sick and I had to return home to help Grandma take care of her."

Lily paused and took a drink. The water cooled the tightness in her throat.

"Then Harold Hanover began courting me. Just before Mama died, she made me promise that I would never allow the Mormons to belittle me into marrying Bertram or any man I did not love.

"After she passed on, the Mormons began putting pressure on Papa to get me to change my mind. But I loved Harold, or thought I did, and refused to buckle into my father's wishes. When Bertram found out about the engagement, he was furious. He waited until Joshua took Grandma into town for a Ladies Aid Society tea, and came to the barn."

Lily stopped.

"It's okay, honey. Just take your time."

"He told me he was going to make it so that Harold, or any other man, would never want me."

Lily clutched the blanket to her. "And he did. After it was over, he told me that now I would have no other choice. I now belonged to him."

Lily began sobbing and Ann hugged her close, letting Lily release the torment.

After the crying subsided, Lily continued. "I remembered Mama's words about how even the slaves were free. I was determined to belong to no one. Knowing the Mormon Danites would never let me leave, I escaped during the night."

"Your mother was right. And so were you. What you did was very courageous. I just wished I would have had your determination when I was your age."

"But I don't feel strong at all. I'm scared, Ann. They are so powerful. I sent an affidavit of what had happened to the attorney general of Illinois, but it only added fuel to the Mormon fire. Now they have charges against me, said I assaulted poor old Joshua and took all his money. I would never hurt him for anything in the world."

Ann handed Lily a handkerchief. "I am leaving in the morning for Washington to meet with some very influential men who are as disgusted with what the Mormons are doing as you and I are. And to be perfectly honest, your story may just be the leverage I need to get things moving in the right direction. But I will need your real name."

Lily hesitated.

"We all have to start trusting again sometime. It's not easy, I know that, especially after being betrayed by someone you thought you loved. But you can trust me."

Lily looked at Ann and knew the woman was right. "It's Lily. But my last name is Hastings. Donovan was my mother's maiden name."

Ann Eliza stood up to leave. "Okay. Best keep with Donovan until you hear back from me. Let me see what I can do. I will send you messages through Myrtle but in the meantime, listen to Bodeen. He has vowed to protect you. I think it would be wise to do what he says. Now get some rest and let yourself heal, not just your body, but your soul as well. I'll be praying for you."

That surprised Lily. "Even after what you have been through, you still trust God?"

"It's my faith that gave me the will to finally leave. And it's His guidance and strength that has given me this mission. Just because there are vile, wicked men, does not mean that all men are evil or that God is corrupt as well. This battle will take more than what you or I can do and I know that only He has the infinite power to provide justice. I am just his messenger. I don't condemn all Mormons because of one person's misguided beliefs, and I certainly don't condemn God."

"I prayed to God to take the baby. But now . . ." Lily's voice cracked as guilt ate at her insides like vile worms.

Ann took Lily's hand. "Don't try to fight your battles alone, Lily. Trust in Him and ask Him to help you. You will never come to peace with it otherwise."

4

"Why are you doing this?" Lily asked Bodeen, as he helped her into a chair on the porch.

"You have been cooped up in that tiny room for over a week. It's time you get some sun on those cheeks." He looked into the cloudless sky. "Nothing heals like sunshine."

Lily had to admit that it was wonderful to be outside again. The warm rays on her cheeks seemed to radiate deep into her soul. But she was fearful that someone passing by would recognize her.

It was as if Samuel read her mind. "Don't worry, Donovan. I went around town and took down any posters I could find."

"You don't have to call me that anymore, you know. And just how did you know what I was thinking?"

"The name fits you. And I know you a whole lot better than you think I do. I can read your face. When you are angry or fearful, you get a crease in the middle of your eyebrows and kind of cluck your teeth."

"I do not cluck my teeth! And you did not answer my question. Why are you taking care of me like this? Do I look like your long lost sister or something?"

He looked at her earnestly, and then smiled. "Let's just say I like a good challenge and leave it at that. You are definitely a challenge, Donovan. Besides, some day you are going to marry me."

"Marry you?" Lily was shocked.

"That's right," he said resolutely.

Lily was overwhelmed. She could never marry anyone. Even now, she could hear Bertram's vicious words just as if she were back in the barn.

"If that is what you are after, Samuel, you had better just leave now," she said firmly.

"Am I that bad? Oh yes, I forgot. I am a . . . what was the word you used?"

"Scoundrel."

"Yes, a scoundrel," he said, as if liking the word.

"It's not you, it's me. I take it Myrtle didn't tell you everything."

"She did."

"So you know why I can never marry. I am, as you put it when you described Mattie's girls on the train, a soiled dove. I am no longer fit to become anyone's wife and have to accept that fact, just as they have."

Bodeen's face grew tense with anger. "And just who gave you the power to judge?"

"What?" Lily was shocked at his sudden animosity.

"Look, 'Miss High and Mighty,' do you think that any one of those girls on the train made it their lifelong goal to be where they are now? Do you think they said as a child that when they grew up they wanted to be a whore, to be used in the most vile way a woman can be used? I doubt it. No, I know it. They aren't there because they want to be, but because they felt they didn't have a choice. And to be quite honest, many of them didn't, for whatever reason it might have been. Maybe they had hungry brothers and sisters to feed, or worse yet, maybe they didn't have anyone at all."

He glared at her.

"But you do. It's one thing to judge others unfairly. It's even worse to let others judge you. But to judge yourself in that way, Lily, that's the biggest sin of all. It's like you are thumbing your nose at the magnificence the Good Lord has made."

He looked west to the Rocky Mountains. "You know, some people look at those mountains and see their splendor. They treasure them for it but lack the tenacity to make their dreams come true of being able to live in the middle of all that wonder. And some look with greed at what they can get out of the mountains, and treasure them in a very different way, but lack the foresight not to destroy their beauty in the quest for the riches the mountains have buried inside of them. And some see only the hard times. They turn tail and run when the going gets tough: the rocky roads, the back-breaking labor and lack of luxuries one has to live with in order make their dreams real."

Samuel stood up and looked hard at Lily. "And then there's me. I see the beauty, both on the surface and inside, but also the hard work it will take to make a dream come true. I don't retreat just because there are challenges that will have to be met. I have the faith to know the hard work will all be worth it one day."

He turned to go. "And I think you are more like me than you are willing to admit. Look me up when you get done with celebrating at your pity party. Just don't wait too long, Lily. I am not a patient person."

As she watched Samuel march down the street, she realized it was the first time he had ever called her by her real name.

Lily went back inside the boarding house and grabbed a knife to help Myrtle peel potatoes.

"He's a good man, Lily," the woman said.

"I take it you heard?"

"The door was open. He's right you know."

"Why does he always have to be right? How long have you known Samuel?"

"Going on ten, no, eleven years. My husband served as a Union soldier. During the Civil War, Union troops were stationed in the Colorado Territory at Fort Garland. My husband, being an officer, was allowed to bring along his family. In 1865 he died of a rattlesnake bite and I found myself alone and with a son to feed. Several days later, Kit Carson was commissioned to take over as commander of the fort and offered me a job as a laundress. I never want to see another dirty cavalry uniform as long as I live."

Myrtle stood up and put a pot of water on the stove.

"Bodeen was just a young second lieutenant then. He took a real liking to my boy, kind of like he has done with Jimmy. When Carson gave his resignation in 1867, Samuel told me it was time for me to go, too. He knew that sooner or later things were only going to get worse with the Indians in the West."

She rose and put the potatoes in the water.

"I would not have this place if it weren't for Colonel Bodeen. He gave me the two hundred dollars it took for a down payment and then convinced the banker to loan me the rest."

"I didn't know he was a colonel. He never said."

"You didn't notice the three stars on his uniform? He's not much for tooting his own bugle but let me tell you, there is no officer in the cavalry more respected than Colonel Samuel Bodeen."

"Does he have a family?"

"A sister, I think. But to be honest, I really don't know for sure. That is something he refuses to talk about."

Lily anxiously waited for Samuel to return. When he didn't show up for supper, she became concerned. Maybe he had changed his mind and decided she was right, she thought, as she waited up. Finally at eleven o'clock she went to bed.

The next morning she found a pile of clothes outside her door. A note was laid on top of a black coat. The words looked as if they had been hastily written: *Important matters to attend to. Can't stay. Ticket on the D&RG is waiting for you at the train depot. Leave at once. Don't take the boy, it's too dangerous. I love you, Lily Donovan. S.B.*

"Do what he says, Lily," Myrtle said after reading the note.

"I'm just supposed to up and leave without knowing anything? What about Jimmy?"

"Hank and I will see to the boy. I would trust Samuel Bodeen with my life, and you would be wise to do the same."

"But I don't even know where I will be going. And am I supposed to wear that?" She asked, pointing to the cavalry uniform.

"There is a leather valise in the closet under the stairs."

Myrtle helped Lily dress. First, the gray undershirt, then the plain black frock coat with a row of nine buttons closing the single-breasted front. It had a standing collar, but was without the epaulettes or shoulder straps she had noticed on Bodeen's coat. The pants were black as well, without the yellow stripe down the side that was on other cavalry issued pants. The hat was shaped in the wide-brimmed Kossuth style Samuel wore, but instead of the brass crossed swords that were on the front of Bodeen's hat, this one had a brass eagle, surmounted by the words United States Army.

Myrtle fingered the black velvet insignia on the sleeve of the coat. The patch contained the figure of a shepherd's stick embroidered in gold. "You, my dear, are now an official United States Cavalry Chaplain."

"Chaplain?"

"He's a smart man. No one would dare question or meddle with an Army chaplain. Your journey will be a safe one. Do you have a Bible?"

"No."

"Every chaplain needs a Holy Bible."

Myrtle opened the drawer of the bureau by the bed and handed Lily the book. "Remember that we will be praying for you."

✝ ✝ ✝

"Donovan, you say?" The agent at the ticket office asked.

"Yes."

"Well, Chaplain Donovan, I do recall there being something here. Ah, yes, this is it. The train leaves in a couple hours."

Lily looked at the ticket. It read 'Pueblo, Colorado Territory.'

What was he doing? Where in the world was Pueblo? She sat on the wooden bench and watched emigrants disembarking from the train she had come to Denver on just weeks ago. Many did not speak English and were dressed in strange costumes. As she watched the children outside the depot begging to carry their luggage for a dime, she could not help but think of Jimmy.

"Watch over him, Lord," she whispered. "And thank you for Hank and Myrtle." Once again, as she had with Joshua, she wondered how she could ever repay them.

About the time the train was pulling out of Denver, two men knocked on the door of the boarding house.

"I'm sorry, we are full up." Myrtle said through the screen door.

"Not looking for a room." The taller of the two held up a poster. "Ever seen her before? Name is Hastings."

"Hastings? No, I can't say that I know anyone by that name." She looked back at the boy who was busy reading at the kitchen table. "Jimmy, do you recall anyone here in the last couple weeks by the name of Hastings?"

"Nope," he said honestly, his eyes still glued in a McGuffey's reader. "But you know what? It starts with 'H', just like Hank, and just like Henry. Isn't that right, Ma'am?" he asked Myrtle.

She smiled sweetly. "You are such a smart boy, Jimmy. Now gentleman, is there anything else? If you will excuse me, I have hungry boarders to feed."

"Mind if we come in and have a look around?"

"Not at all but take off your boots. Jimmy just swept."

The two men looked at each other, then at the boy, then down at their lace-up boots. "Never mind. Seems we were misinformed."

Myrtle shut the door and turned back to crimping piecrusts. Right again, Samuel, she said to herself, with a hint of a smile.

The agent at the train depot was no help either.

"The only passengers who boarded the noon Denver and Rio

Grande were men. Several burly looking miners and . . . well, there was a man who looked something like her. Had the same color hair anyway but it was short and curly. The gentleman was an army chaplain. Sat for two hours reading his Bible until the train pulled out. Even heard him whisper a prayer or two. His ticket was purchased yesterday by a colonel."

The two men looked frustrated.

"Sorry I couldn't be of more help."

As the two men left, one turned and said to the other, "You gave the lady at Silk's place one hundred dollars for this? Next time I suggest you find an informant who is more reliable."

✠ ✠ ✠

Lily got her first close-up glimpse of the magnificent Rockies. They loomed like a fortress west of the railway line. The train did not go directly into the mountains but seemed to ride the bottom rim, winding through interesting rock formations graced with stragglylooking pine and cedar. The day was hot and she felt like she was being baked in an oven, clad in the black flannel coat.

The afternoon passed quickly and the conductor announced they would arrive in Pueblo by supper time.

As she stepped off the train, David Wood was waiting for her.

"So we meet again, Donovan," he said, blue eyes twinkling.

"How did you know? No, let me guess. Samuel."

"Yes, I received a wire this morning that said he was sending a good hand my way. But pardon me, I didn't realize you were an army chaplain."

Lily did not know what to say. So she said nothing. And David Wood, always the gentleman, said nothing more about it as well.

"Let's get you settled in and then have some dinner. I have a proposition for you," Wood said as he led her down the street to a local hotel. He introduced Lily to the proprietor, Walt Wilson.

"My wife is in the kitchen," Walt said. "Should be out in a few minutes. Please, have a seat. Would you like a cup of coffee? Or perhaps a tall glass of water? The train is mighty hot and dusty this time of year."

Lily gratefully took the glass of water. She hastily downed a glass and then poured another from the pitcher Walt had left on the table. She noticed the small restaurant in the hotel was spotless. Heavily-starched yellow and white gingham curtains gave the place a cheery look and bright sunflowers graced all the tables.

David told Lily of his proposition.

"When I got my horses here to Pueblo, a livery and sales stable on the south side of town said they could sell them at once. So I turned the animals over to be sold on commission. I instructed the owner on which to sell and which to hold. I had planned on using the sturdiest to haul the supplies over the mountains, along with some mules I bought in Denver.

"Taking a team and hack, I started for Lake City, a town high in the mountains on the western side of the Continental Divide. It is brimming with miners in desperate need of supplies. My father, mother and sister are already there. After looking over the situation and getting a list of supplies the miners needed most, I returned to Pueblo only to find that the livery stable owner had sold his own horses and was using mine for livery work. He held a bill of $300 against the animals for feed and board."

Wood paused and swallowed a drink of coffee.

"In short, I have been swindled."

"I'm sorry, David," Lily said.

"Minor inconvenience, though I have to admit it was a hard blow. The livery seems to be prospering quite well while I am barely making ends meet."

A slight, fair-haired woman brought plates in from the kitchen piled with fried chicken and mashed potatoes.

"This is Walt's wife, Patricia. She and Walt have been my port in this storm. The good people graciously gave me $300 to start a livery business of my own," he said gratefully, speaking more to the woman serving him than to Lily.

"We were not using it," Patricia said, smiling. "Besides, Walt and I want to see you run that shark clean out of Pueblo. We don't need his kind here. Looks like you could use a few more rolls." She went back to the kitchen.

"And so you see, I am in desperate need of a good hand. Just as soon as I make enough to pay back the Wilsons and pay my debt with the other livery, I will be taking a load to Lake City. Are you interested, Donovan?"

"I have no money, David," Lily said. She did not even ask the price of the room at the hotel. "Is there a place at the livery I could set up as living quarters?"

"Not that I could ask you to stay in. Besides, I already talked it over with the Wilsons before I met you at the train. They will add your room and board to my bill as part of your salary. But please know up front, I can't pay you anything until that first load is safely over the mountains."

"Yes, then I am very interested."

"Bodeen said you would be."

Lily wondered whether Samuel had told Wood that she was a woman. David did not mention the fact. She figured if Bodeen trusted Wood, she would have to do the same.

"Mr. Wood, there is something you should know."

"You are a good hand, Donovan. That is all I need to know. I will be by tomorrow morning and take you down to the livery."

As Lily unwrapped her still sore ribs, she wondered if her body would be up to the hard work she had done at Hank's. It would just have to be. She didn't see any other choice.

David did not say anything the next morning when he saw that she had dressed not in the cavalry uniform, but in jeans and a muslin shirt. As they walked down the street toward the livery, she noticed that Pueblo was a thriving community. The people were well housed, building their homes of lumber, brick and stone. Even in the early morning, the streets were bustling with commerce.

They passed the First National Bank and David said, "It's run by the Thatcher brothers, Mahlon and John. They arrived from the East with several ox teams a year or two ago, unloaded their flour and teams and started the bank. Everyone calls it the Thatcher Brothers Bank. They are progressive men and before long they will build Pueblo into quite a city.

"They are also shrewd businessmen. When I asked them for a loan for the supplies, they said they would be glad to accommodate me, but I would have to pay off my other debts first. They were testing me. That was smart. There are many ruthless, lazy characters in the territory looking to make a fast dollar without earning it. I am determined to earn the brothers trust."

The livery was small but extremely busy. Lily had to learn fast that training mules was much tougher than training horses. By the end of the day the pain in her side was excruciating. She looked at the bale of hay she needed to throw to the mules in the corral and hesitated.

David walked over to her. "You have done quite enough for one day, Donovan. Here, let me get that." He hoisted the bale easily over the fence. For a small-built man he was as tough as nails.

"Why don't you head on over to the hotel and grab a bite to eat. I'll finish up here."

"But . . ."

"Don't worry, I can finish up," Wood said.

Lily didn't have the strength to argue.

July 4th, 1876

The town was packed with citizens watching the Centennial parade. In the midst of the festivities a bundle of newspapers showed up by train. As the news was quickly passed from one to another a strange hush quickly fell over Pueblo and the celebration was over.

Lily had chosen to rest in her room, thankful that Wood had decided to close the livery for the holiday. He knocked gently on the door.

"What's wrong, David?" The man looked like he had just lost his best friend. He came into the room and handed her the copy of the *Rocky Mountain News*. The headline read, "Custer and the Seventh Cavalry Annihilated at Little Big Horn!"

Her hands trembled as she read the article:

> On June 25th, General George Armstrong Custer and the Seventh Cavalry met with the largest gathering of Indians ever assembled in North America. Companies commanded by Major Marcus Reno and Captain Frederick Benteen were also involved in the attack. Tribes from the Cheyenne, Sans Arcs, Miniconjoux Sioux, Oglala Sioux, Blackfeet and Hunkpapa Sioux, overwhelmed the regiments on the south side of Rosebud Creek near the Powder River.
>
> It is noted that General Crook had unexpectedly encountered a band of 1,500 Sioux five days earlier. He had lost nine men in the skirmish and had been forced to retreat and regroup at Goose Creek. His warning to Custer had either been unheeded, or had not arrived in time.
>
> No exact count of the number of soldiers who died is possible at this time as many of the bodies were dismembered or dragged away by the savages. Estimates are between 220 to 265.

The article then stated that a United States Army column under General Terry and Colonel Samuel Bodeen discovered Custer and his men two days later. An editorial column went on to warn Colorado citizens of the dangerous Utes.

"Have you heard anything from Bodeen?" Lily asked as she turned her back to Wood and stared out the window.

"Not since he left Denver," he said, handing Lily a bandanna from his back pocket. She wiped her eyes but the tears would not stop coming. "Let's just pray that he is okay."

But Bodeen was not. It had taken his regiment over a week to bury the bodies. He alone had dug the hole for what was left of the mutilated body of Isaiah Dorman, allowing no one to help him.

And when his job at the Little Bighorn was finished, he returned to his quarters at Fort Lincoln and locked the door. He cursed himself for not being there. He cursed Custer and his frivolous stupidity. He cursed God. He cursed everyone he could think of until the bottle was gone.

The next day when he was sober enough to walk, Colonel Samuel Bodeen marched into headquarters at Fort Lincoln and handed General Sheridan his resignation.

✣ ✣ ✣

Lily was shoveling manure out of a stall in the barn when she saw the man enter.

"Can I help you?" The man tilted back his cowboy hat and she recognized him.

"Bodeen?" It was the first time she had seen him in civilian clothes. He looked as if he had aged ten years.

He did not say anything but held out his arms. She dropped the shovel and ran to him. He held her hard and she gasped with pain. Quickly he let her go.

"God, I'm sorry. I forgot about your ribs."

She smiled and pulled his arms back around her. "Don't let go, Samuel. And the answer is yes."

"You mean I made up my speech for nothing? I practiced it all the way from Denver."

"I want the biggest steak you've got in there," Bodeen said to Patricia, looking toward the kitchen in the hotel. "I'm so hungry I could eat a bear and have room left over. Getting hitched sure works up an appetite!"

Patricia returned with large platters of steak and fried potatoes for Bodeen and Wood. Lily had opted for a bowl of soup. Her stomach still quivered from the nervousness she had felt during the ceremony.

"Now, David, how much did you say you would need?" Samuel asked. He cut a piece of steak and savored its tenderness.

"Well, to do it up right, it's going to take over a thousand dollars," Wood said.

"Consider it done. I'll have it wired tomorrow morning. Get the lawyer to draw up the contract."

"It's a lot of money, Bodeen."

"Yes, that it is. But if our plan works, I'll make twice that much back."

The men discussed the details of their contract over several strong cups of Arbuckle's coffee. Both satisfied with the agreement, Wood said he would leave in the morning to acquire the necessary wagons and supplies in Denver.

"Do you need my help?" Samuel asked.

"No. Anyway, it looks as though you will have your hands full right here." Wood grinned at Lily.

"Sounds good, David. As soon as we get those supplies to the miners in Lake City there will be enough profit to get some good stock to start my herd, and a little left to get Lily here some proper attire."

The men shook hands and Wood rose to go to the lawyer's office to have the papers drawn up.

Samuel looked at Lily and smiled. "Don't think that I didn't mean you don't look quite fine in what you are wearing," he said, staring at the flowered gingham dress Lily had borrowed from Patricia for the wedding. "Still, it would be interesting to see you in a bus-tle," he laughed.

"Don't even dream it, Bodeen. Now that I know how comfort-able you men have been all these years, I doubt you will ever seen me in one of those again. Besides, do you want a wife who will help with the cattle or one to just sit on a shelf and look pretty?" She thought of the shopping trip she and Chipeta had taken in Denver, and her friend's comment about feeding goats clad in organdy and lace.

"Both. But if I have to choose, I guess it would have to be the first," he said, then added, "Actually, I don't really care what you wear, just as long as you're beside me. Come to think of it, I would be happy if you didn't wear anything at all." He took her left hand and kissed the gold band.

"You really are a scoundrel, you know that?" Lily said, looking at the ring. "It was a nice ceremony, don't you think?"

"The best. Short and sweet."

"How long do you think it will take to get everything together?"

"About a week. Think you will be ready to ride by then?"

"I'm ready now."

"They still hurt, don't they?" Samuel asked softly.

"Only when I breathe."

He turned serious. "I don't know what I would have done if I would have lost you, Donovan."

"It's Bodeen. Have you already forgotten?"

"Not for a minute."

✠ ✠ ✠

Samuel shut the door to their hotel room and sat down in the chair to take off his boots. Lily looked at the bed and was suddenly terrified.

"You're clucking your teeth again."

"I am not."

Samuel rose from the chair, took her in his arms and tenderly kissed her hair.

"I lied to you, Lily."

She pulled away and looked at him.

"Remember when we were on the porch in Denver?"

"Yes."

"I told you then that I am not a patient man." Samuel turned away from her and removed his shirt. She looked at the strong muscles in his back.

He unzipped, and then removed his pants. Lily looked away. She took a deep breath, trying to calm her trembling nerves.

"But I am. Look at me, Lily."

Lily slowly turned around. Samuel was in bed, the blanket covering everything below his chest.

"I promise you, Lily, I will never ask you to do anything you are not agreeable to. You just let me know when you're ready."

Samuel watched as Lily slowly unbuttoned the dress. She slid it off and laid it over the chair. But she could not bring herself to take off the chemise slip.

Samuel lifted the covers and she slid in beside him. He kissed her gently on the forehead.

. "I love you, Lily," he said, before he rolled over.

She could feel his warm body next to hers but instead of fear, she only felt tenderness.

"No, Samuel, please don't turn away. I want to look at your face."

He turned back to her and studied her eyes, as if trying to understand the deep, wonderful mystery inside them. "You could have knocked me over with a feather when you said yes. Why Lily?"

She told him about the letters, not just those written by Andrew and Kathleen McCluskey, but of the letters she had written to him during the days she had waited to hear whether he was alive or dead. She had known what Kathleen must have felt, the deep bond and the longing.

She studied the black hair streaked with gray along the temples. She followed the wrinkles on his tan face gently with her fingers and tenderly kissed the cleft in his strong chin. And finally she looked in his soft but troubled eyes. She wanted to kiss away their pain. And wanted him to kiss away hers. She had become one with Samuel Bodeen long before he had placed a ring on her finger to prove it.

The next morning the chemise was on the floor by the bed. As Lily lay in Samuel's arms, she knew it was as God had intended it to be, this love and desire shared so intimately by a man and a woman. For the first time in her life she felt whole and warm and complete. It was a miracle unequaled to anything else the Lord had created, this bringing of two separate souls together into one. It was taller than the mountains, higher than the stars in the heavens, and brighter than the golden light from the morning sun that was beginning to stream through the window.

"Thank you, Lord," she whispered.

"What?" Samuel stirred beside her.

"Nothing. I love you, Samuel Bodeen."

He gave her one of his boyish grins as she leaned over and kissed him again.

✚ ✚ ✚

"Tell me your speech," Lily teased, pulling on her denim jeans.

"What?"

"You said you practiced it all the way from Denver."

"Oh, that." Samuel's mood quickly turned somber. "Let's not spoil the day. Just forget it."

"Was it that bad?"

"Yes. No. The speech? I don't know. Lily, don't ask me about it. Deal?"

He turned and looked out the window. The town was alive with the business of the day. People were hurrying down the street as if there were no tomorrow.

"Samuel, I learned to trust you. Please, remember you can do the same. If you ever need to talk. . ."

"They don't realize," he said, his voice sounding far away.

"Realize what?"

"How very precious life is. That's what I was going to tell you. That life is so very short and we have to grab every moment, not waste a mere second of it. We have to look to the future. To live in the past is slow suicide."

He turned and looked at her, his eyes haunted by the atrocity of what he had seen.

"Isaiah didn't make it, did he?" Lily said gently.

"I was too late. That damned Custer didn't listen to anybody. His quest for immortality killed all his men and now they want to make him some kind of damned hero."

"I'm sorry, Samuel."

"Don't pity me, Lily. I detest pity," he said angrily. "I should have been there for him."

"It takes a strong man to show his own weakness. It's admiration, not pity."

She took his hand. "Any more than you pitied me when you found out about what had happened that night in the barn. You didn't let me judge myself for someone else's mistake. Heed your own words, Samuel. It's not your fault."

As Lily took Samuel in her arms, she didn't think she could possibly love this man more than she did last night.

But she was wrong.

August 1st, 1876

5

et's roll 'em!" David yelled. The six wagons moved out of Pueblo on the same day that President Ulysses S. Grant signed the proclamation admitting Colorado as the thirty-eighth state. The wagons were new, costing $150 each. They were heavily loaded with a wide assortment of supplies: pieces of machinery, shovels and picks, iron bars, building materials, tin cups and frying pans, household items, flour, sugar, coffee and canned goods. The last wagon's contents made Lily a bit nervous. It contained blasting powder. Samuel and David had harnessed only the most reliable animals to it. There were ten mules harnessed to each of the heavier wagons that contained the machinery. Sturdy horses were hitched to the lighter wagons that contained the dry goods and household items.

Lily was riding Henry, her wedding present from Hank O'Rourke. He had the horse shipped to Pueblo on the train after Lily had written Myrtle about her marriage to Samuel. Lily had spent the last week preparing the animal and he seemed up to the journey. He had even stood relatively still when the farrier put shoes on him, as if eager for the trip ahead.

As Lily rode alongside the wagons she thought about the letter she had received yesterday from Myrtle. The boy was doing well though there still had been no word from his grandparents. Hank had posted another telegram to Henry McCluskey in Paradise, Kansas, but they had heard nothing back from him, either. To Lily's dismay, there had also been no word from Ann Eliza Young. Lily wondered if there would be another wedding in the near future. The rest of the letter had been all about Hank.

The first day proved to be an easy ride. The dirt road was wide and soft. Anxious fortune seekers passed by them in droves on their way to the mining country. The rush was on to the San Juan Basin, comprising Lake City, Ouray, and Silverton.

Henry proved to be a sure-footed mount. He took to the ride willingly as if he was as impressed with the country as she was. He looked curiously at the wildlife that was so abundant in the foothills, perking up his ears with every new noise on the trail. Deer and elk herds grazed in the high meadows and birds of many species looked down at the pack train through the trees. Once the horse jumped sideways when a pheasant flew up from a clump of oak brush, but Lily quickly regained control.

"Easy, boy," she said, patting his neck. Her steady hand reassured the horse.

David had a well-planned routine for the train. They started early in the day. The animals were hitched and ready as the sun began to peak over the eastern horizon. They pushed hard until around noon, when the hot August sun began to tire the animals. They then watered, fed the animals a ration of grain, and turned them out in a grassy pasture for two hours rest. Then they hitched the animals back up again and pushed hard until dark. David had scouted the country on his way to and from Lake City and had picked out the best places to stop, those with abundant water and grass.

On the evening of the second day, they made camp on the banks of the Arkansas River. As Lily got down off her horse, Samuel asked, "Are you doing okay?"

"Just fine," she said. "I really don't know what all the fuss is about. The road is quite passable in my estimation."

Samuel pointed to the western horizon where ominous peaks loomed in the distance. "Just be sure to cinch Henry up tight tomorrow. You'll soon see what these mountains really have in store. We made good time these past couple days, about twenty-two miles a day. The going will be slower from now on."

As they crossed over Cochetopa Pass, Lily got her first taste of what the Rocky Mountains were actually all about. Huge pine and aspen trees towered up to the sky. The air was pure, crystalline, the sky a deep, vivid blue. Surely it was the same sky as she saw back in Illinois, she thought, but somehow the blue looked more vibrant, and the clouds looked like puffs of cotton.

The road narrowed and quickly turned rocky and steep. The pack animals became belligerent and fidgety as if anticipating what was up ahead. David halted the train and instructed the mule skinners to grease the wheels and tighten the reins.

It took all day to reach the Continental Divide. Lily was astounded at the vastness of the mountains and the incredible beauty, but she felt like a child when she asked Wood, "How much farther?" The hard ride was reminding her of muscles she never knew she had.

"Four more days if the weather holds. Just pray it doesn't rain when we come down off Slumgullion Hill."

As Lily crawled into her bedroll that evening, she told Samuel, "Do you know how much I would give right now for a hot bath and Myrtle's soft bed?"

He kissed her goodnight and said, "Is that your way of complaining? You've been a real trooper, Lily, as good as the best soldiers in the cavalry. I'm proud of you. As soon as we get to Lake City I will personally see you get anything you want."

"Anything?" She said teasingly as she watched him crawl in the bedroll beside her. She missed his warm body next to hers. Far off on a distant hillside she could hear the calling of a wolf to its mate. She snuggled in close and listened to a hoot owl instead.

✦ ✦ ✦

Slumgullion Hill was a toll road built by Otto Mears, and had been shamefully misnamed. It was no "hill" at all. The long route wound down around the side of the biggest mountain Lily had ever seen. David told her it had been so named because it had been nothing but slumgullion until Mears had corduroyed it. Going up the backside of the mountain had been hard enough but coming down the other side made Lily's hair stand on end. The wagons bumped precariously as they coursed their way down the jarring, steep side. Just before getting to a circling hairpin turn, David instructed his men to lash a downed tree to the rear wagon containing the blasting powder.

"Take it slow and easy," he told the driver. "There's enough powder to blow us to eternity." The mules, as well as the driver, were played out when they finally reached the bottom.

Everyone on the wagon train sighed with relief. They rested the animals and gave them water and a large ration of grain.

At a small trading post called Branum the road branched. One fork went to Lake City and the other to Ouray, the town named after the Chief of the Utes. Samuel rode up beside her. "Next spring we'll take this other fork. Our place is about fifty miles southwest of here."

"So the deed was good?"

"Good as gold. The boundary lies on the border of the reservation set up by the Brunot Treaty three years ago.

"That's wonderful!"

Samuel looked at her seriously. "I'm afraid you may find that many Utes will not think so, Lily. I'm afraid there are those not near as cordial as Ouray and Chipeta."

"So I will have to wait until spring to see my new home?"

"I'm afraid so. Not knowing what is there, I would be foolish to take you now. We sure can't live in a tent in these mountains all winter, and with autumn just around the corner, I don't think there would be time to build you a proper house. The prospector had said he built a small cabin on the place, but there's no telling what kind of shape it's in. David said snow can start falling as early as the middle of September and also advised that before I bring cattle to this country, I will have to build some good solid fences to keep the Utes from taking off with them."

"But we are so close, Samuel. Couldn't we at least check it out before we head back to Pueblo?"

"I thought you would be tired of riding by now. That would mean an extra three or four days of hard travel. Are you sure you are up to it?"

"Absolutely," she said, ignoring the pain in her ribs.

"I could go and check things out while you spend a few days in Lake City resting up," he offered.

"Not a chance. What's a few more miles. I don't want to spend the winter wondering what we will be up against. I would rather spend it planning and dreaming of our home. I'm as anxious to see it as you are."

"Well, all right then," he said with a grin, once again thankful for the woman he had married.

It was a slow, arduous climb from the fork up to Lake City, but it had been just as David had said, seven days altogether. There were at least two hundred tents and cabins set up, and very little commerce to accommodate the needs of the miners. It only took an afternoon to sell all the goods on the wagons. David gave Samuel his share of the profits and offered to take them to his parents' house for dinner.

"Thank you for the invitation, David. But I think what Lily would like is a good hot bath and a soft bed," Samuel said as he watched Lily climb painfully down off her horse. He then told David of their plans to leave early in the morning to scout out their place.

"No sense in making your way back to Lake City. I'll meet you at Branum's Fork in four days. There's a good place down on the north edge of town called Izzie's. She serves up a great elk stew and her beds are the softest in town," Wood said.

Samuel and Lily could smell the homemade bread before they entered the small inn. The clerk led them to a room that was small, but comfortable. There was no bathtub, so Lily made do with a washtub and soft, white towel. It was heavenly to feel clean again.

The stew was warm and filling. As Lily slathered butter and wild honey on a thick slice of hot bread, she noticed a black woman watching her from the kitchen doorway.

When the apple pie was brought out, Lily looked up and saw the woman looking at her again with a puzzled look on her face. The woman ducked behind the door when she saw Lily looking back at her.

"Who is the lady in the kitchen?" Lily asked the Mexican woman serving the pie.

"That would be Izzie. She runs the place. "She's got the biggest heart in all the Rocky Mountains. Took me in when I had no place else to go."

"Give her my compliments," Samuel said. "This is the finest apple pie I have ever tasted."

"You better not let Myrtle hear you say that," Lily whispered. "Isn't that what you told her?"

Izzie came out of the kitchen with another piece of pie.

"Carmen told me I have another satisfied customer. Thought you might be interested in this last piece," she said to Samuel. "Name's Izzie Royce. If there is anything you need please let me know." Once again she look oddly at Lily.

"Samuel Bodeen," he said. "And this is my wife."

That face, Lily thought. She tried to remember where she had seen the woman before.

"Have we met?" Lily asked.

"No, I don't think so. But you do remind me of someone I knew a long time ago. It was nice to meet you both."

Izzie turned and hurried back to the kitchen.

"See? Works every time," Samuel said with a wink, and then took a big bite of the second piece of pie.

✤ ✤ ✤

The next morning they went to the livery where Samuel purchased a couple of sturdy-looking geldings, having decided to rest their own animals for the trip back to Pueblo.

David was waiting for them and agreed to bring their horses down to Branum's Fork with him. "Good idea, Samuel. That ride took a real toll on Lily's horse." He waited until she had gone to the barn to check on Henry before he told Samuel the news.

"My father said last night that the Utes have been acting up again. You might want to rethink your decision. You two will be like sitting ducks in the middle of a pond."

"I don't think I can talk her out of it. She's as anxious to see the place as a mama with a new baby."

"There's an alternate route, a pass that will take you through the mountains and drop you right into the town of Ouray." He drew Samuel a map. "It's a hard ride but you might have less chance of running into any bucks that way. You will still need to watch your backside."

Samuel took the map and told David he would give it a try.

"If you don't meet me at Branum's Fork, I'll come looking. Have a safe trip," Wood said.

Samuel and Lily started up the route that paralleled Henson Creek, then began ascending the precipitous Engineer Pass. rocky pass. Uncompahgre Peak loomed high into the clouds to the north.

They climbed up and out of the dense forest, reaching a point where there was no vegetation at all. Samuel explained to Lily that they were at timberline. The air was so thin that even sturdy pines could not exist. They stopped every half hour to rest the horses, but still the animal's sides heaved under the strain of the climb and thin air. Finally, they could feel themselves descending and just as quickly as the vegetation had refused to grow, it came back. Tiny yellow flowers popped out of crags in the rock, and Lily was amazed at their hardiness.

The aroma of the air was intoxicating and the view breathtaking. Lily could see that Samuel was as impressed with the country as she was. The mountains peaks were mysterious and awesome and Lily's heart raced with every new turn. They passed a herd of strange-looking creatures that Samuel said were Rocky Mountain bighorn sheep. Two large rams with thick curled horns fought for their rights to the ewes. The sound of their horns hammering together echoed like the blast of cannons. They saw deer and elk in abundance, and Samuel pointed to a tree that had been marked by a bear.

In the late afternoon they set up camp by a small stream. Lily unsaddled the horses and Samuel hobbled them. The meadow grass was belly high to the animals and they ate heartily after the long, difficult trek.

It only took Samuel a few minutes to catch a number of small trout that he called 'brookies.' He rolled them in cornmeal and then fried them in hot bacon grease.

"Now this is the life," he said, looking completely satisfied as he turned the fish in the pan. "What more could a man ask for?" For dessert they feasted on wild raspberries Lily had picked in a shady glen while Samuel was fishing. They ate until their appetites were saturated with the taste of the wild freshness of the country.

Lily had never seen stars as bright, glittering like God had tossed handfuls of diamonds across the vast sky. They were so close she thought she could reach out and touch them. Even in the large, infinite wilderness, with the threat of bear and mountain lions lurking in the dark timber, she felt safe with Samuel. She watched him pour another cup of coffee from the pot on the fire.

"Samuel, what are you thinking about?"

"Have you ever had a dream, Lily? I mean, one that comes back over and over, not just when you're asleep, but wide awake?"

"No, not really."

"I have fantasized of a place like this. When I was out on the plains, so hot that I couldn't sleep, I would lay awake and dream of this. The reality is even more amazing than the dream ever was. I don't know when I've ever been this happy. Should have quit the cavalry a long time ago."

"But maybe you would not appreciate it as much as you do now."

"And I wouldn't have you. Sure, it's nice to dream alone, but when you have someone to share it with, that makes it all the more special. You're an amazing lady, Donovan."

"You mean Bodeen."

"Yes. But to me, you will always be Donovan, that strange illusion I first saw on the train in that ridiculous hat. I loved you from that first moment I saw you, clucking your teeth as you wondered how to shake my hand."

They sat drinking coffee as they looked up at the brilliant heavens, each immersed in separate thoughts, but still connected.

Finally Samuel broke the comfortable silence. "I don't know what we are going to find tomorrow. For all I know, the place will be a living nightmare. Promise me something, Lily. If it gets to be too much, don't cover it up. I've seen even the best and strongest of women buckle under to what the pioneer life brings. Once when I was in Wyoming I came upon a woman alone on the prairie. She was covered in blood. She had gone plum crazy and killed her own baby. She kept asking me to stop the wind. But I couldn't."

The night air turned cool and Samuel put another log on the fire. Golden embers shot up into the velvet black sky.

"I love this land already, Samuel. There's a passage in the Bible that says something like, 'I will look up to the mountains from whence comest my help.' There is a godliness to this country. Everywhere I looked today, I saw his majestic wonder. And though I feel so small in such a vast, untamed country, I have never felt more alive and more courageous than I do right now."

"Don't kid yourself, Mrs. Bodeen. It won't always be that way. We still have a long road ahead of us. And I'm afraid that this is about as close as we'll get to a honeymoon for a good long time."

"Then lead on, Mr. Bodeen," Lily said as she leaned over to kiss him.

They got an early start and by mid-morning they dropped down into the town of Ouray, a settlement in the midst of growing pains. Structures were being hastily assembled to accommodate the growth. Samuel went to the land office and asked for directions to his land.

"Fine piece of land you got there, mister. Head north following the Uncompahgre River about ten miles. Then head west, across the river about four more miles until you come to Dallas Creek. Your place starts on the other side of it."

The road sloped gently downward out of the San Juan Mountains. The trees around Ouray had been aspen and pine. The trees changed, not towering like the large pines in the mountains, smaller but still with pinecones.

"Piñon," Samuel said. "The Indians put blankets under the trees in the fall and then shake them. The nuts are quite tasty. And that scrub oak over there will make good firewood. It burns long and hot. But it's hard as nails so it is a real tough wood to cut."

When they reached the draw and headed west, it took only a few minutes to reach the river. The water was low and they crossed over easily. "I can see I'm going to have to build a bridge as well. I don't imagine we'll be fording it during the spring runoff," Samuel said, eyeing the wide riverbank that was dry this time of year.

They rode several miles until they came upon a lush, green valley surrounded by high mountains. The massive San Juans stood like sentinels on the southern horizon.

Lily's heart sank when she crossed the creek and noticed the small dilapidated cabin near a large cottonwood tree. There were no windows and the roof was completely caved in on one side. The door hung precariously by one hinge. They tied the horses to the tree and entered. She could hear the mice scurry for cover.

"Needs a little work, I'd say, but the logs are sound."

"Samuel, surely you don't think we can live in this." The kitchen in Illinois was larger than the small, one room hovel. There was a rusted iron stove in one corner, but the door had been broken off and was lying beside it. Animal droppings covered the dirt floor.

"What did you expect, the Markham Hotel?" Samuel's laugh echoed against the walls until he saw the dismal look on Lily's face.

"No, Dear," he said. "I'm only kidding. But it will make a mighty fine tack shed when I get it fixed up. Let's go back outside and envision your dream home."

They picked the spot for the house about fifty feet from the cabin. Lily began walking off the walls of the house. "I want the west wall here. That large cottonwood tree will block the hot afternoon sun."

As Samuel watched her, he took a pencil and notebook from his front pocket and started a list. It grew long as she talked over everything they would need.

"A large, sunny porch here. Let's see, a parlor here, with a fine horsehair settee and a warming stove. And the bathing room here, with a large white enameled tub. And a big cookstove here in the kitchen, with cabinets on this wall. And a large picture window here in our bedroom that will face south toward the mountains. I want to be able to look at them first thing every morning."

Lily had a wonderful time dreaming. Then she looked at the long list.

"Samuel, can we afford all that?" For the first time she wondered about money. She thought about how generous Samuel had always been with everyone. Even with a colonel's pay, he could not have saved enough for everything she had just envisioned.

"Maybe not right now but someday. Don't worry about it. Just keep dreaming."

But the fantasy had been replaced with reality.

"Seriously, Samuel. I don't want to impress my false hopes on you," Lily said quietly. She had felt foolish for going on so, knowing she didn't have enough funds of her own to even buy a frying pan.

"Lily, when you're at an army post out in the middle of nowhere, there's not a whole lot to spend your pay on. I've saved up a tidy nest egg," he said, looking down at the ground. But even with his words, for the first time since she had known him Lily had a deep suspicion that he was not being honest with her. She felt like there was an awful lot she didn't know about her husband. And she didn't like the feeling at all.

"I can do without the settee, Samuel."

But she sure wanted the picture window.

They went back to the river and swam in the cool water, then lounged in the warm sun. When the sun finally dipped in the west, Samuel started a fire and heated up a can of beans, then made a batch of biscuits and coffee.

"Not much of a dinner celebration, " he said. "Too bad I missed that sage hen."

"It was fine, " Lily muttered.

She washed out the pan while Samuel took out the bedrolls to spend the first night on their land. They crawled in and looked up at the wide sky.

"Lily, what's the matter? You hardly said two words all afternoon. Are you having second thoughts?"

"Tell me about your family."

He grew uneasy. "Not much to tell."

"I need to know."

"Is this about the money?"

"Some, yes. But more than that. You know all about my past. But I realized something this afternoon, never once have we talked about yours."

Samuel was silent.

"Do you have any brothers or sisters?"

"Yes, a sister. She lives in New York."

"Do you ever see her?"

"Not much."

"What about your parents?"

"My mother is dead. I don't know where my father is."

Lily could hear the hostility in his voice and wondered whether she should press him further.

Finally he spoke. "Lily, I will always take good care of you. You don't need to know any more than that." He turned his back to her and went to sleep.

✤ ✤ ✤

It was a four-mile ride north to the Los Pinos Indian Agency They passed the agency which consisted of the agent's house, a large storehouse and underground vegetable cellar, and a mess hall and a building to house the Mexican laborers who had been hired to teach the Utes how to farm. There were a number of Mexicans harvesting a field of corn nearby while several Ute braves watched.

Samuel and Lily didn't stop but rode another ten miles north to Ouray and Chipeta's farm inside the Ute reservation.

The women hugged warmly.

"Please, come in. I wished I'd known you were coming. I would have been more prepared," Chipeta said, putting a kettle on the stove for tea. Ouray had taken Samuel out to look at a new foal and to show him the farm.

"I am happy for you, Lily. Samuel is a fine man. I could see how much he cared for you when we were in Denver."

"You have a wonderful home, Chipeta." Lily looked at the carpets on the floors and lamps on the tables. The tea was served from a delicate porcelain pot painted with pale pink roses. Even though Chipeta was an extremely gracious hostess, Lily could tell the woman was not entirely comfortable in her surroundings

"You have a very beautiful home," Lily said.

"I must say it is very different than the tepee in which I grew up. Even with all this, there are days I miss the old ways. I wake in the morning and feel like I am living in a cave, surrounded by these walls and heavy roof over my head. I can't hear the birds like I did in the tepee. I can't feel the breeze. There is a strength one gets from living beside nature. I do not feel that strength in this home."

Lily thought of the power she had felt the night they had spent in the mountains.

"I feel myself growing soft in this house, though in the winter I am quite thankful for its warmth," Chipeta said. "In trying to teach our people this new way of life I am afraid we are becoming outcasts. Many of my people resent this way we are living, not understanding that much of what we have has been forced on us. We can't change it, any more than we can change the seasons. There is a deep sadness in me for I know that someday it will be forced on them as well."

Lily could hear loneliness in Chipeta's voice and thought of how she had felt when the church had disowned her.

"I am thrilled that we will live near each other. It will be good to have a friend," Lily said sincerely.

"Yes, it will," Chipeta said. "Sometimes it is hard living in two different worlds. I am thankful to have another woman to talk to. One who understands."

"Someday, Chipeta, your people will understand as well," Lily said.

Ouray was somber as he and Samuel looked at his horses grazing in the pasture. "I am glad you will be here, Bodeen. Maybe you will be able to help my people realize the inevitable. They grow more agitated every day when they see the wagon loads of whites entering our territory. Both the whites and the Utes will respect your words. I envision only trouble in the future." They started back to the house.

"You could stay here for the winter and get a good start on your ranch. I am sure Chipeta would be happy for Lily's company."

"I am grateful for your offer, Chief, but we have no supplies, and Mr. Wood is expecting our help. Have you received any cattle?"

"A herd of two hundred straggly looking range steers arrived about a month ago. They will help get us through the winter months but it will not be enough."

After a wonderful supper of elk steak and wild greens, Chipeta led the couple to the extra bedroom. The iron bed was covered with a brightly colored, woven wool blanket. The bed felt as soft as down to Lily's weary body. Samuel told Lily of Ouray's offer after they settled in. They decided it would be more beneficial to return to Pueblo for the winter, and besides, it was too long a time to take advantage of their friends.

"I will see that wagons of supplies will arrive before winter," Samuel said, already planning on whom to speak to at the Bureau of Indian Affairs. But he knew it would not be enough to stop the inevitable.

Ouray offered to accompany them back to Branum's Fork. He harnessed a matched team of fine-looking sorrels to a buckboard, and tied Samuel and Lily's horses to the back. Lily and Chipeta sat in the back of the wagon and gaily planned out the new house.

"Your land is a good land." Chipeta said. "Lush green grass, good water, and protection from the winter's winds. I have always thought of your valley as such a pleasant place," Chipeta said.

"That's it!" Lily replied excitedly. "Last night Samuel and I tried to come up with a name. Samuel, what do you think of the Pleasant Valley Ranch?"

"I like that," Samuel said. "The Pleasant Valley Ranch."

Though the Chief did not say as much, Samuel got the distinct feeling Ouray's decision to accompany them had not been just for an outing. His suspicions were confirmed when a group of ten braves overtook the buckboard in the Cimarron Valley. The Indians looked surprised when they saw that their chief was driving the wagon.

"Colorow."

"Ouray." The two men stared at each other for several moments. It was Ouray that broke the taut arrow of silence.

"These whites are our friends. I expect them to have safe passage back to Pueblo."

Samuel could see the anger on the other Indian's face. The brave was fierce looking, even without the scowl. But he could also see the respect Colorow gave to his chief and knew that the band would not go against Ouray's wishes.

Colorow jerked his horse and rode swiftly away, the other braves following in his cloud of dust.

David was waiting for them when they reached the fork just as night was falling. The relief on Wood's face was transparent. He invited Ouray and Chipeta to stay the night in the camp and dished them up some of the grouse he was roasting over the fire.

Ouray looked displeased when David told him of his plans to start a transportation line to provide supplies to the mines. The chief never interrupted, but listened with patience.

He then spoke with dignity and repose, but his face was stern.

"I understand you motives, Mr. Wood, even if I don't agree with them. Every day wagon loads of men pass by our farm on the way to the mountains. My people call the San Juans the Shining Mountains, not because of the silver they hold inside of them. We admire them for their magnificence. The forests have fed my people for generations and we have healed our bodies in the hot springs that bubble forth from inside their depths. I know we can't change what will be and it makes my heart heavy. I am fearful of what the white men will do to our mountains in their quest for riches. They do not respect them as the Utes do. I earnestly hope they do not destroy them." But there was much he left unsaid. Deep inside he hoped the white greed would not destroy his people as well.

The next morning, Ouray waited until the wagons had all been hitched, then stated to Samuel and Lily, "I look forward to seeing you in the spring. Please remember our door will always be open to you."

Chipeta hugged Lily, and then used the same words she had spoken in Denver. "I will think of you with smiles and good thoughts. May the Great Spirit watch over you until we meet again."

"Take care, Chipeta. I will miss you."

As the wagons pulled out, Lily looked back at the couple and wondered what the future was to hold for all of them.

Thanksgiving, 1876

6

I t was the first time Lily had entertained company in her own home. She and Samuel had rented a cabin next to the livery in Pueblo for the winter. It was small, but tight and warm against a brisk autumn wind that was blowing in smoky gray clouds and the smell of snow in the air. Once again she opened the oven and looked at the turkey slowly roasting to a golden brown.

"The bird's never going to get done if you keep opening that door," Myrtle said with a smile. Having never cooked a turkey by herself before, Lily relied on Myrtle's detailed instructions.

"I just want it to be special. My mother had made this all look so easy," Lily said. "I never realized how much care goes into preparing a holiday dinner."

"A labor of love. It will be wonderful, dear. Now stop fretting and don't beat that cream until it turns to butter."

"So tell me about your wedding," Lily said, straightening the coffee can and leaves centerpiece on the wooden plank table and wishing she had a lacy, crocheted tablecloth to hide the knots in the wood.

"How I wished you and Samuel could have been there. It would have been just perfect then. But it was fine just the same. Hank surprised me with a fine jade green organdy gown to wear, along with a matching hat. He said it matched my eyes. I didn't know he had such good taste."

"He chose you, that's mighty good taste in my opinion," Lily said. "I'm sorry Myrtle, but under the circumstances, Samuel and I thought it would be better if I did not go to Denver. I'm still waiting to hear more from Ann Eliza."

The most recent correspondence from the woman had not been encouraging. Ann Eliza had spoken to the governor of Illinois and two senators, but without Lily's testimony in person, Ann Eliza had offered little hope of an acquittal. There was still a warrant for Lily's arrest.

Jimmy came into the kitchen and put his finger in the bowl of sweet cream Lily had whipped.

"Pumpkin pie, my favorite."

"You skedaddle on out of here, boy, and help Hank and Samuel with the chores," Myrtle said with a gleam in her eye. "Dinner will be ready in an hour. You won't waste away to nothing by then." She tousled his hair and handed him a warm roll.

"He has grown so much. I didn't mean to put him on you like I did," Lily said as she watched him run out the door.

"It's been a joy and he has become the apple of Hank's eye. Not ever having children of his own, he dotes on that boy like a dog with a pup and Jimmy follows him around like a shadow. The boy is always happy about one thing or another, and I swear it's catching. I don't know what will happen if the uncle ever shows up."

"So you never heard back?"

"Not a word. Hank did some checking. Seems Jimmy's grand-parents both passed on last spring. Hank checked with the sheriff in Paradise and was told that his Uncle Henry had lost his place and no one seems to know where he and his family have gone. Rumors had it they were coming to Colorado but the sheriff didn't know quite where. Nowadays it seems everyone is coming here. It wouldn't bother me a bit if we never hear from him. I have a nagging night-mare that one day I will open the door and it will be Uncle Henry coming to take the boy away. I don't think Hank could bear that. He's got a sharp little Welsh pony all picked out for Jimmy for Christmas."

As they held hands and said grace, Lily could feel the tears building in the back of her eyes. It was the first time she had ever had a holiday away from her family. But she looked at these new friends, David, Myrtle, Hank and Jimmy, and her fine husband, and she knew she had been richly blessed with a new one.

After their fine feast, the men sat by the fire while Myrtle and Lily cleaned up the kitchen.

"So the trading was good?" Hank asked, lighting his pipe.

"We couldn't have asked for better," Samuel said. "Even the weather cooperated. David and I were able to purchase four more wagons and take three loads to Lake City before the snow closed the passes. We lost one wagon and several mules in a slide on Slumgullion Hill, but otherwise our proposition yielded a tidy profit. Lily stayed here and did a fine job managing the livery while we were gone."

Samuel had deliberately failed to tell Lily of the dangerous encounter they'd had with a band of Utes who had chased them over the pass, forcing them to recklessness. Instead, he had chosen to blame it on an autumn rainstorm when she had asked about the missing wagon.

"Denver is getting too darn big for my taste. Sometimes I think of packing up and heading for the mountains myself," Hank said. "Seems like every cutthroat west of the Mississippi has decided to hole up for the winter in Denver. And Myrtle is tired. She deserves to be pampered, not spend her life cleaning up after boarders."

"Would you consider Pueblo?" David asked. "I will be leaving for Ouray in the spring to start the transportation line. I could sure use a good man like you to manage the livery here. Don't think I can talk Lily into it," he said with a grin as she handed him a cup of coffee.

"I don't know, David. I've worked for myself for so long I don't rightly know if I could work for someone else," Hank said.

"I admire that. That is why what I would be offering is a partnership in the transportation line. I would handle the end of the business in Ouray, and you could manage this end, securing the supplies to haul and acquiring good stock. I can't be in two places at once, now can I? I offered it to Samuel here, but he has his mind set on being a cattleman."

Hank grew serious and the two men spent the next hour discussing the proposal.

"Let me talk it over with my wife. If she agrees, it looks like you've got yourself a partner," Hank said, shaking David's hand.

Myrtle did not share in their enthusiasm.

"Sell the boarding house?" Just the thought made her uneasy. It had been her security for almost ten years.

"It would bring a good price, especially right now during the boom," Samuel said.

"I don't know. Kind of hate to get rid of the place. It's been home to me for a good long time. Cleaned every nook and cranny at least a thousand times."

David offered an alternative. "I know a lady in Lake City by the name of Izzie Royce. Runs a small but very nice inn."

"Yes," Lily remembered. "We stayed there when we took that first load." The black lady's face still haunted her.

"She's a fine woman. Good cook and honest as the day is long. Last time I was up there she mentioned something about moving back to Denver. Winters are mighty long and lonely up in the high country. Maybe she would be willing to manage your boarding house."

Myrtle looked relieved. She just wasn't quite ready to let go of the place.

"I'll post a letter tomorrow and ask her. Funny thing, Lily," David said as he put on his coat to leave. "Izzie seemed quite taken with you. I was a bit surprised that out of all the boarders she had over the summer, she distinctly remembered you. When I was up there on that last trip she asked me your name, and got the strangest look on her face when I told her. You sure you don't know her from somewhere?"

Try as she might, Lily could not remember anyone by the name of Izzie Royce.

That night after her company left, Lily went to the bedroom and reached in the drawer where she had placed the letter from Anne Eliza Young that Myrtle had brought with her. She read it and then handed it to Samuel.

"Do you think I should go?"

He read the letter over several times.

She walked back over to the bureau, picked up her hairbrush and began nervously running it through her hair, which grown to shoulder length. She wondered whether she should cut it again. One decision would determine the other.

"Do you want to?"

"I'm scared." She crawled into the bed beside him and he held her close.

"Lily, I need to tell you something. I got a letter yesterday. Now seems as good a time as any to show it to you." He got up, took the letter from inside his shirt pocket and handed it to her. The envelope was elegant pink onionskin, and the writing on it was just as fine.

"Go ahead, open it. It's from Victoria."

"Who is Victoria?" Lily asked, fingering the wax on the back of the envelope.

Samuel did not answer.

The letter was an invitation for Samuel to spend the Christmas holidays in New York with her. The words were very formal and brief. It was simply signed, Your sister, Victoria.

"I wasn't going to say anything. But if you want to go east to Washington, it would be a fine time for you to meet my sister in New York."

As they lay in bed, Samuel listened to Lily impatiently clucking her teeth.

"Don't worry, I'll be right beside you."

"So you think I should do it?"

"Only you can answer that, Lily. But I will tell you this, the anticipation of fighting an enemy is usually worse than the battle itself. And I would rather face them head-on, rather than spend my life looking over my shoulder," he said. "Well, Indians anyway. Victoria is entirely a different matter."

"Tell me about her. Will I like her?"

"I'll let you form your own opinion."

He knew Lily's decision had been made and as he thought about the last encounter with his sister, he wondered which one of them was going to be fighting the bigger battle.

✢ ✢ ✢

Samuel insisted that Lily purchase a new wardrobe in Denver for the trip back East. She gasped at the cost of the gray serge traveling suit, but Samuel handed it to the owner of the elite dress shop. She also purchased a brown wool coat, a princess slip, a purse, hat, mitts, and a pair of button shoes. She looked at the bustles and corsets, but decided against them. After being comfortably attired the past months she was not about to go back to that imprisoning and uncomfortable way of dressing.

Samuel picked out a fine burgundy gown and added it to the pile.

"I really don't think so, Samuel," Lily said, looking at the price tag.

"Trust me, you are going to need it."

They spent a wonderful evening at Myrtle and Hank's before embarking on their journey. Lily noticed a change to the boarding house. Hank had built on a fine bedroom, and Myrtle had her own private bath.

"I'm as spoiled as a rotten peach," Myrtle said, as she showed Lily the fine new brass bed. "How about you, Lily? Are you happy?"

Lily paused before answering. "Yes, I am."

"But?"

"Just nervous I guess. Samuel is so supportive of me. What if I give my testimony and it does no good. I could be arrested. I've been mighty lucky it hasn't happened before now. What would Victoria Bannister think of her sister-in-law then?"

✛ ✛ ✛

The agent at the station was dressed in shirtsleeves with fancy sleeve garters above each elbow. "First class to Washington? That would be three hundred and forty dollars for the two of you."

Samuel pulled out a roll of bills, which the agent stared at from beneath his paper eyeshade.

"Really, Samuel. First class? It would be half that amount if we took the second-class car," Lily whispered.

"I would like to see Victoria's face when we got off with all the emigrants, smelling like sausage and cabbage," he said coldly. He motioned for the porter who came quickly to pick up their new valises. "I told you Lily, that I would take care of you. Just this once, don't worry about the money. I want this trip to be special for you. Deal? Consider it the honeymoon we never had," he said, leading her to the luxurious Pullman car. She looked down at her fancy new traveling dress and Samuel in his new suit. Already he was tugging impatiently on the stiff, starched collar.

Once again she questioned whether the trip was going to be a huge mistake. She tried to lighten the tenseness.

"I don't know, Samuel. I think we had the best honeymoon ever. Remember the wild raspberries?"

He smiled and took her hand. But the frown lines on his face only deepened.

And her own apprehension grew with each passing mile. The fields of Kansas looked barren and foreboding, covered with the cold, icy snow of winter. The train moved fast and easy, but with each stop Lily wanted to get off and head back to the safety of the high mountains where she could so easily hide from her past.

It took five days for the train to reach Washington D.C. They pulled in at ten o'clock on a dank, gray morning. Ann Eliza was waiting.

"I'm sorry, Lily, but you will have no time to rest up. The committee is waiting for you, anxious to return to their home states for the Christmas holidays. The buggy is just outside."

Lily was almost relieved that she would not have too much longer to know her fate. She just wanted to get her testimony over with and discern what the future held. She was astounded when the buggy pulled up in front of the White House. President Grant was standing on the steps waiting to greet them.

"Colonel Bodeen, good to see you again!"

"Good to see you, too, sir," Samuel said, shaking Grant's hand. "It has been a long time."

"And this fair lady must be your wife." The President kissed her hand graciously. It took Lily a moment to catch her breath.

"Come in, please. Let's get this business out of the way and then you can tell me what you've been up to. I was sorely disappointed to hear of your decision to leave the cavalry." He ushered them into a conference room where a number of men were seated around a large mahogany table.

The committee consisted of several United States Supreme Court justices, and the Honorable Judge McKean, attorney general for the Utah Territory.

President Grant attempted to put Lily at ease. "I know this won't be easy for you, Mrs. Bodeen. We are extremely grateful you have taken this long trip to try to set the record straight. Please, just take your time and tell us exactly what happened in Illinois."

An aide poured her a glass of water and she sipped it slowly before beginning. She then told the men everything, just the way it had happened.

The men sat in silence for several minutes, and Lily grew more apprehensive. She spied a guard standing by the door and she wondered if he was there to take her away.

Finally Grant spoke. "Before you arrived, I had a top detective from the Pinkerton Agency check into the allegations made against you," he stated, looking over a detailed report in front of him. "The black man, Joshua I believe his name to be, was not able to say much. He seems to be in poor health after the assault. He was able to say that he did not know who had accosted him. But there was more than one, and they had come at him from behind. He was able to corroborate just what you have told this committee. Your stories fit like kid gloves."

The chief justice looked at Lily with kind, understanding eyes. "It looks to me like Mrs. Bodeen has been railroaded, do you agree, gentleman?" The men nodded in agreement.

Judge McKean added, "If there is nothing else, I move to have the charges against Mrs. Lily Hastings Bodeen rescinded, on the grounds there is a complete lack of evidence."

The vote was taken that gave Lily back her future.

"I will notify the governor of Illinois," McKean said.

"That is something I would sincerely like to do myself," Grant stated with a satisfied smile. "I'm sure he will be more than willing to inform the Chief Justice to drop the charges. Now then, I think there is a fine lunch waiting for us."

Samuel stood up. "Just a minute, gentleman. To date, there have not been any charges brought against Bertram Ellis, is this true?"

"Yes," McKean said.

"I have done some checking of my own and it is my understanding that Mr. Ellis now resides in your fair state of Utah. Therefore, you would have the jurisdiction to arrest this man for the crime he committed against Mrs. Bodeen. That is, if she is willing to pursue charges." Samuel looked at her.

"Absolutely." Though Lily just wanted the matter over with, she knew it was the right thing to do. She would not allow her circumstance to happen to anyone else.

"Consider it done," McKean said. He then turned to the aide. "I would like a copy of the woman's testimony by tomorrow morning before I leave."

The president thanked Lily for her courage as they sat down to an exquisite meal. "Your testimony is key to what I have been saying all along. Several times Utah has asked for admittance into the Union, but until polygamy is outlawed in the state, I will see to it that they remain a territory. Maybe it will twist their arm enough to make the necessary changes. It seems, Ann Eliza, that our labors in this endeavor will not be in vain."

The woman nodded in agreement. "Thank you, Lily. I don't know if you realize just how much you have helped the cause."

A fine-looking Hansom carriage was waiting to take Samuel and Lily back to the depot. There was just enough time before boarding the train for Lily to post a quick telegram to her grandmother to tell her she was safe.

"How did you know Bertram was in Utah?" Lily asked, after they had selected their seats on the Pullman car to New York.

"I was a soldier for a long time. Let's just say that the code of the West is different than in the East and with some of my connections I was able to retrieve the information. Sometimes a man has to make his own rules and his own form of justice. Sooner or later, I was going to make sure Bertram Ellis was going to pay."

"You don't mean. . .?"

"I abhor injustice of any kind. Don't you think I noticed how scared you were to walk down the streets, afraid of being recognized? That's no way for even a dog to live. You were not the criminal; you were the victim. And when I think of what he did to you that night in the barn . . . "

His eyes grew dark and menacing and Lily could feel a chill crawl down her spine.

"No one hurts the people I love. One way or another, I was going to be sure justice prevailed. Ellis had just better thank his lucky stars it's McKean who will be picking him up, not me."

Samuel squeezed her hand. "Now then, onto the next battle. I'm afraid, my dear, my sister will be every bit as challenging."

✦ ✦ ✦

The station in New York was packed with people of every race and origin. A stern-looking older gentleman with silver white hair greeted Samuel and Lily. He was dressed in a fine black waistcoat and breeches.

"Mr. and Mrs. Bodeen, I believe?"

Samuel looked suspiciously at the gentleman. "Yes?"

"My name is Jiggs. Mrs. Bannister has instructed that I ask you to accompany me. I will be providing your transportation to Bannister Manor." Without further hesitation, he picked up their bags and walked away. They had no choice but to follow.

He opened the door to a fine white Concord carriage. The seats were made of plush red velvet, and the entire coach was lined with silk tassels. After they were settled in he placed a soft blanket over them and put warmers at their feet.

"We shall be at the residence in approximately one hour," Jiggs stated before latching the door.

Lily felt like a princess. "Samuel, you never told me she was rich."

"That's because she is not. Don't be fooled, Lily. She has everything that money can buy, that is true. But unless she has changed, she is one of the most unhappy people I have ever met."

They passed through high wrought iron gates and the carriage stopped in front of an elaborate mansion. Even her grandfather's plantation in the South had not been nearly as refined. Two huge concrete lion heads with mouths opened and teeth protruding stood guard at the front entrance.

The heavy doors opened and hastily a butler in a white uniform retrieved the valise Lily had in her hand. A large chandelier illuminated the large foyer tiled in gray marble but the room seemed cold and impersonal.

"Sir, Mrs. Bannister is waiting for you in the library. This way, please."

Volumes of books lined every wall of the large room from floor to ceiling. Victoria was seated in an overstuffed leather chair, reading a book. Without looking up, she stated in a terse voice, "You are late, Samuel. I expected you yesterday."

"You didn't get my telegram?"

She put her book down on the table beside her and took a sip of tea. "I had planned on you yesterday. Jiggs, show the couple to their room. Dinner will be at eight o'clock. I trust you both to be properly attired by then." She looked Lily up and down with a stern glare and then dismissed them with a wave of her hand.

They were led up a wide spiral staircase covered in stark white carpet. Their room overlooked at vast expanse of lawn that was covered with ice and snow. The branches of the many trees were bare.

Lily stared out the window. "I'll bet it's pretty during the summer."

"Don't kid yourself, Lily. It could be springtime, and the place would still feel as cold as a dungeon."

"How could a person with all this still be so miserable?"

"Life has not been easy for her," Samuel said.

"Did you grow up here?"

"Lord, no. We were born and raised in New Orleans. Then came the war, and let's just say . . . well . . . we both went our separate ways. I joined the army and she came East."

"Is there a Mr. Bannister?"

"You will likely meet him at dinner."

There was a faint knock on the door. "Your bath is ready," a frail black maid said meekly. She led Lily to a large bathing room that held an enormous white bathtub with gilded gold faucets. The water was steaming hot. The woman started for the buttons on Lily's traveling suit.

"Please, I can undress myself." Lily pushed the woman's hands away.

"But the missus says I'm to help you."

"Tell you what," Lily said, unfastening the dress. "I won't tell if you won't."

The woman smiled, then sat down on a pink velvet settee and waited while Lily enjoyed a long, hot bath. But even after soaking until the water turned tepid, Lily could not get rid of Victoria Bannister's cold stare.

✠ ✠ ✠

They sat down to dinner just as the grandfather clock in the hallway began to strike eight. A fire had been lit in the massive fireplace in the dining room. China and fine crystal glowed in the firelight.

Victoria was dressed in a dark blue silk gown. A necklace of fine sapphires and diamonds glittered around her neck.

"You have a very lovely home, Mrs. Bannister," Lily said, trying to erase the silence between Samuel and his sister. She was thankful her husband had insisted on the burgundy dress.

"I'm sure it is different than what you are used to out in the god-forsaken wilderness of Colorado." Victoria sipped her soup daintily from a silver spoon. "Jiggs, this bread is cold. You know I detest cold food."

The butler swiftly swept away the bread and took it to the kitchen.

"Oliver is not dining with us tonight?" Samuel asked.

"He's not feeling well and has chosen to take supper in his room."

Jiggs returned with a plate of steaming bread. "The cook apolo-

gizes for the mistake, ma'am. She will see it does not happen again."
He returned to his place by the door.

"Be sure it doesn't. And I am assured that Mr. Bannister's is warm as well?"

Jiggs went back to the kitchen.

Victoria took a slice and buttered it lavishly. "Now then Samuel, I noticed in the last bank statement that over one thousand dollars was wired out of our joint account. Is there an explanation for this?"

Samuel told her of his recent business venture with David Wood, and then carefully added, "You will notice, Victoria, that the money was replaced in November. We received a handsome profit from the supplies."

A maid rolled in a cart from the kitchen. It contained a platter of roast beef, a large bowl of fluffy mashed potatoes, and a smaller bowl of glazed carrots.

The bowls of soup were whisked away.

"Shall I serve, ma'am?"

"That will be fine. Just a small portion for me." Victoria took a small bite of the beef while the servant waited. "Inform the cook there is too much onion."

"Yes ma'am."

Lily took a bite of the roast. It was tender and juicy, melting like butter in her mouth but she forced herself to eat slowly. Samuel quickly devoured his and asked for more.

"Tell the cook this is the best darned cut of beef I've ever tasted," he said, grinning at the servant. She stifled a smile.

"I told the cook that if she served beef and potatoes every night during your stay, you would be satisfied. I see I was right. Don't you get tired of the same menu, Samuel?"

"Victoria, I've eaten so many beans and biscuits over the years that a good cut of beef is about the best dinner I could ask for."

"That was your choice, not mine. You have not changed, Samuel."

"Nor have you, Victoria. Still as pretty as a jewel," he said with a grin.

A faint smile graced Victoria's face, and then quickly vanished. Her face was quite beautiful when she smiled. Her skin was as smooth as silk, her dark hair thick and lustrous. The sapphires brought out the dark blue of her eyes and the tailored cut of her gown was careful in revealing just enough of her buxom figure with good taste.

"Still a lady's man, full of bluster. And I would presume that you still smoke that filthy pipe. See that you do it out on the veranda."

"So what wonderful plans do you have for our stay, dear sister?"

"We will be attending the governor's holiday ball tomorrow night. I trust that your wife will be wanting to purchase an adequate gown for the occasion." She looked at Lily's dress. "I will take her into the city tomorrow and see if we can't find something suitable."

The servant brought in an elegant cherries jubilee, but Lily could not eat a bite, feeling suddenly ill at the thought of spending the day with Victoria.

Victoria, too, declined the rich dessert. "If you will excuse me, I need to check on Oliver. Jiggs, I will be needing your assistance." Before she had risen from her chair the butler was at her side.

✤ ✤ ✤

"Stop clucking your teeth, Lily."

"I'm not," she said, taking a sip of fine English tea.

"She likes you."

"She never even looked at me. Nor did she ever address me by my name."

"If she didn't like you, she would have had a clothier come to the house with a selection of dresses. I have the distinct impression she wants to get you alone and check you out to see if you are good enough for me. Never did trust my judgment with women, and probably for good reason. Besides, she wants to show you off tomorrow night."

"I am not a bauble to be put on display, Samuel."

"So tell her that. The best way to deal with my sister is to attack her directly, right up front. She respects that."

"You mean put her in her place."

"That, too. Just remember she is as apprehensive of you as you are of her. She will test you, feel you out. She is like a mother hen, very protective. Other than Oliver, I'm the only family she's got."

✤ ✤ ✤

Once again, Samuel was right. On the carriage ride into the city, Victoria bombarded Lily with questions, wanting to know about her childhood, her family, and her education. Then came the most pointed question of all.

"Jiggs tells me that the train came in from Washington D.C. What were you doing in Washington, Lily?"

Lily got the strange feeling that Victoria already knew. She had no choice but to tell the woman the truth.

Victoria turned away and looked out at the snow falling from the leadened sky. "Are you ashamed of what happened?" she asked, her tone remote, as if she were a million miles away.

"I was, but not anymore. Your brother made me realize the attack was not my fault. I can't change what happened. The past is just that, the past. I can only change how I face it and do everything I can to make sure it does not happen to anyone else."

"That must have been hard for you," Victoria said sincerely. "It takes a great deal of courage to own up to one's past. Life can be terribly cruel, Lily. I'm sorry."

"I appreciate your understanding, but I don't want your pity, Victoria," Lily stated firmly.

They sat in silence for the rest of the ride into the city.

They entered a boutique where Victoria was instantly recognized, and two clerks quickly came to her assistance. They were seated in elegant winged chairs covered with fine tapestry. Tea and pastries were served before the show began.

"We want to see the finest gowns you have," she said to the clerk.

Lily could not decide. Each gown was more beautiful than the last.

"With your coloring, may I suggest the amber brocade? Or even the fine winter white. You are blessed my dear. Most woman are not able to wear white, but your fine peaches and cream complexion enhances the color," one of the clerks advised. She was much too discreet to comment on Lily's strange hairstyle. Lily had cut it again before the trip. It made her feel more protected somehow.

Lily was taken to the fitting room and assisted into the amber brocade. The material was coarse against her skin. Victoria shook her head. The winter white crinoline made Lily feel like a dressed up Dresden doll, with the full skirt requiring a bustle and a stiff under slip. Thankfully Victoria was as unimpressed as she was.

Lily gasped at the last gown presented. It was a deep emerald green velvet, with delicate ivory French lace around the bodice and sleeves. The cut was simple and straight. When she tried it on it fit perfectly, enhancing her small waist.

Victoria nodded her approval.

"We will have it hemmed and delivered by four o'clock this afternoon," the clerk said. She brought out a pair of green velvet slippers that matched.

Lily hoped Samuel had given her enough money as she reached for her purse.

"Put it on my account, Esther," Victoria said, signing the sales slip.

Lily started to argue.

"Merry Christmas, Lily," Victoria said with a hint of a smile. The resolute look on her face told Lily there was no sense in arguing.

They had a late luncheon of salmon soufflé and champagne at the Ritz Carlton. Lily was surprised to find that she was actually having a good time. She and Victoria talked about books and Lily respected the woman's vast intelligence. She, like Lily, had a deep love of English poetry.

Their next stop was an elegant salon where the stylist did her best with what auburn hair Lily had. She trimmed just enough to bring her natural curls to life.

"By next week, half the women in New York will have cut off their long hair," Victoria said approvingly.

The carriage was waiting when they left the salon. They visited several more shops where Lily purchased presents for her grandmother, father and Joshua. The clerks graciously wrapped them for mailing.

"Thank you, Victoria. I had a wonderful time today," Lily said honestly, as the carriage drove them back to the Manor. She had seen the same qualities in Samuel's sister that had so endeared her to him. Victoria was blunt and to the point, unwavering in her opinions. But she was also a careful listener. Her qualities were just hidden deep inside the woman by a wall of self-preservation.

"How much has Samuel told you about me?" Victoria asked.

"Not much. He told me I would have to form my own opinion of you."

"That sounds just like my brother. As a matter of fact, that's exactly what he said about you. So have you?"

"Yes. Have you?" Lily said.

"Yes," Victoria said with a satisfied smile. "I admire your courage and your honesty. If there is one thing I abhor, it is self-pity. That is part of the rift between my brother and me. Has Samuel spoken about our father to you?"

"No, it is something he refuses to talk about. He seems so angry, Victoria."

"You have to understand that Tyrone Bodeen went against everything Samuel holds dear. Our father left us when the war started. Samuel was fourteen and I was sixteen, and little William, Bodie we called him, was thirteen. Just after Father left, Mother became sick. Poor as church mice, Samuel took every odd job he could get, as did I. When I turned nineteen, I took a job in a local tavern. One night Samuel came in just as a filthy-looking man was trying to grope me."

Victoria paused at the memory. Lily took her hand and patted it with understanding.

"When Samuel saw the five dollars I held in my hand, he beat the man to a pulp, grabbed my arm and took me home. The next morning he enlisted in the Union Army, sending his pay home to support us. Mother died a year after he left. When Bodie turned fifteen, he enlisted in the war as well and was killed in the battle to take Atlanta."

Victoria's voice cracked as she fought off her tears.

"After the war, our father came back with a carpetbag full of money, but when Samuel found out how he had earned it, running guns and selling out to the highest bidder, he threw it back in our father's face. I had never seen my brother angrier. He blamed Father for Bodie's death and I thought at one point he was going to kill him. Our father was gone the next morning but he had left the money on the table. I caught Samuel just as he was putting it in the fireplace, and suggested that we spend the money on doing good things for others in an attempt to set our father's actions right. After quite a fight, we agreed to put the money in the bank. Then Samuel re-enlisted. Soon after that I married Oliver."

"Have you seen your father since then?"

"He contacted me several times. Last year I finally agreed to meet with him. I tried to get Samuel to accompany me but he flatly refused. He was furious that I would agree to it, and even more furious when I took some of the money to place Father in an old folks home. Tyrone Bodeen is now a senile, lonely old man. In trying to do what he had thought was best for his family, he destroyed it."

Victoria sounded sad and full of regret.

"So you see, Lily, we all have a past we are still trying to overcome.

Secrets that are hard to accept. I just wish Samuel would stop blaming our father and get over feeling sorry for himself that his father was no hero. You know, this is the first time I have ever told anyone this. I hope it will help you to understand my brother better."

"It does," Lily said. But it also gave her a better understanding of his sister. "The war destroyed so much for my family as well. My father will go to his grave still fighting it. But Victoria, it is never too late to work toward peace. A family is not like a building. It can be damaged, but never destroyed. Maybe it is time for both of you to talk about the past so you can finally start to remove the rubble and build a new understanding."

As the carriage pulled up to the mansion, Victoria laughed. "Won't Samuel be surprised to learn that we didn't kill each other!"

Samuel had not only been surprised, he had been shocked. He had spent the past hour nervously watching for the carriage from the window and worrying about how he was going to settle the skirmish he was expecting. But instead of seeing two women ready to tear each other limb from limb, he saw two friends enter the house with arms full of packages and hearts full of laughter.

"Samuel, could I see you in the library?" Victoria asked as she handed the maid her bundles.

He looked at her strangely, then at Lily. Yes, these were the same two women who had left this morning, he was sure of it.

"Go on Samuel," Lily coaxed. "I have a bit of primping to do before the ball and I surely don't want you underfoot." She smiled at him and kissed his cheek.

Victoria took the first step toward peace, toward rebuilding what the bullets of the past had so brutally damaged. The pair talked for over an hour, cleansing old wounds so they could finally begin to heal.

7

The maid came to the room to assist Lily with dressing, but she had already slipped on the gown, anxious to show Samuel. "Won't that be just the frock to tame unruly mules in!" Seeing the nervous look on her face, he quickly added, "You, my dear, will be the loveliest belle at the ball," Then he gently kissed her lips.

"The missus asked me to bring you this." The maid handed Lily a soft white ermine jacket. "Said you might be needing it. I swear the governor always plans the Christmas Ball on the coldest night of the year."

Lily had not even considered a coat. All she had was the brown wool that she had bought in Colorado. The fur was soft and luxurious.

Victoria was waiting at the bottom of the stairs.

"You look beautiful, Lily, but I think the gown is missing something. Samuel?"

He pulled a long black velvet box from inside his coat. Lily opened it to find a fine rope of pearls, with a large, single emerald glittering in the middle of the strand.

Lily gasped. "It is perfect," she said. "How did you know?"

"Good ole' Santy Claus. Merry Christmas, dear."

Victoria grinned as Lily removed the necklace from the box, and then assisted with fastening the clasp. The pearls set off the lace of the dress, and the emerald matched the color of the gown exactly.

"You two have been conspiring, haven't you?" Lily asked, looking at the pair. She realized that they truly were related, both sharing the same teasing grin. She also could see the intense love they had for each other in spite of the obstacle they seemed to have in communicating.

"What's all the laughter in here? Am I missing the joke?"

Jiggs pushed a wheelchair into the foyer. Even though the old man in the chair was pale and frail, his voice boomed from his body.

"Samuel, you remember Oliver?" Victoria asked.

"Good evening. You are looking well," Samuel said, putting out his hand.

"Dear, are you sure you are feeling up to this tonight?" Victoria asked. Lily noticed that she spoke to him with kindness and respect.

"As bad a liar as you ever were, Sam my boy. Haven't missed the Governor's Ball in fifteen years, I'll be damned if I start now! And who is the fair maiden gracing my presence? Surely you didn't agree to hitch up with this rebel?" Oliver asked Lily with a twinkle in his eye.

"Mind yourself," Victoria chided as she straightened his tie. "Lily, this is my husband, Oliver Bannister."

"Pleased to meet you, sir." Lily said, stunned. Victoria's husband looked to be at least thirty years older than she was. His hair was silver white and curled down around his collar. But he had a beaming smile, the kind that put a person immediately at ease. Lily instantly liked him.

"You're even more beautiful than Victoria described," he said. "I hope you will not be too embarrassed to accompany a crotchety old man like me."

Samuel assisted Jiggs in lifting Oliver into the waiting carriage. There was a specially built box on the back for the wheel chair.

The governor's mansion was even bigger and more elaborate than Bannister Manor. Never had Lily seen so many exquisite gowns and glittering jewels in one place. And all the women, whether young or old, seemed to know Samuel.

Lily could feel her jealousy rising as a woman in a revealing red gown came over and hugged him close, crushing her ample bosom up against his chest.

"Samuel, my sweet. I heard you were in town, " the woman purred, kissing his cheek.

"Madeline. You look as lovely as ever," Samuel said, returning the kiss.

The woman fairly swooned. "Don't forget," she said, "I expect to have at least one nice, long slow dance with you." The words dripped like honey from her painted lips.

Victoria stepped in. "Madeline, I would like you to meet my sister-in-law, Mrs. Lily Bodeen." She emphasized the word Mrs. with a firm tone.

"Charmed, I'm sure," Madeline said coldly, before fluttering off to the next potential victim.

"Samuel, behave yourself tonight." Victoria spoke to him as if he were a boy.

"Oh, I was just having some fun. Have to do something to lighten up this stuffy bunch. You have to admit, it was kind of entertaining to see the look on Lily's face. See what a catch you got, my dear?"

"If you're not careful, Bodeen, I'll throw you back," Lily teased.

"Come, the governor is anxious to meet you," Victoria said, taking Lily's arm.

Oliver and Samuel enjoyed themselves immensely, bantering and arguing politics with anyone who would listen, but Lily soon realized that much of the glitter and glamour in the vast ballroom was superficial. Many of the carefully coiffured women seemed to live only for the next ball, the next gown, and the next potential admirer. The men spoke of nothing but making money and the upcoming election.

Samuel and another gentleman with a full dark beard came over to the table where she was trying to keep her attention on a conversation Victoria was having with a matronly old lady about an upcoming fundraiser for a hospital.

"Lily, I would like you to meet Otto Mears. This is my lovely wife, Lily."

He took her hand and graciously kissed it. "It is indeed a pleasure, ma'am." He had a stern face with deep-set eyes that looked directly into her. He was dressed in a fine black wool suit, crisp white shirt and black string tie.

"I don't know who was more surprised, Otto or myself when we saw each other across the room."

"What brings you to New York, Mr. Mears?" Lily asked.

"I am making plans to establish a railroad in western Colorado. I am sure you find the stage service as uncomfortable as I do," he said. "If you will excuse me, I would like to speak with Oliver Bannister before he leaves."

Lily was relieved when Victoria stated it was time to leave. The heavy cigar smoke and the din of constant chatter had given her a headache. She had forgotten how tedious social events could be.

Oliver fell asleep on the way back to the manor. Lily wished she could do the same, but her mind whirled with the colors of the gowns at the ball and too much champagne.

✛ ✛ ✛

"Tell me about Otto Mears. How can he be planning to build a railroad on Ute land? Wouldn't the Utes have to approve it?" Lily asked Samuel as she slipped into her flannel nightdress.

"Strange man, isn't he?" Samuel said. "Likable enough, but something a bit cock-eyed about the man. He's never given me a good reason not to trust him. I guess I must think him a bit too bottom dollar. He's always looking to make a profit.

"He's a smart one. He speaks Spanish and the Ute language fluently. I guess that is what makes the Indians trust him so much—that and the gifts he gives them. He was instrumental in getting Ouray his house. Otto speaks Russian as well. He immigrated with his parents to California. They died, and he was left to find his own way at an early age. And he's done right well for himself, I must say that."

Samuel sat down on the bed and lit his pipe. "After a stint in the Civil War and fighting the Navajo with Kit Carson, he opened a store in the Conejos country. Soon he had a wheat farm and two mills. Then he started building roads to get his goods to the miners in Leadville. Made a pretty penny off of them with his inflated prices. But they bought it."

✢ ✢ ✢

There was a faint knock at the door.

"How I wish that maid would just leave me alone," Lily said to Samuel in a weary voice. "She follows me around like some kind of loyal dog."

But it was not the maid, it was Victoria, dressed in an elegant peach silk nightgown and matching robe.

"I've instructed Esther to make a nice pot of tea. Would you two care to join me?"

"Not me," Samuel said. "I'm ready to hit the hay. Lily?"

The tea sounded like just the prescription she needed to calm her jangled nerves. She also detected a hint of loneliness in Victoria's voice. Lily followed her to the library.

"That will be all, Esther," Victoria said after the maid brought in the silver service.

They sat in silence for several minutes, enjoying the warm fire Jiggs had built up in the large fireplace. They seemed such an unlikely pair, Lily thought, she dressed in her flannel gown and Victoria in silk.

Finally Victoria spoke. "You are a lucky woman, Lily."

"Yes, I am. So are you. Oliver seems to be a wonderful man. If you don't mind my asking, what happened to his legs?"

"He received a bullet in the back during the war and was lucky to have lived at all. The stubborn old man should not have been fighting in the first place. I nursed him back to health, astounded at his determination. He repaid me by asking for my hand in marriage."

Lily could hear regret in Victoria's voice.

"Please understand, I am not complaining. Oliver has been very good to me. He is kind and generous."

Victoria poured more tea from the ornate silver pot.

"My husband's wound made him all the more determined to be successful. He envisioned the West opening up and invested heavily in the railroads. Quite obviously the investment has paid off. He shows his love for me in the only way he can. I have everything his money can buy."

"But it's not enough." Lily said.

"I am thirty-six years old. I want a child. Unfortunately that is the only thing he can't give me. And he is not well. Last year he fought back from a severe attack that left his heart weakened. He spends most of his days sleeping and I wonder just how much fight his fragile body has left. The doctor tells me to prepare myself, it could be anytime. I don't know what I'll do when . . .he's all I've got."

Victoria twisted an embroidered hankie into tight knots.

Lily reached over and held her hand. "Remember that you have us, too. When that day comes, Victoria, please know that you will be welcome to come to Colorado with Samuel and me."

"Oh, heavens, me out west? The savages, the desolation, the harsh, cold land—just the thought of it makes me shudder."

"It's really quite beautiful. And I met a Ute Indian woman, the wife of Chief Ouray, who is one of the kindest women I have ever met. Just know that the invitation is open."

Lily patted her flat stomach. "Besides, little Bodeen here is going to need his, or her, Aunt Victoria."

"Are you saying . . .?"

"Yes. And I am going to be needing you too, come next summer."

Victoria's eyes lit up. "I'm thrilled, Lily. Does Samuel know?"

"Not yet. Mrs. Claus will have a few surprises of her own on Christmas morning."

Oliver was feeling poorly on Christmas Eve, so they chose to stay at the manor instead of going to church. Everyone, even the servants, drank mulled cider in the library and Lily read the beloved Christmas story from the Holy Bible that Myrtle had given her, thankful she had decided to bring it along. The miles that separated her from her family melted away as she thought of her grandmother's soft voice reading those same words to her when she was a child.

Lily slept very little, eager with anticipation. The next morning after the rest of the presents had been unwrapped, she handed Samuel a small box. When he saw the pair of tiny booties, he whooped and hollered as he spun Lily round and round. He said it was by far, the best present anyone had ever given him.

But Samuel had a few surprises of his own. "I hope you didn't mind that I sent a telegram to let your grandmother know where you were spending the holiday." He handed Lily a letter.

> Dear Lily,
>
> My prayers have been answered and I thank God you are safe. We are well. Your Christmas box was just the medicine Joshua needed. He got out of bed and went to the barn for the first time yesterday to try out his fine leather gloves. I pray the present I have prepared for you will come in handy some day soon as well. I'm anxious to meet your husband. He seems to be fine man. Love, Grandma.

Samuel handed Lily a box he had carefully hidden behind the immense Christmas tree. She opened it to find a lovely quilted blanket, just the size for a baby. Lily quickly recognized the material; the pieces had been cut from the dresses Grandma had packed away in a trunk after Lily's mother had passed on. Each square had a special memory.

"I wonder how she knew?" Lily whispered as she ran her fingers over the exquisite seams. But then she remembered how her grandmother had always seemed to know what she had been thinking. Grandma had always had the right words of comfort to ease Lily's growing pains. And if she did not have them, she searched her well-worn Bible for them. And they always came.

Samuel reached in his pocket and gave Lily one last present. It was a ticket to Nauvoo and home.

✣ ✣ ✣

As Lily lay in her old bed at her grandmother's house, she realized it was no longer home at all. Everything, even the clock on the wall, had its familiar chime, but she was now just a visitor.

It had been hard walking down the streets of Nauvoo, seeing Mormon wives and their large broods of children buying goods at the market. It had been hard to face her father's cold eyes. They had not changed. But hardest of all was facing Joshua's blank ones. The twinkle was gone, replaced with a vacant stare, as if he was trying hard to remember something but couldn't. Several times she caught him calling her Isabel and talked to her as if she were a child.

Lily was thankful to see that her grandmother was as feisty as ever. As Lily heard the mantle clock strike five a.m., she knew the sound that would soon follow, the sound of the whistling teakettle.

Lily rose, careful not to disturb Samuel. She put on her robe and descended the stairs. Her grandmother was sitting in silence, a teacup and Bible sitting on the table just where Lily knew they would be. She watched her grandmother as she "centered down," as she had called it. Many times Lily had tried this Quaker way of greeting the morning. Her grandmother had encouraged her not to pray, but simply to listen. But Lily had never been able to empty her mind long enough to let the voice enter. Lily sat quietly at the bottom of the stairs, careful not to disturb the old woman's quiet time.

After several minutes, her grandmother opened her eyes.

"Good morning, dear." Grandma Donovan's eyes held the peace that Lily had so often envied.

Lily poured a cup of tea from the pot and sat down at the kitchen table.

"You will be leaving today," her grandmother said in a knowing voice.

"Yes. We have been gone almost a month. There is much to be done before spring."

"It's not easy to come home again, Lily, especially with your father still so afflicted. You must pray for him and remember that in his own way he loves you very much."

"Then why doesn't he say so?"

"Because he is angry with himself. But 'vengeance is mine', sayeth the Lord. You must forgive him. It is the beginning of a new year, a good time to start. You have a new life ahead of you. Don't let the old one be a burden."

"But how do I forgive?"

"First you try to understand. That does not mean to make excuses, but to accept the weakness in others. And if you can't, ask the Lord to help you. Some, like your Grandfather Hastings, will never know that true peace until their last day. You must ask yourself if that is how you want to live. Some choose to see life's bitterness and some choose to see life's blessings. Only you can choose which one you want to see."

"I love you, Grandma," Lily said, as she rose to hug the woman, this fine lady who had spent her life seeing some kind of blessing in everything.

"I know, dear. And I love you, too."

✦ ✦ ✦

As they passed through the fields of Kansas, Lily repeated her grandmother's words to Samuel. Several times during the last few days of their stay in New York Victoria had tried, yet again, to convince him to see his father, but Samuel had flatly refused.

"Then at least write him a letter and tell him how you feel," Lily said.

"I have nothing to say to the man."

"Samuel, you may not have much longer. Victoria said he is not well."

"What did you say to your father, Lily? Thanks, Dad, for betraying me?" His voice was angry.

"No, Samuel. I simply told him that I wished him well. And it felt good, like I was releasing all the torment. I can't change him, but I can change me."

"Well, just maybe I don't want to change, Lily. Maybe I'm happy just like I am."

"Then do it for the baby," Lily pleaded. "Do you want your child to grow up as unforgiving as you seem to be?"

"I would never do anything to hurt my child!" Samuel shot back.

"Maybe not deliberately. But sooner or later, we as parents will be bound to make the wrong decision for our child, one he or she may not agree with. Just maybe if we try to forgive our own parents for any wrongs they may have committed, our child will grant us the same forgiveness as well."

"You do what you have to, Lily, to ease your mind about your father. Just don't preach, and let me do what I have to in order to ease mine."

He rose and strode down the aisle to the smoking car, and once again, Lily felt shut out of his life.

✛ ✛ ✛

Lily was thrilled to see Hank, Myrtle, and Jimmy as she got off the train in Denver.

"I got to get out of school and everything!" the boy beamed.

"I swear you have grown a foot," Samuel said as he tousled Jimmy's hair.

Myrtle had baked a ham and a delicious caramel custard pie to celebrate Samuel and Lily's homecoming, and Lily's newfound freedom.

"So are you going to let your hair grow back? I declare I won't know you without that fine head of short curls. Hardly recognized you anyway, without your britches," Hank teased.

Lily laughed. "I really don't know yet. This style is so much easier. Just wash it and go. And to be honest, I can't wait to get back into a pair of jeans and boots. And these ridiculous shoes—I'm lucky I didn't fall flat on the ice."

"My dear," Samuel said, "in a few months the only pants you will be able to fit into will be mine."

Lily could see that Myrtle and Hank were confused by his remark and she told the couple about the child they were expecting. They were thrilled, but no one was more pleased than Jimmy.

"Oh, boy! A baby?" But his elation quickly turned to sadness.

"But if you are leaving this spring, I won't never get to see it."

"But of course you will," Lily said.

"Lily, come to the bedroom, I want to show you the fine comforter Hank got me for Christmas," Myrtle said. Lily followed her to the bedroom.

Myrtle shut the door and whispered, "We heard from the boy's Uncle Henry just before Christmas. He and his family are in Central City, where he is employed at one of the mines. His letter said that just as soon as he is able, he will be coming for the boy. Hank and I knew it was bound to happen sooner or later. We told Jimmy as gently as we could."

Lily could see the deep disappointment on Myrtle's face.

"We will just have to pray the man will change his mind, especially when he sees Jimmy so happy and well taken care of," Lily said.

"Maybe it's for the best," Myrtle said, trying to convince herself more than Lily. "The boy needs other children. He needs a family, not two aging people like Hank and me."

"You have given him the best home, the best family, that any child could hope for," Lily replied. "Henry will surely see that. Then Jimmy's uncle has other children?"

"Four. Jimmy is anxious to meet his cousins, but I think he is a bit fearful as well. His schoolwork has dropped and I've caught him crying in the night."

"How soon do you think it will be before Henry comes for him?"

"I haven't the faintest idea. And I can't help but wonder that if Henry does not have the funds to come to Denver from Central City, how will he have the money to feed another hungry mouth?"

"You know, Myrtle, where there's a will, there is always a way, my grandmother used to tell me," Lily said. "It's Friday. Jimmy does not have school tomorrow. Samuel and Hank will be spending the rest of the weekend traveling to several ranches to acquire stock. So what is stopping us from boarding the train in the morning for Central City ourselves? It is only a two hour ride."

"You mean take Jimmy to see his uncle?"

"Why not? And when Henry sees how happy the boy is and meets you in person, he is sure to change his mind and let the boy stay."

"You're right, Lily. Why not? It's worth a try. And won't Hank be tickled to come home and find that the boy is ours for good? Even if it doesn't work out, at least Jimmy won't be wondering about it anymore."

"Or you. Henry will agree, I just know it," Lily said confidently.

Henry McCluskey's home was little more than a wooden shack, with deep snow piled up around the solitary window. But even in the bare coldness of the room, Lily could see that it was neat and clean. Sarah McCluskey, Jimmy's aunt, was kind and gracious.

"Please excuse the cold, ladies. We burned the last of the coal two weeks ago. The crew boss promised to have a load delivered last week, but we have yet to see any. Wood just does not keep the room warm, no matter how many times I fill the stove."

She took the kettle from the stove and poured boiling water into two chipped cups.

"It's so good to see you, Jimmy," she said sincerely. "Henry is at the mine and won't return until dark. I was saving the last of the tea for a special occasion. I see no occasion more special than this."

She placed a cup of tea in front of Lily and Myrtle. Lily noticed that Sarah did not pour any for herself.

"Sugar?" Sarah placed the near empty bowl on the table.

"Please, Mrs. McCluskey, have my tea. Nothing seems to settle well on my stomach these days," Lily said.

"Well, if you are sure," Sarah said. She took the cup, added a bit of sugar, and handed the cup to the oldest girl sitting quietly on a bed in the corner. The children shared the tea eagerly.

Myrtle pulled several peppermint sticks from her bag. "Here, Jimmy. Maybe you would like to give these to your cousins." He went to the corner and shyly offered them the candy.

"Wanna play dominoes?" the boy closest to Jimmy's age asked.

"I don't know how."

"I'll teach you. My name's Danny, what's yours?" the boy asked as he sucked on the peppermint stick.

Soon they were playing like they had been best friends forever.

"Please know, Sarah," Myrtle said, "Hank and I have come to love Jimmy very much. And he has been through so much in his short life. It would be a crying shame to uproot him again. That is not to say that you and Henry could not see him whenever you wish. My son is all grown, and Hank never had any children. We are willing and able to give the boy a good, stable home. And if you don't mind my saying so, it looks like you have a pretty full house already."

"Yes, you're right, Myrtle. It's hard to feed the children we already have. But family is family, Henry says. He feels a duty and obligation to his brother to take care of Jimmy."

"And I truly admire that. Surely I do. But what it really boils down to is what is best for Jimmy. Hank and I can give him everything he will ever need."

"I'm afraid you will have a hard time convincing his uncle of that. He is a very proud man. Please, stay tonight. We will find the room somehow. Tomorrow is Sunday and the mine will be shut down. You are welcome to come to the church services with us in the morning, and then you and Henry can talk of this afterward."

"No, we don't want to put you out," Lily said. "I noticed a boardinghouse just down the road, we would be glad to stay there." Lily could see from the bare shelves that Sarah would have a hard time feeding two extra mouths.

The church service was held in the back of the general store. It was packed with weary-looking miners and their weary looking families. But even in the cold, they sang the hymns warmly and with reverence. Lily could see that their faith is what held them together in the bleak conditions of the mining town.

Lily was thankful that Myrtle had stopped at the store on their way to the boardinghouse and purchased a ham, a wheel of cheese, and a sack of flour. The children ate heartily after the service.

Unfortunately, Henry did not seem nearly as pleased and ate very little. "Just as soon as we find that vein of ore, we will all be living 'high on the hog.' Should be any day now, the crew boss says we are getting closer all the time. And the owner of the mine has offered those of us who stick it out a cut of the profits. Just as soon as that happens, I'll be able to pay off the bank in Kansas and get the farm back."

Myrtle thought of the many boarders who had told her that same story, only to be disappointed when it did not happen.

"I'll make a deal with you, Mr. McCluskey. When that day comes, Hank and I will joyfully let you take Jimmy with you. But in the meantime, let us provide for him. And I will even do you one better than that. How old is your daughter?"

Myrtle had noticed the girl singing at church. So had a lot of lonely miners.

"She'll be fifteen next month."

"I am in dire need of good kitchen help. I can offer her room and board, along with a salary of fifteen dollars a month. Of course I will see to it that she goes to school during the day. I will give you and your wife some time to think it over."

Myrtle put on her coat. Her eyes advised Lily to follow her. They went outside and helped the children stack firewood against the side of the shack.

The walls were thin and Lily could hear the couple arguing inside.

"It's a dream come true, Henry. Didn't you hear the preacher this morning? Pride goeth before a fall. Just for once put your stubborn pride aside and think of what is best for Mary. This is no place for her. Already she's had at least five proposals by men you wouldn't even let near her. And she needs schooling if she is going to get any-where in life."

"Are you forgetting, Sarah, you were just sixteen when I asked you to marry me? Or maybe you do remember and have lived to regret it. This surely is not the life I promised you."

Lily could hear the utter feeling of failure in his voice.

"I don't regret even a single day. I love you, Henry McCluskey. I'm behind you through thick and thin. I always have been, and always will be. But you can be the most bull-headed Irishman I have ever met. You know as well as I do that Mary will be leaving us someday soon, one way or another. She is almost a woman now. Let her leave having a better chance than what we can give her right now. My father gave me that chance when he agreed to give you my hand. But if you remember, he made us wait until I finished my schooling. And when we lost the crop, we would never have got through the winter without what I made teaching. Now it is up to you to give that chance to her."

"What about Jimmy?"

"Who better to represent our family to the boy than Mary? She can be our connection to him. She will make sure he is well taken care of."

The voices in the house were silent for several minutes.

"I just can't do it, Sarah. I'll work more overtime. Mary stays. So does the boy."

"You already work fourteen hours a day. The children don't even know who their father is anymore. The only time they see you is on Sundays."

"My decision is final, Sarah."

Myrtle boxed up Jimmy's clothes. She included his favorite books and the soft brown teddy bear he had slept with since he had found it under the tree on Christmas morning. The boxes were sitting by the kitchen door when Samuel and Hank walked into the boardinghouse on Sunday evening.

"What's all this?" Hank asked.

"Jimmy's gone." Myrtle ran into Hank's arms and wept inconsolably.

Lily told Samuel and Hank what had happened in Central City. "We wanted to surprise you, Hank, but instead it was us who ended up with the worst surprise of all."

"Sounds to me like you went about it all wrong," Samuel said. "Sarah warned you that Henry was a proud man. By taking his family the food, you put McCluskey on the defensive from the start. And he saw right through your offer to take his daughter as well. Sounds like you put him right between a rock and a hard place. The only way not to give into his wounded pride was to protect what little of it was left."

"He never even thought about what was best for Jimmy," Lily brooded.

"That's where you are wrong. I think that is all he thought about. He could not in all good conscience leave his brother's boy with strangers, ones I might add, who tried very subtly to buy him. He must be a good man to take his obligation so seriously."

Lily was furious. "So you are saying it is better for five children to go hungry rather than for a man to admit he can't take care of them properly?"

"Not at all. Bad thing is, though, McCluskey will likely work himself into an early grave rather than admit it. Seems to me, Hank, we have a bit more traveling to do."

The men took the early train on Monday morning.

On Tuesday evening they arrived back at the boardinghouse, but they were not alone.

After Myrtle had put Jimmy to bed, and had seen to it that Mary was safely settled in her new room, she and Lily coaxed what had happened out of Samuel and Hank.

"You were right. Henry McCluskey is one of the proudest men I know. And that is what finally made him give in."

"What are you talking about?"

"Proud men are proud of two things, their families, and their work. We simply convinced Henry that he was much too good a man to be mucking mud out of a dark, empty hole. And he's a farmer, born and bred. Farmers only want to do one thing—farm. They have as much respect for the land as Chief Ouray does. The last place a farmer wants to be is under it. They crave the sun like a newborn calf craves its mama's milk."

"So what did you do, Samuel?"

"Gave him what he wanted most. A farm."

"You bought him a farm?" Lily was shocked.

"Not exactly. You remember that nice stretch of flat ground a few miles down from our place?"

"The one that you said would grow good corn and hay for cattle if you could somehow irrigate it with water from the Uncompahgre River?"

"Yes. Like our land, it lays just outside of the Ute reservation. Last fall it was for sale for a song. I told McCluskey that if it's still for sale this spring, I would like to purchase it. But I told him, 'Shoot Henry, I don't know the first thing about farming. I could sure use a good man like yourself to work the place for me, someone who knows farming and irrigation.' Said I'd put up the purchase money for the land, a sturdy plow and a good set of workhorses, and he could pay me back in feed for my cattle. In five years he would own the place free and clear, but he would still have to give me first option on buying his corn and hay."

"Then his wife asked about whether there was a house on the place," Hank said.

"I told her there were enough good pine logs in the nearby San Juans to build a fine, sturdy house. It's going to take a lot of work, I said. Well, Henry said, I'm not afraid of hard work. Then he showed me the calluses to prove it."

"You should have seen the look on those kids faces when he asked them what they thought." Hank added. "I think they hate the mining camp every bit as much as Henry does."

"I told McCluskey that we can't do a thing until the spring thaw in a couple of months. Said it might be best for the boy if he stayed in Denver to get a bit more schooling before they head over the mountains," Samuel said.

"And I told Henry I would be mighty grateful to him to ease Myrtle's burdens by allowing Mary to help her out until we can get someone to take over the boardinghouse this spring and move to Pueblo. Said he would be doing me a real favor," Hank added. He did not tell them about the comment of Myrtle not getting any younger.

"I have to hand it to you both, I never dreamed anyone could change a stubborn Irishman's mind once it is set," Myrtle said, winking at Hank.

"From now on, ladies, you best leave the surprises to us men," Samuel stated in his most manly voice.

"Well, there is one surprise you men will never be able to perform," Lily giggled, as she stroked the small swelling in her tummy.

"Yes, my dear, " Samuel said with a satisfied smile, "but remember, I had a bit of a hand it that, too."

May 1, 1877

8

Making biscuits was next to breathing for Izzie Royce. She poured flour into a bowl, then cupped her hand and measured out the perfect amount of baking powder. She made an indention in the mixture and added fresh, sweet buttermilk, then stirred the mixture, careful not to beat it. She set the dough out on a well-used breadboard and kneaded it ten times. The secret to light, flaky biscuits was not to overwork the dough, and to be as gentle with it as a newborn baby.

A baby. The lady was upstairs resting, having spent the afternoon shopping for supplies for her new house and a layette, accompanied by that Indian woman. Izzie had recognized Lily right off in Lake City last fall, but after meeting once again, there was still no sign of recognition on Lily's face. Izzie should have been relieved, not hurt, but she was. That fact bothered her more than just a little bit.

Izzie had always known that Lily would grow up into a fine figure of a woman. After all, she had been such a beautiful child with deep, laughing amber eyes highlighted with gold flecks. So different than Izzie. Where Izzie's nose had been broad and flat, Lily's had been like a pixie's. Izzie's body had been large and cumbersome, with feet to match. Lily had been as petite and as graceful as a fairy. Izzie's hair had been, and still was, kinky and coarse. Back then Lily had shiny lustrous flaxen hair that had perfectly matched the palomino filly Lily had received on her ninth birthday. Even short, it was still silky smooth with just enough curl to halo her creamy complexion. And now that Lily was with child, she glowed like the morning sun on a bright bunch of daffodils.

Izzie cut out the biscuits, carefully laid them on top of the simmering chicken stew in a heavy Dutch oven and set the pot in the stove to bake. She knew and accepted the fact that, unlike Lily Hastings Bodeen, she was not much to look at, but everyone in Denver knew Izzie Royce made the best chicken pot pie in all of Colorado. And wasn't that worth something?

"Off with your boots now," Izzie caustically told one of her favorite boarders as he walked through the door. "This ain't a barn you know."

He gave her an apologetic grin. "Sorry, Izzie. It just smells so danged good in here I plumb forgot myself. Forgive me?"

"Oh, go on with you now and wash up," she said, handing him a couple of lemon cookies. "Supper will be on the table in about a half hour."

She should not have taken her rainy day out on the man. Hell's fire, she shouldn't even be seeing any clouds at all, Izzie thought, as she looked at the sun streaming through the kitchen window. Hank and Myrtle had appreciated her domestic skills and after being in their employ for just six weeks they had generously upped her salary to thirty-five dollars a month, plus they had given her one of the nicest rooms in the boardinghouse. It was the most money she ever made in her life and surely the nicest room.

No sense in being unhappy at all, she chided herself as she set out the plates on the long wooden table in the kitchen. Course, if she wouldn't have given handouts to all those down and out miners in Lake City, and wouldn't have put up her savings for Kip Whipple to stake his claim, she would have had enough to keep her own place going. Surely her small inn had not been nearly this fine and only had three rooms, that was true enough. And surely Lake City had been no place for a woman, what with the men outnumbering women fifty to one, and the winter lasting eight months with snow hip deep. But the inn, no matter how modest, had been hers free and clear.

As it was, she was lucky to have come out of Lake City with enough to pay her bill at the general store and funds to buy a broken-down old mare to get her back to Denver after she received Hank's offer. But thankfully Myrtle was a good woman, and this boardinghouse was clean and respectable, unlike some of the baudy houses Izzie had cleaned and cooked in since she was sixteen years old. And it was warm—tight and cozy with plenty of wood in the pile, already split and chopped. Hank had seen to that. Lawd, it felt so good to be warm again, Izzie thought.

But even with the fine position, she was back to working for somebody else and that fact didn't sit very well either.

Nope, your problems have been entirely of your own doing and there's no sense, no sense at all, in frettin' or kicking your own behind for it. And the good book surely does warn a soul about coveting what other's have, Izzie said to herself as she neatly laid out the silverware.

But as she wiped the already spotless counters, she could not erase the woman from her mind. Lily Hastings had everything Izzie ever dreamed of as a child. Izzie envied her back then and envied her now. And once again, years later, nothing much had changed. Lily still had all Izzie could ever hope for. Sure, the hopes had changed a bit. Izzie no longer yearned for a fine pony of her own as she did back then, especially after that cold, back-bending ride down from Lake City. And after seeing what happened to those pretty women in the brothels, no longer did she care about being beautiful. God had protected her by making her plain.

But the most important hopes had not changed at all. What Izzie wanted the most now, just like then, was a family and a place to call home. And once again Lily had what Izzie could only dream of.

"And still I don't got either one," Izzie thought with a downhearted sigh. She opened the door to the oven and checked on the pot. The biscuits had risen and baked to a deep golden brown.

But you still make the best pot pie in Colorado, Isabel Hastings Royce, and that fact will just have to do for now. She brushed away a lone tear and forced a smile to her face, hoping somehow the smile would hit her heart.

✤ ✤ ✤

It had been the lemon cookies that had finally given Izzie away. The pot pie had been familiar, but those wonderful cookies . . . Lily knew the minute she took that first bite. She was instantly taken back in time to hot, lazy August afternoons out on the veranda. She was not sitting on a wooden chair in a boardinghouse in Colorado, but on a white wicker settee sipping a tall, cool glass of spring water laced heavily with mint and sugar, munching one of Lucinda's tart lemon cookies. No one before or since then had made lemon cookies as flaky and delicious as Lucinda Hastings, Isabel's mother.

"Are you feeling all right?" Chipeta asked when Lily grew pale and quiet. One minute she had been eating enough for two, and the next minute she looked as though she had seen a ghost.

"I'm fine, just a bit tired. I think I'll go get some air."

"Would you like me to go with you?" Chipeta asked, as Lily awkwardly rose from her chair.

"No, please, just enjoy yourself."

What Lily needed was some time alone to think. She sat down in the rocking chair on the porch and watched the sun just beginning to set in the western sky. It lit up the horizon like a forest fire.

Why hadn't Isabel said anything?

Deep down Lily knew why. She had seen the cool, if not angry looks Izzie Royce had given her when she thought Lily wasn't looking.

And Isabel had every right to be angry, Lily thought dismally, still tasting the tartness of the cookies, and the sourness of the past.

＋ ＋ ＋

Joshua Hastings and his family shared the same last name as Lily's family only because slaves had been given the last name of their owners. Joshua had been Grandfather Hastings' plantation foreman in South Carolina before the fall of the Confederacy and the family had been forced to move to Illinois to live with Grandma Donovan.

Up until the war, Lily had the best life any child could hope for. Looking back, she could say she had even been quite spoiled. Her early childhood had been full, content, and secure.

Even all these years later she could clearly recall that giddy, girlhood feeling of laying under the pink lace coverlet on her canopy bed, whispering her best-kept secrets to her best friend Isabel. She was just nine then, and though Isabel was three years older, they fit together just like salt and pepper. Though black and white, they were a set. Joshua had called them his belles of the south—Isa Belle and Lily Belle. They'd been best friends forever, and promised each other it would always be that way.

But nothing is forever. The day Isabel was taken away so long ago played over in Lily's mind as the darkness of evening closed in around the present.

She and Isabel had been in her bedroom rolling bandages cut from old sheets. Grandfather Hastings came in, took Isabel by the hand and said she had been sold to a man in Charleston in need of a kitchen maid. Isabel quietly rose to leave with him. Her father had warned her early in her childhood that this day might come, saying he had been sold when he was just ten.

The thought had scared Isabel to death. She would wake in the darkness of night, sure the plantation overseer was putting chains around her ankles. She would kick and fight until she was awake enough to realize it was only a blanket.

When Isabel had confided her fears to Lily, her best friend reassured her by saying that Grandfather was a good man, a respected owner, and would never do such a thing as break up a family. Joshua, Lucinda and Isabel weren't just property, they were family, she said, trying to calm Isabel's fear.

Then Lily took it one step further by asking Isabel to take a blood vow and become her blood sister, assuring that their hearts would be together forever. Each took a sharp knife and cut a forefinger. Then they sat in silence under a blooming magnolia and held their fingers together for a full hour, sealing their vow. The bad dream had never come back until the moment when it became a reality.

Lily had blocked the door, then begged and pleaded and even kicked her grandfather in the shin trying to stop him. But he would not change his mind, saying that two hundred dollars was more than a fair price for the girl, and besides, the money was needed to help the war effort. Grandfather brushed her aside like a pesky flea on a dog.

"The money could help buy your father and the other soldiers a hot meal. Don't be so selfish child!"

Lily cried for days, clutching the rag doll Isabel had handed her from the wagon before it started down the lane. But never once did Lily ever see Joshua shed a tear. Nor did he cry when they laid Lucinda in the ground several months later. After the funeral Lily overheard Joshua tell her grandfather that his lovely Lucinda had died of a broken heart and empty arms.

Then Joshua had walked away into the woods. Grandfather had not tried to stop him and Lily feared that Joshua would be shot as a runaway slave. But Joshua did not run. He chopped on live oak trees from dawn to dusk, and sang old spirituals in his deep, baritone voice.

When he returned days later, he said simply, "I done left it all to the Lawd. You chile, gotta do da same. Cain't change it. No, suh. Cain't bring dem back. Lawd I wished I could. But I cain't. Dat's jus' the way things be."

After the war Joshua spent two years trying to find Isabel but she had disappeared without a trace. Lily's father, as she had known him, had disappeared as well. A stranger that looked a bit like him came home and took over his chair. Papa had lost his leg in the battle at Vicksburg, as well as his will to live. Day after day, he sat in the oak rocker by the fire complaining about how cold it was in Illinois and sipping what was left of his Tennessee whiskey.

And so to fill the deep emptiness in both their souls, Joshua became Lily's surrogate father. He had taught her to handle horses, to whittle, to skip rocks and to fish. Things he should have taught Isabel.

And in return, Lily became the daughter that had been taken from him. She blessed him with the gift of time that, once again, had rightfully been Isabel's to give.

Together Joshua and Lily spent their days in the barn, and their evenings reading her Bible. Whenever she would come to a passage on forgiveness Joshua would sigh and say, "Read dat 'gain, Lily Belle." Then he would read it himself with a little coaching from Lily, repeat the words as if branding them into his heart and fervently ask, "Oh yes suh, sweet Jesus. Teach me dat."

And Jesus did. Joshua received the courage to learn to let go of blame, to accept without bitterness, and to truly forgive without malice, something her father had not the strength to do. Instead he had chosen to follow in the path of Grandfather Hastings, who had drank himself to an early grave, fighting a battle he could not win alone, and too weak and angry to ask for help.

How much of her father was in Isabel? Lily wondered. Was a forgiving heart something a person inherited, like the color of their skin? Or was it a learned trait, taught by those who found the art of forgiveness by trial and error? Had Isabel inherited Joshua's compassion? Had twelve years of his teaching somehow planted that seed of absolution?

Would Isabel be able to forgive as well?

"Excuse, me, ma'am, but the night air's getting a bit damp. I brung you a wrap. Not good for that baby to get chilled."

But the cool tone of Izzie's voice was even more chilling than the night air.

"Thank you, Izzie," Lily managed to say. "Please, would you like to sit with me for a few minutes?"

Izzie looked rigidly at Lily and contemplated the offer. "Nope. Don't think so. Got a kitchen to clean." She went back inside the kitchen and firmly shut the door.

The next morning Lily stood silently while Chipeta graciously accepted the lemon cookies Izzie had packed for their long trip back to the Western Slope. Lily knew it would be wrong to leave without offering some sort of explanation, some sort of apology. But mere words never replace hurt and betrayal. She knew that only too well.

So she never said a word and felt like, once again, she had let her best friend down.

✤ ✤ ✤

On the way to the stage station, Samuel pulled the buggy up beside a large corral at the Denver Stockyards.

"Well, what do you think?" he asked, looking as excited as a kid on Christmas.

One hundred Hereford cows looked at Lily through their soft, wide, brown eyes. Calves darted to and fro amidst their mothers, kicking up their heels in playfulness.

"It's the beginning of our future, Lily," Samuel stated proudly. He then explained that he would be staying on in Denver and would start driving the cattle over the mountains to the ranch by the end of the week.

"Soon as I round up some help, we'll have these critters on their way. Shouldn't take more than a month," he said.

Only Chipeta noticed the look of dismay on Lily's face.

He then pointed to a stocky brown and white bull in a pen. "And that magnificent beast is sire of the Pleasant Valley Ranch herd," he added, stating that Victoria had the curly-haired bull shipped all the way from England. The animal was named with an illustrious title to befit his position: King Ferdinand, but Samuel had chosen to simply call Freddie.

"Can't have grand offspring without a grand sire!" Samuel said cheerfully, as he patted Lily's rounded abdomen.

"How much was he, Samuel?" Lily asked.

"Now, don't you worry about it. Victoria and I worked it all out. Besides, the deal has already been made. You just worry about keeping yourself fat and sassy until I get back. There's plenty of supplies at the ranch, and Ouray promised he and Chipeta would check on you every couple of days. He has to stay in Denver to meet with the governor, but will be returning by next week. I'll be along with the cattle and supply wagons just as soon as we get things squared away with the Bureau of Indian Affairs."

Only when Lily turned her head away and bit her lip, did he notice her fears.

"I know this is not the best timing, but I just couldn't pass up the cattle. They're prime stock. And the business with the Bureau just can't wait. You'll be just fine. You are the toughest, most self-reliant woman I've ever met. It's one of the things I loved about you from the very start." He handed her the bill of sale. "I'd hate to lose this in a stream somewhere on the trail. It will be safer with you; be sure not to lose it." She folded it without looking and put it in her satchel. She did not really want to know.

At the station Samuel gave Lily a gentle kiss and promised to be home by the middle of June, and further promised he would be sure the baby's room would be finished in time for its arrival the first part of July.

As Lily boarded the coach without Samuel, she was horrified at the mere thought of being in the vast country alone. She was also terribly frustrated. Samuel had taken a very expensive step and never once had consulted her about the enormous purchase. Even with Victoria's backing, they were taking on a huge and risky investment.

But what bothered Lily even more was Samuel's lack of concern for her and the baby. He had passed off her fears as if they were a child's nightmare. And she was bothered by the lack of him treating her like an equal. Yet, she was expected to be strong. Expected to be self-reliant. Expected to be a good wife and mother. But she had the uneasy feeling that Samuel would never expect her to truly be his partner.

✣ ✣ ✣

The wheels of the stagecoach creaked as it bounced over the hard, rocky ground and dust swirled into the windows. Chipeta disliked this white way of travel, but the silence from Lily was even more uncomfortable than the ride. She tried to concentrate on the scenery as the coach headed up into the foothills of the vast Rockies. Wildflowers were just beginning to bloom in the bright spring sunshine: bright blue lupine, crimson Indian paintbrush, buttery yellow lazy Susan's. Several does with their fawns grazed in a grassy meadow, pausing to look up at the coach. But even the beauty of the day did not lighten the heaviness she felt from Lily.

"Are you worried about Samuel?" Chipeta asked.

"A little." Lily did not want to answer any questions. She was as furious at herself as she had been at her husband. Mad that she never even tried to get on equal footing with Samuel. And even more irritated that she never told Isabel that her father was alive. She rubbed the faint scar on her finger.

"She is not any different from other woman, you know, just darker skinned," Chipeta finally said.

Lily realized that Chipeta thought she was upset because Izzie was a negress. "It's not what you think. I knew her a long time ago."

"And she did something to hurt you?"

"Actually, we were best friends."

The uncomfortable silence continued for several more miles.

"Lily, is this problem with your friend a canyon that can't be crossed, or merely a gap where there needs to be a bridge?"

"I don't know."

Lily opened up and told Chipeta all about Joshua. And she also told her about the animosity she felt toward Samuel for not being included in his decisions.

Lily felt a welcome release when she had finished venting her frustrations. They had spewed from her like steam from a cauldron. And Chipeta, in her usual quiet way, pondered all Lily had said before finally speaking.

"Sometimes the men in our tribe think my husband is wrong in letting me speak my opinions. Indian women are not supposed to be able to think and are considered inferior when it comes to tribal matters. And though Ouray values my opinion, sometimes it makes my heart heavy when he speaks to me of the hard decisions he must make concerning our people. I don't know which would be worse, Ouray not speaking to me of the problems he faces, or the cumbersome burden of having to worry about them as well. My heart grieves with his. Maybe your husband just wants to spare you from worry."

"But what he doesn't realize is not knowing is even more worrisome."

Chipeta smiled at her with understanding. "Yes, I suppose that would be true."

"You and Ouray seem so devoted, so close. You share such a deep love for each other and your people. Were you raised in the same tribe?"

"Actually I was not born a Ute. I was Kiowa Apache. When I was very small, both my parents were killed in a raid and I was taken in by the Utes. When I turned fourteen, I was asked to become a surrogate mother, what the white people call a nanny, to Ouray's son, Queashegut. Ouray's first wife, Black Mare, had died during child-birth. Ouray called the boy Paron, which means 'apple.' Paron had two deep dimples and a round face like an apple." Chipeta's face lit up when she spoke of the boy.

"Two years later Ouray and I married. We have been together seventeen years."

"And Ouray's son? He is grown now?" Lily had never heard Chipeta speak of the boy before.

"By the time Paron was five he could ride like the wind, and stalk and shoot game. He loved to hunt. Then when Paron turned six years old, Ouray took him on his first buffalo hunt on the eastern plains. They spent two weeks having a wonderful time and a very successful hunt. But the night before they were to return home, one hundred Sioux warriors attacked their camp. The Sioux killed three Utes and stole half the horses.

Chipeta's velvet eyes clouded to a deep darkness. "Ouray tried to hide the boy under some blankets but the Sioux warriors found him. When they rode away with Paron, Ouray tried to follow but he was outnumbered and he had to return to protect the main camp."

"Was he able to get Paron back?"

"Ouray searched for ten years trying to find his son . . .our son. Then four years ago as part of the negotiations of the Brunot Treaty, the government promised Ouray that they would find Paron as part of securing his approval of the treaty. Brunot wrote all the Indian agents and was able to learn that Paron had been sold by the Sioux to Neva, brother of Chief Friday of the Northern Arapahoe. When Neva died, Paron was then sold to the Southern Arapahoe. Having been raised in a different tribe myself, I ached for what the boy must have gone through."

Chipeta fingered the dust on the window of the coach.

"When Ouray met with Brunot early in 1873 concerning the treaty, Brunot again promised to have the cavalry find Paron and was to deliver him back to us in August. But by September sixth when the council for the treaty began, Brunot had still failed to find Paron. So instead of giving him back his son, Brunot promised Ouray one thousand dollars a year for ten years as 'salary' for working with the government. And Otto Mears promised Ouray a house and 160 acres of land."

Chipeta's voice became bitter.

"It had gone with the Brunot Treaty just as it had gone with the Hunt Treaty of 1868. During those earlier negotiations Ouray had made a statement that crossed through my mind a thousand times during the 1873 negotiations, like a deep rushing river that slowly cuts away at a riverbank. In 1868, Ouray had said, 'The agreement an Indian makes to a United States treaty is like the agreement a buffalo makes with his hunter when pierced with arrows. All he can do is lie down and give in.'"

"Once again, my heart had been pierced, but this wound went very deep. I was tired of having to be put in a position of laying down and giving in, especially where Paron was concerned."

Chipeta brushed the coarse dirt from her hands. Her normally serene face turned to a deep scowl.

"Ouray signed the treaty, with the promise from Brunot that he would continue looking for Paron. Having thought of Paron as my own child, I was sorely disappointed in my husband's decision. I had encouraged him not to sign until the boy was indeed back to us. I thought of the money, house, and land as a bribe, especially when I felt that the land they were 'generously giving' us, was ours in the first place. It had been Ute ground for centuries."

Lily wondered if Chipeta and Ouray had argued over his decision.

"Brunot promised the government would set aside a large sum of money for the Utes, and that interest on the money could be drawn annually by the tribe to use for food, clothing, and supplies. To this, my husband said that he would rather have all the money in the bank to be allocated by the Tribal Council as needed. And here it is three years later, and the tribe has not received a single dime."

The stagecoach continued its ascent into the Rockies. Lily, by now used to Chipeta's long silences between conversation, waited impatiently while Chipeta gathered her thoughts together before continuing.

"In October, Brunot brought an Arapahoe boy to us and once again, I hoped for the return of our lost child. The boy was seventeen, as Paron would have been and he favored his left hand, just as Paron had.

"The boy called himself Friday. There has been a long-standing resentment between the tribes and being brought up as an Arapahoe, Friday had an intense hatred of the Utes. And he seemed to have an extreme dislike of us as well. His animosity toward Ouray was most unbearable.

"Brunot said there was a distinct resemblance between Ouray and Friday, but I could not see it. Maybe if I would have been the boy's birth mother I would have felt something, but I felt nothing. Nor did Ouray, and that troubled him. It still does. We offered to take the boy with us but he chose to return to the Arapahoe people. We do not know to this day if Friday is indeed, Paron."

Chipeta's voice went from bitterness to a sadness that seemed to come from deep within.

"And you and Ouray never had children of your own?"

"I am not able to bear children. Ouray, being a chief, would have every right to take another wife but he has chosen not to do this. We did, however, take in three children and raise them as our own. They have been a joy but will never fill the hole in my heart, or in Ouray's, that was left after Paron was taken from us."

Chipeta turned and looked at Lily sincerely.

"My friend, I tell you all this because I feel deeply that you need to repair whatever wrongs you may have with the black woman who was once your friend. If there is a way you can give back what was taken from her, you must find a way to do it, not just for her or for

Joshua, but for you as well. We can't change the past, however good or bad it has been. But we can make the best of what we have today, and try to make things right for tomorrow. I feel strongly that you must do this before your baby is born."

Chipeta smiled and the composed look returned to her face.

"And Lily, even after all these years, Ouray and I are still not always of one mind. But we are of one heart. You and Samuel will have this as well. It just takes some time."

✦ ✦ ✦

Lily was exhausted by the time the stage pulled in the next afternoon to the town of Ouray.

Chipeta's half brother, Piah, was waiting for her at the station.

"Your husband is not with you?" he asked, looking inside the coach.

"He stayed on in Denver to speak with the governor."

"And he allowed you to come home unguarded? Once again, I suppose he feels the company of whites is more compatible and important than of his own people."

Lily could hear the caustic bitterness in his voice. Chipeta chose to ignore the comment.

"This is my friend, Lily."

Piah gave Lily a bitter stare but did not say a word. He didn't have to. The look had said exactly what he felt toward Lily, and to all whites he felt were intruding onto Ute land. Lily had seen him riding a majestic-looking blood bay stallion on their land earlier in the spring just after their arrival in late March. Piah had not come down to speak to them, but had stayed high on a hill to the north, watching as Samuel and Henry McCluskey unloaded wood from a wagon for the house.

Piah thrust a pair of reins into Chipeta's hands. "We go now."

Chipeta handed the reins back to him. "Lily and I are going to rent a buggy. She will be staying the night with me and I am going to take her home tomorrow."

Piah's eyes narrowed and he grabbed back the reins to the mare he had brought for his sister to ride.

He looked down at them. "Sister, you are too kind and trusting. Just because your husband has forgotten, don't you forget who your people are." He whirled the horses around and left Lily and Chipeta standing in his dust.

On the way to the farm, Chipeta explained Piah's resentment toward the whites and toward Ouray. To her brother, and to many of her people, treaties meant nothing, as they felt that the land could be owned by no man. It belonged to the Great Spirit, as did the great bear, the eagle, the elk and deer, the birds of the air, the fish of the waters, and all the other animals that inhabited the land.

In 1872, during the early negotiations with Brunot, Ouray and Piah had gotten into a heated argument over the mere thought of bargaining with the whites. Her brother had failed to see Ouray's deep sincerity and purpose in trying to protect the Ute people from what he felt was inevitable. After his visit to Washington D.C. in 1868, Ouray had seen first hand the immense power of the Great White Father, and the formidable army that was at his disposal.

But Piah disagreed vehemently with Ouray and felt the Ute people were being sold out by their chief. Brother-in-law or not, Piah had attempted to murder Ouray. Ouray had reached for his knife while holding Piah by the throat. Chipeta intervened and grasped Ouray's knife from its sheath, thereby saving her brother's life.

"I fear not only for my family but for all my people as well. There are many like Piah who strongly disagree with my husband. You must take care to protect yourself Lily. I don't know what the next few years will bring."

Lily was thankful for Chipeta's offer of a soft bed. The four miles to Ouray and Chipeta's home had felt like ten. The muscles in her back were knotted and coiled like a rope after the long day stagecoach ride from Denver, and though the seats of the stagecoach had been uncomfortable, at least they had offered a back rest and a bit of padding. The rickety buckboard, the only transportation that had been available at the livery, had been equipped with neither.

Chipeta made Lily a cup of soothing spearmint tea, but Lily was too tired to finish it. As she stretched out on a bed covered with a brightly colored woven wool blanket, the baby began to kick unmercifully, finally having room to move. Lily prayed that her little person would be content in the womb for at least another month. Already she could feel her stomach muscles tightening in preparation for birth and her breasts were becoming heavy with milk.

This child is every bit as impatient as its father, Lily thought. But she had to admit she was getting anxious, and more than a bit nervous as well.

As tired as she was, sleep did not come. Lily thought of the fear she had heard in Chipeta's voice when she spoke about the growing discontent among the Ute people. She thought about Joshua's kind, empty eyes, and Isabel's cold stare.

She got up and lit the oil lamp Chipeta had left by the side of the bed. She took a pen and paper from her dusty traveling bag and began to write. When she finished hours later, she went to put the letters in her satchel. It was then that she noticed the bill of sale for the cows. She slowly opened it and gasped at the price Samuel had paid for King Ferdinand. But she also noticed something else. Her name was on the bill of sale as well. She and Samuel were joint owners.

The next morning Chipeta tried to talk Lily into staying with her until Samuel returned, but Lily kindly declined the invitation, anxious to return home and begin to complete her nest. They hitched up the wagon and headed south.

Henry waved to them from a field he was plowing into long, straight rows. Samuel had told her that planting would have to take priority over the house and she felt a keen sense of anticipation to see if any progress had been made on their new home. She hoped that at least the walls would be up so she could start working on the baby's room.

They crossed the Uncompahgre River, which was running swift and muddy from the spring runoff. The first thing Henry and Samuel had done in early March was to build a good sturdy bridge before the snow had started to melt in the high mountains. It had been a wise thing to do.

As the buggy rounded the bend to the house, Lily tried to hide her disappointment. It looked as if nothing had been done since she and Samuel had left for Denver two weeks earlier.

Samuel had tried to hire carpenters in the town of Ouray but no man had been willing. The mines were paying a sign-on bonus to lure in workers. Samuel had warned her that Henry would be spending the next few months working to get in two large fields of good grass hay and corn, and would only be available to work on the house if the weather turned wet, and he would be needing to work on his home as well. His family was living in a hastily constructed one-room log cabin, sturdy, but only a bit larger than the mine shack they had lived in while at Central City.

The logs Samuel had cut were still piled beside where the house was to be. A rock foundation had been laid but the walls on the house were only up about five feet. Lily realized she would be spending yet more nights in a canvas tent, but this time Samuel would not be beside her to provide the sense of security she had come to rely on from him. Yet she was determined that her child's first sight would be a roof, not a cottonwood tree. The house would be finished by the first of July even if she had to do it herself.

"Are you sure you do not want me to keep you company until Samuel gets back?" Chipeta offered before she climbed back onto the seat of the buckboard.

"No, thank you anyway. But I would be grateful if you would post two letters for me at the Los Piños Agency." Lily reached in her satchel, took out the two carefully written letters that had taken her half the night to write, and handed them up to Chipeta. But as the buggy pulled out of sight and the heavy stillness of the vast country closed in, Lily wished Chipeta would have stayed.

A lone black crow teased her from the cottonwood tree. She grabbed a broom and began to whisk away at a mouse nest in a corner behind the new cast iron cookstove still covered by a wooden crate. "Besides, I'll have plenty to keep me busy," she said aloud to the crow that gazed down at her from the cottonwood tree to inside her roofless house. Her voice echoed back at her, sounding lonely and alone. The crow flew away without answering.

The rest of the day passed quickly. Lily found a shovel and dug holes for the slips of lilacs she had dug up from around the bushes at the boardinghouse. She hauled buckets of water from the river and gave them, and herself, a good, long drink.

As she spaded out a spot for a vegetable garden, she had the uneasy feeling of eyes on her. Several times she looked up but could see nothing move but a few tree branches in the morning breeze and an occasional hawk. She planted corn, beans, carrots, lettuce, spinach, and peas and hauled up countless buckets of water. By the time she had finished with the garden spot, the sun was beginning to sink into the western horizon.

Too tired to light a fire, Lily opened a can of beans, ate them cold, then opened a tin of peaches and ate them warm. She then laid out the bedroll in the tent, exhausted from the day's toil and last evening's lack of sleep.

The floor of the tent was cold, damp and uncomfortable. Her back hurt miserably and she tried to turn, groaning out loud when she did. She felt something crawl up her arm and she smacked it away, grateful that in the dark night she could not see what it was.

Tiny feet scurried over the canvas and Lily shivered. Somewhere far off in the night she heard a screeching scream, like that of a wounded animal. Then came muffled tramping sounds of footsteps outside the tent. She was too frightened to look out and see what was just on the other side of the flimsy tent flap. She tightened the ties on the flap, and piled her few belongings in front of the door. But still she felt like the canvas walls of the tent offered no more protection than onionskin paper.

The sound of breaking branches crackled and popped. Then came footsteps again, louder and closer this time. Lily hovered down in the bedroll and covered her head, all the while thinking of Ouray's small boy Paron, whisked away from his family by angry savages with wrathful scowling faces like Colorow and Piah. The faces were covered with war paint. Their bronze arms wielded devilish tomahawks and long shining knives glittered in the night as they took them from their sheaths tied to their rugged, dirty brown legs.

She thought of the butcher knife in the box stored in the wooden shed. Samuel had fixed the roof to protect the supplies they had brought in March and compared to the tent, the shed was a fortress. But there was no way Lily's shaking hands would ever be able to untie the knots she had put in the door of the tent. Nor would her jelly-filled legs ever be able to carry her even that far in the dark, moonless night.

Another screech, another howl. More cracking branches, as loud as the sound of gunfire. More footsteps.

Lily burrowed deeper into the bedroll and waited. She held her hands over her protruding stomach, as if trying to shield her unborn from the savages when they finally swooped into the tent to carry it away. She prayed loudly, hoping her words would protect her from the demons outside . . . and the demons within.

When the faint, pale rose rays of morning started to stream in between the seams of the canvas tent, Lily finally had the courage to untie one knot and look out. Deer tracks and droppings surrounded the tent, the telltale signs of last night's intruders.

She rolled back the canvas door and looked at the high rugged mountains looming gray and bleak in the faint light. Stone cold pinnacles looked like peaked noses of ghosts, glaring down at her through dead, evil eyes. Great deep chasms of gullies gaped open like mouths taunting her, with ravines of broken teeth. Standing groves of aspen trees at the base of the mountains shivered in the early morning light, as if yearning for the sun to warm their leaves in the crisp morning air. Lily shuddered as well.

She walked over to what was to be her new home. But she did not see the dream of what it was going to be; she saw reality. The slips of lilacs she had carefully planted and watered just outside the door had been chewed down to a stub. A mouse nest was once again in the corner behind the stove.

Lily Hastings Bodeen, joint owner of one hundred cows and an over-priced curly haired bull named King Ferdinand, self-reliant rancher and pioneer woman, sat down in the dust beside her dead lilacs and cried.

Then ever so quietly, shadowy pale pink rays reached out to the dismal ashen faces of granite. Wan, sunken cheeks flushed lightly as the early glow of the sun warmed them. Then pale tangerine, then deeper salmon, and finally a bright vermilion, just before the life-giving warm radiance of sunlight burst upon them.

The aspen leaves, the pine, the cedar, all became a vivid, brilliant green, illuminating the sharp early morning sapphire sky. As the heavens turned a deep aquamarine, the last stars of night disappeared.

Lily rose slowly and brushed away the dust from her skirt, the tears from her eyes, and then grabbed a bucket to gather water for her lilacs.

✛ ✛ ✛

The first pain came as she was carrying a full bucket back from the river, a dull aching throb deep in her back. She set the bucket down and took a deep breath. The second one came later when she bent down to gather dry sticks for a fire. Then came another as she poured water into the teakettle.

Then again during her midday meal, so strong that she dropped her teacup. It sliced through her like a sharp, long edged razor, reaching from her back to around her tight, rock hard stomach. She clenched her teeth and doubled her fists. Finally, it subsided to a dulling throb in her back but fear gripped her heart. There was no horse to ride for help, and even if there would have been, it was eight miles to the McCluskeys' and fourteen back to Chipeta's.

The pain came again, sharper and harder and longer this time. She doubled over and cried out in agony. Beads of perspiration broke out above her lip. She waited for the pain to subside, then slowly made her way to the canvas tent. Already the intense noonday sun had raised the temperature to a stifling warmth inside the tent. Lily tried to move the bedroll outside but just as she reached the doorway the pain seized her again, enveloping her like a dense fog. Then again, and again. Lily writhed on the bedroll, turning one way, then another, trying to escape the torment. Flies and mosquitoes swarmed around her face and sweat rolled between her heaving breasts. She tried to breath, but the air was hot and heavy inside the sweltering tent.

Somewhere a deep, stern voice called out to her from the fiery fog.

"You must walk."

Lily opened her eyes. A shining silver armband glistened on copper skin. It was Piah. Lily screamed. "No, please, no!"

"You walk!" another Indian commanded to her in English. He then turned and spoke to Piah, but Piah argued back. The Indian, much bigger and stronger looking, sternly gave the command again and Piah mounted his horse and rode away swiftly.

Strong arms forced her to an upright position and then lifted her to stand. He forced her to walk, stopping when the pain became too intense for Lily's weak legs to carry her. She leaned on him for support. His eyes were kind and he looked to be almost as terrified with what was happening as she was.

The hot sun was nearing the western horizon when Lily heard the whinny of horses. She looked in their direction, but all afternoon the sweat had streamed into her eyes, stinging them like nettle and making it hard for her to focus. The sound of hooves came close, then the sound of hurried footsteps.

The voice was soft and reassuring.

"It's okay, Lily. It's Chipeta. I'm here. Sapiah, you go now."

With a look of great relief, the Indian walked away and grabbed the reins of his horse.

Chipeta softly brushed the sweat from Lily's face with a cool cloth as Lily fought her way through another contraction. After the pain subsided, an old woman lifted Lily's skirt, pulled down her pantalets, and felt inside the birth cavity.

The old woman's shrill voice spoke sharply to Chipeta in Ute.

Chipeta nodded and urged Lily to walk to the shade of the large cottonwood tree.

"You must bend down now, Lily," Chipeta said. "No, like this." Chipeta crouched down, legs wide apart.

Lily bent down and grabbed Chipeta's arms, clutching them tightly. The old woman placed a brightly colored woven blanket between her legs, covering the tufts of wild columbines and violets that were blooming in full splendor. Then the old woman placed a long stick of smooth, hard wood between Lily's lips.

"Bite down, Lily, " Chipeta said. "Look to the Shining Mountains and push your baby from the spirit world."

Lily clenched the stick between her teeth and pushed.

When the pain eased, Chipeta took the stick from her mouth. "Breathe deep, Lily."

The pain hit again. Somewhere deep in Lily's soul a dam of inner strength broke free. Determination flowed through every cell of her body. Chipeta put the stick back Lily's mouth and she bit down hard, leaving deep dents in the wood. She gripped Chipeta's arms and pushed relentlessly, feeling the life slide from her womb.

The old woman barked at Chipeta.

"Again now. . ." Chipeta commanded. "Push!"

A limp, lifeless form lay blue and transparent on the colorful blanket. The old woman carefully lifted it, cleared its tiny mouth and tried to breath her air into the child. It lay still in her wrinkled hands.

The old woman clucked her tongue and muttered.

"Too small, too soon," Chipeta interpreted.

The old woman gently turned the baby over and massaged its fragile back. Then once again she cleared the tiny mouth and attempted to breath her life into it. The spirits waited to take the child back to their world.

But little Rose Kathleen Bodeen proved to be a fighter. She gasped, choked and then began to wail loudly, flinging her arms and tiny bantam legs as if trying to swim away from them. She blinked her swollen eyes, as if searching out the bright blue of the sky and the magnificence of the snow still clinging to the high peaks of the Shining Mountains. Then she kicked and squirmed and screamed in the warm sunshine, fighting off the spirits.

An hour later, little Rose's delicate, yet determined heart-shaped mouth nudged greedily at her mother's breast. Finding what she was looking for, she suckled voraciously at the life-giving sustenance.

Slowly the spirits slid back into their world, after beholding the spunk and determination of Rose Kathleen Bodeen to stay in hers.

Los Piños Agency
May, 1879

9

I don't understand this, my friend, the white man's ways. And sadly, Mr. Meeker is doing nothing to try to understand ours," Chief Ouray stated.

Bodeen had been trying to explain to Ouray and the many other chiefs and sub-chiefs of the various Ute tribes gathered at the Los Piños Agency for the annual Spring Bear Dance, the reasoning of Nathan Meeker, new Indian agent at the White River Indian Agency recently built in the northwest corner of Colorado. But how could he explain Meeker to the chiefs, when he didn't understand, or even care for the man himself? Secretly, Bodeen had been as disappointed with the appointment as Ouray had been.

Samuel had first met Meeker in Greeley in 1870 when Nathan was just establishing the Greeley Colony about one hundred miles north of Denver. Samuel had taken an instant dislike to the man. Maybe it had been his eloquent nature of speech, using lofty words that made Samuel feel like he was constantly being preached to. High and mighty were the words Samuel thought of when assessing Meeker. Maybe it had been the feeling he got from Meeker that he was just a bit better than everyone else. It had been easy to surmise from the Ute chiefs that Meeker had not changed.

Nathan Meeker was honest and dedicated, that was true enough. He was a well-educated man, especially knowledgeable in the field of agriculture. In 1870, he had convinced his friend and benefactor, the famous newspaperman Horace Greeley, with an idea for the perfect Utopia, the Colorado Territory. Horace financed Meeker's dream and in return the new settlement was christened Greeley.

Meeker had proved to be a tireless worker, devoting himself, as well as his life savings, to the welfare and growth of the colony. He started the *Greeley Tribune*, sending flowery articles depicting the magnificence of the West back to Greeley to publish in the *New York Tribune*. Dreamers flocked to the new settlement like starving immigrants to a free banquet, not realizing that they in turn were to sell their souls to Meeker.

Nathan Meeker was also quite egotistical. He built the most expensive house in Greeley, borrowing heavily from Horace to finance its construction, with the understanding that he would repay his debts when financially able to do so.

Unfortunately for Meeker, Horace Greeley died in 1872. The new owners of the *New York Tribune* refused his articles, and the executor of his friend's estate ordered his debts be paid or Meeker would face court action.

Nathan's troubles surmounted when the colonists experienced grasshopper plagues, lack of rainfall, and other misfortunes known to farmers. Their hard work and dreams blew away like dust. The promised milk and honey never came and once again they found their children's faces gaunt with hunger.

Meeker's worst traits began to surface. He became more obnoxious and tactless than ever, insulting colonists in public and preaching about the sins of drinking, gambling, smoking, and laziness. Disillusioned and desperate, one by one the pioneers crept away into the night, afraid of facing Meeker in the daylight.

In 1877, Meeker applied for the position of Indian agent at the White River Agency, hoping the $1,500 per year salary would help pay his debts and keep him out of court. His appointment was confirmed in March of 1878.

In May of 1878, he traveled to the remote agency, bringing his wife Arvilla and daughter Josie. They were appalled at what welcomed them. The Agency consisted of a few small shacks with dirt roofs. Undaunted, Meeker looked over the lush green valley and realized the potential of the region. The pastureland on which the Ute ponies grazed was prime for raising crops.

Once again Meeker's eloquence paid off. He asked for, and received, invaluable assistance from the Secretary of the Interior. He was promised an allotment of $20,000 to start a model farm, with the hopes he could turn the nomadic Utes into farmers. He secured rations for the Utes. Flour, oats, and even plug tobacco were distributed on a weekly basis. But the soft-gloved, giving hand hid Meeker's iron fist. Nathan also resolved he was given the authority to give the Indians orders that must be obeyed or face his punishment.

Just as he had been in Greeley, Meeker was brusque and abrupt. Though he was well-read in many fields, he had no understanding of diplomacy, of Indians, or the Ute way of life.

✜ ✜ ✜

The two principal White River Ute chiefs, Douglas and Jack, complained to Bodeen that Meeker was trying to rule the tribe by threats, insisting the Indians become self-sustaining farmers. He firmly told Chief Johnson that the Ute ponies must go, threatening to plow up the racetrack located next to the agency. To show his resolution, he brought in whites to build roads and bridges on the Ute land and hired surveyors to project routes for canals.

Last month he used money allotted for Ute supplies to build a boardinghouse, blacksmith shop, and living quarters for his employees and their families. He ordered a threshing machine, a gristmill, and two wrought iron plows.

Most recently, Meeker had further outraged the chiefs by stating that the Utes did not own the valley and could only stay there as long as they did his bidding and his work.

"Adams, do you believe this as well?"

The air in the room grew tense as Charles Adams, agent at the Los Piños Agency, rose to answer.

"I believe as you do, that the land has been set aside for the use of the Utes as stated in the Brunot Treaty. If you choose to farm the land, any harvest is to be used to feed your families."

Several chiefs seemed satisfied with his answer.

"Ouray has found that farming greatly increases the Tabeguache tribe food stores for winter," Bodeen added. "Maybe if you..."

Chief Douglas stood up angrily. "Black men came to us years ago from the South with stories of the white men's brutality, of torture, of working like beasts. Just as with them, we know the crops grown on White River land will not be used to feed our tribe's families, they will be used to fatten Meeker's pockets with paper. We will become slaves to no man!" He banged on the table with his fist, and the White River sub-chiefs yelled in agreement.

Chief Jack retrieved a newspaper clipping from inside his pocket and handed it to Samuel.

"Read!"

"I've already seen it," he said.

The article that had appeared in the *Greeley Tribune* stated, "The Utes Must Go!" The chief stated that he had accused Meeker of writing the article, an accusation that Meeker had denied.

"Even if these are not his words," Jack stated, "they are of his mind. He has planted the seed in the heads of the white people."

Samuel encouraged Douglas and Jack to ride to Denver and speak to Governor Pitkin.

"You go, too," Douglas stated firmly.

Samuel declined, stating that he could not leave his ranch. The mother cows were calving, and he had corn and oats that needed planting.

"I will go," Adams said.

"And I will do this," Samuel stated. "I will write of your concerns to the Bureau of Indian Affairs, and to Pitkin as well. And as soon as I am able, Charles and I will attempt to speak to Meeker."

But the chiefs were not satisfied. The tension had been drawn as tight as an arrow on a bowstring. The room grew hot in the stale afternoon air.

Ouray stood up. "Come," he stated. "Let's join in the festivities. We will speak more of this later."

✚ ✚ ✚

Chipeta explained to Lily the significance of the Bear Dance.

The Utes loved singing and dancing almost as much as they loved their children and their horses. Human passions such as love, hope, anger, and fear, were all found in dance. It was through dance that the Utes explained the meaning of life.

She explained that dances were held to celebrate all-important occasions: new campsites, old campsites, hunting, courage for battle, and celebrating victory or grieving over defeat. Dances were held to drive away hunger or famine. And sometimes they were held simply to keep warm in winter.

"The spirit that sings, must also dance," she said.

The Mamaqui Mowats, or Bear Dance, was one of the Utes' major social events of the year. All tribes of the Ute Nation gathered to celebrate. It was the oldest of all the dances, performed every spring. The celebration and dance lasted three to four days, and including dancing, socializing, music, eating, and trading between the tribes.

The origin of the dance, she said, was that many, many moons ago, a Ute brave had a dream in which he came upon a great bear who had not yet awakened from his winter hibernation. The brave knew that it was late in the season for the bear to still be sleeping, and if not awakened, it would soon starve. So, the Indian woke the bear and as a reward for his kindness, the bear took the boy deep into the woods where the other bears were celebrating the end of winter. The bears taught the boy their special dance, and he returned to teach it to his people. The dance signified lasting mutual friendship. It was also a mating ritual of courtship between the young people.

Lily watched, entranced by the colorful antics of the dancers. The drums, flutes and rasping rhythm of the morache or bear growler, with its sound created by a hard stick being drawn across a roughly notched surface of a animal's jaw bone, was hypnotic. Her heart seemed to beat in time with the bear chant, which had been handed down to special singers for generations. The chant was to wake the bears, considered one of the most sacred animals by the Ute people.

The dance was performed several hundred yards away from the agency, inside a circular wall enclosed with six-foot cedar boughs. The single opening into the enclosure faced the spring morning sun to the east. Men and women were lined up in parallel rows, men stood on one side, women on the other. It was up to the women to ask the men to dance. Refusing to accept a dance invitation was considered an insult and was not tolerated. A dance leader, usually a medicine man or tribal elder, was armed with a willow whip. He used it on reluctant males who were slow in accepting an invitation.

The women wore colorful shawls over their shoulders. The steps were simple, three steps forward, three steps back, in time to the beating drum or morache.

At the end of the dance, the singers thanked the elders for allowing them to sing and play the sacred music.

A great feast followed the dancing. As usual, Rose Kathleen was in the middle of the festivities. She had never learned to walk, having gone directly from crawling to running.

"Rose Kathleen!" Lily said.

Jimmy jumped up. "I'll get her Lily," he said. After Henry and Sarah McCluskey had graciously allowed Jimmy to stay and help with the baby that first summer, he and Rose had developed a deep and unbreakable bond. He had just returned yesterday from Hank and Myrtle's to spend the summer helping his aunt and uncle.

The boy had the best of both worlds. Winters were spent attending a good school in Pueblo with Hank and Myrtle, and summers were spent with his cousins, where he worked hard, but played hard as well. The McCluskey boys taught Jimmy to hunt and fish and he was able to teach his cousins some of what he had learned at school. Sarah made sure that Jimmy spent at least two hours teaching reading, writing, and mathematics to his cousins.

Jimmy was quickly turning into a fine young man, Lily thought, as she watched Rose throw her arms around him. He was still small for nine years old, but was smart as a whip and had a heart of pure gold. Mary was to return at the end of the month, having spent the past year at a fine college back East studying nursing, courtesy of Victoria.

Lily wondered about her sister-in-law, having received a letter last week stating Oliver had passed away peacefully in his sleep the first of April. Lily had written back with her condolences, and with an invitation to come to Colorado. But secretly she hoped that Victoria would stay in New York.

Over the past two years Victoria had become a thorn in Lily's side. Samuel constantly wrote and asked his sister's advice on business and ranch matters, advice he never sought from Lily. She knew she should not feel resentful, that she should be glad that Samuel and his sister had patched up their misunderstandings. Deep down, Lily hoped that Samuel would begin to include her more in his business decisions. Maybe she would not feel so insulted and more like a partner, not just a hired hand.

Lily watched Samuel as he came from the agency. A Ute woman filled a plate for him from the heavy-laden tables. As the chiefs quickly made a place for him, Lily noticed the respect they had for Samuel. Guilt washed over her like a downpour. Was she too selfish? She searched her heart for an answer but once again came up empty.

She hoped he would finally have some time to spend with her and Rose. But as was the Ute way, the men ate separately from the women. Samuel walked over to where Ouray was sitting, never looking her way.

Several times during the past two years the cavalry had asked Colonel Samuel Bodeen to return to the cavalry. With each offer, Samuel would retreat into himself and spend days pondering the commission. Lily's insides would quiver until he would write and turn the post down.

Then last fall the army had asked him to take the post as Commander of Fort Lewis, a garrison in the southernmost part of Colorado that was to keep the Southern Utes in check. Without so much as a moment's discussion, he told Lily he was going to take it, stating that maybe he could make a difference in the outcome of what was to happen to the Utes.

They argued for days until Lily flatly refused to go. Disappointed, Samuel turned the offer down and though he never said as much, Lily knew he had been frustrated with her over it ever since.

But the guilt was easier than the thought of Samuel's life being hacked away by an angry tomahawk. Still, she felt the terrible remorse of knowing that she had forced Samuel into being something he was not. Some men were born to be farmers, others shopkeepers. And deep down she knew that Samuel's heart and head would always be with the army. He was born to be a soldier. It was what he loved. It was a fact that came to her every night he came in after plowing a field, looking dusty and dejected. He was not a rancher, a fact that she knew every time one of King Ferdinand's calves died. Samuel took each death as his weakness, not the animal's.

And even though she and Samuel had finally agreed that he should take a seat on the Bureau of Indian Affairs Board, she knew it was small consolation for him giving up the high post at Fort Lewis.

The past two years on the ranch had taught Lily something about herself that Samuel did not seem to see. She was a rancher. She thrived on the rugged life, even when the harsh winter winds whipped around her. Instead of weakening her, it only served to make her tougher and stronger than she had ever been before. She had come to love the land and the life almost as much as she loved Samuel.

✟ ✟ ✟

Rose was tired and getting fussy. Lily was tired as well and ready to go home. She impatiently waited for Samuel, and then decided to catch the horses to save time.

Chipeta found Lily as she was starting to harness the horses to the buckboard.

"Samuel wanted me to tell you that the men have decided to resume their discussion and to go on home without him."

Lily turned and watched as the men rose and started walking back to the agency as dusk began to close around the encampment. Samuel was among them.

"He couldn't take five minutes to tell me himself, or to help harness the horses?" Chipeta felt Lily's anger and knew her friend was scared of only one thing. Lily detested the dark.

"I'm sorry, Lily. Here, let me help you. Better yet, why don't you just stay the night? You can stay in the tepee I set up in the grove of aspen down by the river. Ouray has asked that I sit in and listen at the powwow, so you and Rose will have the tepee to yourselves, as I expect they will talk far into the night," she said.

Lily was grateful for the offer, having dreaded the drive back to the ranch alone, even though a full moon was rising. The McCluskeys had left earlier to get back in time for evening chores. Lily should have left then as well. She should have known better than to stay and wait for Samuel.

After thanking Chipeta she looked for Samuel to tell him of her change in plans but he had already gone inside the agency. Besides, she thought, what does he care?

She picked up Rose, who by now was as cranky as her mother felt, and walked down to the river. She took the child inside the tepee and tried to take off her tiny moccasins.

Rose screamed, "No! Me want them on!"

"Okay fine, but you need to lay down and go to sleep." Lily lay down on an elk hide with Rose but the child fussed and squirmed.

"I wanna count stars! I not tired!"

Lily was too tired to argue. Counting stars was a game Lily had made up with Rose when she didn't want to go to bed. The cool night air always made Rose grateful to crawl under her nice warm quilt.

Lily lit a fire in the pit outside the tepee and sat down on a log. Somewhere in the far off night a coyote howled. She shivered and hugged Rose close.

"One," Lily said as she and Rose searched the sky for the first stars.

"One."

"Two."

A man's figure quietly walked out from among the falling shadows in the trees and sat down next to Rose on the log.

"Chawee!" Rose pulled away from her mother and snuggled into Sapiah's arms. Around the valley Sapiah was known as Buckskin Charlie, but Lily preferred to call him by his Ute name, knowing that he preferred it as well.

"You are not with the men?" Lily asked.

"No, I have heard enough talk for today. It hurts my ears and my heart. All the talking on earth will not change what is to come," he said sadly.

"Three, four . . ." the child sighed deeply.

Even Rose was calmed by Sapiah's presence and seemed content to let the game end.

They sat in silence and watched as the mountains turned from burnt orange, to cinnamon, and finally to a dull gray. Lily felt her anger slipping away with the sun and felt comforted as the night slipped into velvet blackness. There was a softness that she felt with Sapiah, and with most of the Ute people. There was no finger pointing, no condemnation, just acceptance. Acceptance of what was, of what is, and of what would come to be.

"Fute?" Rose asked. Sapiah grinned and handed the child back to her mother. He pulled his flute from the inside pocket of his buckskin jacket.

Lily rocked Rose as Sapiah played softly into the night sky. The glow of the firelight danced like fairies among the child's golden curls. Soon Rose's vivid blue eyes grew heavy, and she quietly drifted into the place of bliss that only a child knows the way to.

Lily took the child inside the tepee, laid her on a soft elk hide and covered her with a warm beaver pelt.

She went back out and sat next to Sapiah. He put down his flute and stood to go.

"Please, don't stop playing," Lily said.

Sapiah had played for her many times in the past two years, stopping by to check on her and Rose when Samuel was in Denver on business, which this past winter had been often. Sapiah came not as the other braves who looked for a handout of food and sugar. He came with gifts for Rose: a perfect apple, a leather cache bag of wild strawberries, a cornhusk doll. In summer he and Rose counted stars. In winter he would sit by the fire and whittle the child horses out of cedar or pine or aspen. Each was different, and each was polished to a high gloss and was as smooth as glass.

And Sapiah sometimes brought Lily gifts as well: a perfect seashell he had found high in the shining mountains, the first wildflowers of spring, or nuggets of gold and turquoise.

He brought Pagosa, the old medicine woman who had breathed her life into Rose. The old woman had spent many hours walking the land with Lily, pointing out valuable plants and teaching her what they could cure. And she pointed out which to avoid. She taught Lily the Ute language and Lily taught her English. Lily learned that in the Ute language the woman's name meant healing water. The name fit. The woman's wisdom and companionship had become treasures to Lily as well. Lily had grown to love the woman dearly.

Sapiah always brought his flute, a welcome relief from the sound of the lonely winter winds. And he brought the best gift of all— friendship. With Samuel, Ouray and Chipeta gone much of the time, and the McCluskeys working from dawn to dusk, Sapiah was the one on which Lily had come to rely. He helped her feed the cows, chopped wood, and always seemed to be around just when she needed someone to talk to.

But tonight Lily could see it was Sapiah who needed a friend. He was normally strong and self-assured but tonight his shoulders were slumped as if he were carrying a heavy burden. The laugh lines around his brown eyes were gone, replaced with deep lines above his strong brow. He put his lips to the flute, but the notes were disjointed, as if the breath had been squeezed from his chest. He put down the flute and sat in subdued silence. When the fire had burned down to glowing embers, he spoke. Like Chipeta, his voice came low and thoughtful.

"There are no words in the Ute language that speaks of material things. When a Ute says he is rich, he means that he has many friends. When he speaks of being poor, he means that he has few. We do not understand greed."

He got up and stirred the fire, watching as embers rose and crackled in the night sky.

"Everything the white man touches, he wounds. He searches for Mother Earth's beauty inside the mountains and leaves gaping holes in her side. He kills the buffalo, taking only the tongue and hide and leaves the rest to rot in the sun. Then he gets paper for the hide and says he is rich."

Sapiah added a log to the fire and put out his hands to the warmth.

"He burns the land, leaving it scorched and sore. Then he tears it up, peeling away its blistered body layer by layer, so he can plant corn, not to share with others, but to sell to the highest bidder. Once again he says he is rich. I do not understand this."

Sapiah sat down beside Lily and searched her eyes, as if pleading for an explanation.

There was none.

"The language of the white man is as smooth as ice. They can make the right way sound wrong . . . and the wrong way sound right. We slide along on the words, trying to keep our footing. But underneath these smooth words, there is a cold river. I can feel it rumbling underneath my feet."

Sapiah shut his eyes and put his lips back to the flute. But the sound was different now, mysterious and haunting, as if he and his music became one. He played as the water on the river, sometimes soft, sometimes spirited, sometimes as angry as the spring runoff over mighty boulders.

The music spoke in harmony with Lily's heart. She shut her eyes and absorbed the sounds from Sapiah's flute. The music took her back to the day of Rose's birth, and all the emotions she'd felt: apprehension, pain, suffering, gripping fear, and love. Love so intense, so overwhelming, so passionate, so overpowering.

The music turned soft and somber, caressing Lily's soul. She saw the bear dancers before her, shawls tantalizing, eyes alluring. Deep in her heart she knew she had been privileged to witness what would likely never come again. A thousand years passing never to be regained. The ritual of the coming of a people together . . . and the destiny of separation. Three steps together, three steps back. Her body rocked with the rhythm.

It had been Sapiah that had sent Piah for help. It had been Sapiah that had stayed: comforting, supporting, and giving her his strength. Without him she would not have the most precious treasure to her on earth. Without him, she would be poor.

The music began to fade. Soon, the dance would be over. The ice was beginning to crack. Soon, it would split wide open.

Lily felt the deep sadness of it all. She felt the mountains and the coyote and the bear cry as well. Lily opened her eyes and looked at Sapiah. His eyes met hers, brimming with kindness and tears and grief. She knew he felt it as well. She heard it in his music. She saw it in his eyes.

Sapiah stopped playing. He walked to the river's edge and placed the flute in the water. They watched as the river slowly carried the music away and around the bend into the unknown.

As was the Ute way, there would be no regret, no finger pointing, and no condemnation. There would only be acceptance. Acceptance of what has been, of what is now, and of what will have to be. Their hands and hearts became one as together they celebrated and mourned a night that would never be again.

10

The sun beat down without mercy. Lily packed a light lunch of bread and cheese and two quarts of sweet tea. She grabbed her fishing pole and dug a few fat worms from beneath the rich soil of the garden.

Lily had hired two cowboys to help with branding last spring when Samuel's business meeting with the Bureau of Indian Affairs had been extended from a week to three because of problems with the Nez Perce. Both hands had agreed to stay on and watch over the herd. Now that the cattle were in good hands and Lily's work load had lightened considerably, she spent an hour or two every afternoon at the Dallas Creek, fishing for speckled trout while little Rose sailed stick boats and made mud pies, and then would lay down on a quilt under a large cottonwood and take her nap.

The afternoons were a peaceful time for Lily, a time to think or rest or even doze beside Rose. Many times she brought along a pencil and tablet, and sketched the landscape, flowers, and animals. She had loved to draw as a child, and though she was still a bit rusty, she enjoyed this favorite pursuit of trying to capture the beauty that surrounded her.

Besides, she reasoned, the heat in the house was like an oven by early afternoon and it was impossible to do any housework without feeling half-baked. The large picture window that she had asked for facing south, did provide a beautiful view of the Shining Mountains, and in the winter it provided cozy light and warmth, but in the summer when the sun was unforgiving, the picture window heated up the house like a tin box. Lily had made a curtain for the window, but it did little to keep the heat out.

Still, Lily was immensely pleased with her home. It blended in perfect harmony with her lifestyle and her personality. It was simple, with a kitchen, living area, bedroom and bath area downstairs, and a loft upstairs for Rose.

The rock fireplace in the living room had been formed from the colorful smooth stones from the riverbed. Each was unique in color: grays, creams and whites, along with hues of greens, blues and grays. One even looked like a face, complete with a crooked nose. Until Lily had assisted an old mason in the construction of the fireplace, she had thought of them merely as rocks. But as they had laid each one in place, each stone had taken on a distinct personality. The mason had been right in stating that laying a fireplace was like putting together the pieces of a puzzle and when finished, it would create a beautiful picture. And it did, especially when Sapiah had found the perfect piece of aspen wood for the mantle. Lily changed the decorations on the mantle as Mother Nature changed the seasons. In spring there were wildflowers and pussy willows, in summer it could be an abandoned robin's nest, in the autumn were colorful autumn leaves and cattails in a hollowed-out tree limb. Even in winter, there were bright red dried berries among sprigs of fragrant evergreen.

The colorful wool blanket Pagosa had given Rose, the same blanket on which she had arrived on earth, lended a bright splash of color to the brown leather settee, and the chairs on either side were made of sturdy brown leather with wide oak arm rests. A drop leaf desk in the corner completed the furnishings in the living room.

The bedroom contained a large bureau and matching four poster bed, sent by Victoria as a belated wedding gift. A quilt her grandmother had made that matched Rose's, topped the bed.

The kitchen was small, but efficient, with a heavy oak table and benches in the middle, a well organized Hoosier cupboard on the east wall, and large pantry room on the north side. Lily was particularly pleased with the indoor water pump and large tin kitchen sink on the west wall. Otto Mears had stopped by one afternoon when she had been hauling water. He had taken a forked stick to determine the best place to dig a well by the house, and had stopped just several yards from the back door. He then devised a plan to pipe the water directly to the kitchen, and the bath area when funds were available to purchase a cast-iron tub. For now the small room held a water closet and a tin tub. Mears had made the tedious job of hauling water from the creek obsolete, and Lily was extremely grateful to him for that.

The loft upstairs contained two windows: one facing east, so Rose would be blessed first thing in the morning with bright sunshine, and one facing south, so she could see the mountains as well.

The front door faced the south, but it was the back door facing west that was used, as it led directly to the barn and garden area.

Lily thought it the perfect home: simple, uncluttered, bright and sunny, and cozy in winter. And it was easy to clean, allowing her to spend her time outside working with the horses she had been breeding and gentling. It was now, as it was when she was a child, the much-preferred place to spend her time.

Lily had established a daily routine to the long summer days. She would rise early, before the sun, bathe, and enjoy a cup of tea out on the porch while watching the sun make its way over Courthouse Peaks. Rose and Samuel woke with the crowing of the rooster and Lily would fix breakfast. She gardened in early morning, before the insects and the sun were completely awake, while Samuel watched Rose. It was exclusive father/daughter time. Rose "helped" with the chores in the barn, and was proud now that she had her own chore to do. She was responsible for feeding the mother cat a large bowl of fresh milk after Samuel was through milking Ginger. They had acquired the large, gentle, caramel-colored milk cow by trading three of Ferdinand's best offspring the year before.

Lily cherished the early morning when Samuel was home, as she listened to his and Rose's laughter in the barn. And it gave her a few minutes to herself before going out to weed, prune and pick whatever had come to fruition in the garden. She would then tend her small flock of hens before cooking breakfast. Next she would spend a few minutes cleaning up the house before going out to spend the rest of the morning with the horses.

She fixed a substantial noon meal for her family and the ranch hands, making sure there would be enough left for a light, cold supper. After the meal, which they ate outside under the umbrella of the cottonwood, for even by noon it was cooler than the house, Lily finished her household chores, replenished the water barrel and stacked wood for the fire she would have to light in the stove later in the day to do the canning. Then it was off to the creek.

Lately she had been accompanying Samuel every morning on a ride to the high pasture to check the cattle. Even though the fence was only two years old, there always seemed to be a new hole in a new spot. Very few days went by that they did not have to stop and repair the fence.

On Sundays, the McCluskeys allowed Jimmy the afternoon off, and Lily could depend on him riding his Welsh pony over after the family church service. Lily knew by Sarah's critical looks that the woman thought the time Lily spent at the creek was wasted time, not just for the boy, but for Lily as well. Several times Lily had asked her to stay, but Sarah always had "chores" to do.

"We're not so graced to have our work done for us by others' hands," Sarah had said pointedly when Lily had asked her last week to visit and have a picnic to celebrate Independence Day. She then looked critically at Lily's attire—blue dungarees, a wide brown leather belt and a cotton shirt.

Lily had decided that long skirts in the West were not only uncomfortable, but also entirely impractical and even a bit dangerous. Once while running to head off a herd of cows, she had tripped on her long skirt and had nearly been trampled.

Where Lily had once admired the McCluskeys for their work ethic, she now pitied Sarah and the rest of the children. It seemed Henry's favorite saying was "gotta make hay while the sun shines." But even on rainy days, the McCluskey family worked like mules, with Henry firmly at the reins. Sarah always looked harried, as if the whole world depended on whether she got the wash out before seven in the morning. Even with the older children to help with the day-to-day work, Sarah never seemed to have a moment to herself. But neither did she complain about it.

Lily was immensely grateful for Gus. Since his arrival, she no longer had to clean the barn, chop wood, fix fence, help with plowing, planting, or harvesting the oats and hay, as she did the first two years. And many times he even filled the water barrel before she was able to get to it. Without Gus, she would not have had the luxury of afternoons at the creek.

The deep lines in Gus Crenshaw's face told the man's age, and the hard life he had led. His gnarled hands ached painfully when cold but he bragged that he could still ride anything that ate grass. His blue eyes tucked into the deep creases were still vivid and he could spot a missing calf from clear across the meadow. He told colorful tales of driving longhorns from Texas to Kansas, and later to Montana. With his full white beard and catching smile, Rose had thought him to be the Santa Claus that she had heard about last winter. Lily had instantly liked him as well.

Laslo Burns, however, made Lily's skin crawl. He was sneaky, like a spider that crept into view and then quickly crawled his way back into the shadows under the eaves. Laslo never had much to say with words, but his eyes, ever looking downward, seemed to hint of a deep and haunting dark secret, too gruesome a story to tell. Even the cattle were skittish around him, as if they didn't trust the man either.

When Lily had spoken of her concerns to Samuel, he said just to watch him closely, that Laslo would have to do until he could get someone more trustworthy. Plus, Samuel reasoned, he would be gone by the end of the year. A man like Laslo wasn't the type to stick in one place very long.

But after a year and a half, he was still around. And Lily did have to admit Burns was a hard worker, having finished the barn and bunkhouse without much help from Samuel or Gus, who were always busy putting up more barbed wire fence, more to keep the Indians out than the cattle in.

✤ ✤ ✤

Lily felt a mild jerk and she reeled in the line. The silver scales on a small fish glistened in the sun as she gently removed the hook. The fish was no bigger than a brook trout, only about six inches long. Lily laid it back in the water and watched it swim away. It gave her a strange kind of pleasure to watch the creature swim to freedom.

Lily caught a grasshopper, baited the hook, and cast the line. She joined her daughter on the blanket spread under the tree by the bank and rubbed Rose's back until the child was asleep.

The air was still. Even the mosquitoes, so vicious in the coolness of twilight, had enough sense to rest in the heat of the day. The cool water beckoned. Lily reeled in her line, removed her boots and socks, rolled up her dungarees and stepped gently into the creek. The rocks were slippery with moss and the water was so cold it made her toes tingle. On impulse, she waded back to the bank and removed her hat and the rest of her clothes. She walked to the rocky part of the creek where a streaming flow of water washed over heavy gray boulders, creating a deep, still pool of water that came waist high when she stood. She sat down on a rock under the waterfall and laid her head back, letting the cool liquid rain down over her hair, her face and her breasts.

The sound of hooves on the bridge jerked Lily from tranquility. She looked quickly at her clothes in a heap on the creek bank and knew there would no time to make a run for them. She crouched down in the water, waiting for the rider to come around the bend and into view. It was Chipeta.

"Thank heavens it was only you," Lily said, laughing as Chipeta removed her doeskin dress and joined her for a cool soak. "I thought for sure it was either miners, Utes looking for biscuits and sugar, or that awful Laslo. And me swimming here like a duck with no feathers."

"This does feel wonderful," Chipeta said, laying her head back and letting the water wash over her as well.

They sat in silence until the coolness of the water forced them to a spot on the warm sandy bank. The arid air quickly dried their skin. Lily checked on Rose, and then began to dress. She reached in her bag, pulled out a horsehair brush and ran it through her hair.

"Here, let me," Chipeta said, as she finished tying a beaded belt around her slim waist. "I am glad you let your hair grow. It glitters in the sun like shiny glass beads."

Lily's hair had grown quickly and the sun had bleached golden streaks into the auburn mane. Chipeta braided it into thick plaits and wrapped the ends with strips of buckskin.

Even after the refreshing swim, Chipeta looked tired. The water did not wash away the dark circles under her eyes, or the worried lines above her brows.

Lily poured two tin cups full of sweet tea from a mason jar and handed one to Chipeta.

"Is Ouray all right?" she asked.

"His stomach is worse. We have been to white doctors and medicine men. No one can seem to help him. He tires easily now and eats little or nothing, but yet his shirts get tighter."

Chipeta took a stick and drew in the soft, warm sand.

"I am as worried about my husband as he is about his people. The White River Utes are angry—angry with Ouray, and angry with Agent Meeker. The tribe has been accused and blamed for setting large fires that are destroying the timber and northern grazing land.

White people all along the Bear River are asking for their soldiers to come in. If that happens. . ." Chipeta's voice grew soft as she looked up to the shining mountains.

"Did the Utes set the fires?" Lily asked.

"Honestly, I don't know," Chipeta answered. "Who can know what Colorow and his followers have done, or will do? Every day more settlers come onto Ute land. Every day Colorow and the northern tribal chiefs get more frustrated. With no rain in over two moons, and the hot dry winds, it could have been lightning. One thing is certain, there is no end in sight to the fires. They rage out of control, just as the fate of my people."

Chipeta looked at Lily. "I am afraid, my friend. Many of the White River Utes do not believe as Ouray does. But then they have not seen firsthand the devastation that can be caused by white soldiers as Ouray has."

Chipeta took a long sip of tea, and as was her way, sat silently for several moments, as if putting her thoughts into order before speaking.

"Though his mother was a Tabaguache Ute, Ouray's father was Jicarilla Apache. Ouray was born in Taos, New Mexico and was raised by a Spanish family. In 1847, when Ouray was fourteen, the Pueblo Indians and many Mexicans revolted against United States rule in New Mexico. White soldiers were brought in to squash the rebellion. The Indians' and Mexicans' old muskets and bows and arrows were no match for the big guns of the white man. One hundred fifty died in the slaughter.

"And then there was Sand Creek in 1864 where white soldiers massacred over two hundred Cheyenne in a village. They shot and then mutilated the bodies. All were women, children, and old men. No one cared. The soldiers had the full support of the fathers in Washington. Ouray was in Denver and watched as the whites cheered and shouted, as if the soldiers had done a great and brave deed.

"In 1868, the United States gave us a treaty, and established boundaries. In 1873, they wanted more. We went to Washington to speak of peace with President Grant. He assured us of every effort to keep the peace, and soldiers would provide protection not just for white settlers and miners, but also for Indians. Ouray believed in the white father's promise. And Grant believed in Ouray's promise as well, that he would do everything in his power to keep the Utes from retaliating on those who crossed over the boundary lines. It was through this mutual respect and trust that they were able to work together but unfortunately, the other white chiefs do not share Grant's philosophy.

"These three things laid the foundation of Ouray's commitment to keeping peace. He realizes that attempting to fight against the whites will mean certain destruction for our people. And Ouray does not make promises that he does not intend to keep. For the sake of our people, and the sake of the whites, Ouray sees no other way but to trust they will keep their word. It is the only way to survive. But many of our people don't understand this and call him a traitor or a coward. And many are angry that Ouray is neither full-blooded Ute, nor was elected as Chief by the tribes. It was the government that appointed him to the position. More and more we are becoming outcasts among our own people. But what they do not realize is that it was Ouray's talks with Grant that kept the government from taking what was left of our land."

Chipeta spoke with great respect for the man who was not only her husband, but also protector of her people.

"What worries Ouray now is that the new white father, President Hayes, does not share the same commitment to peace as Grant, or Secretary Schulz. He seems to be providing Meeker all the ammunition he needs to create a war that, in the end, no one will win. Colorow has become very suspicious and agitated. There has been a regiment of buffalo soldiers traveling along the White and Bear Rivers for over a month."

"It is my understanding, Chipeta, that the regiment is there to impose the northern boundaries and turn settlers away who cross the line. There are also plans to build a fort south of Red Mountain Pass to enforce the southern boundaries."

The look of sheer dismay on Chipeta's face spoke for her.

"It is for your people's protection, as well as the whites," Lily said, wondering whom she was really trying to convince.

"Do you really believe that? Every day more and more silver is pulled out of the mountains. You see the steady stream day after day of settlers' wagons, not turning back but moving forward. No one tells them the Great White Father has said they are not allowed here. In many ways I understand my people's frustration. What if it was not the white, but the Indian who was trespassing? What if one of my people went on a white man's land, butchered his cattle for food, dug riches from his soil, and put up his tepee to spend the winter?"

Lily took the point to heart.

"And still we are told not to fight." Chipeta set her jaw. "All I can do is trust in the judgment of my chief, and in that of yours as well."

"The fort should be able to help with that. The soldiers will see to it that the boundaries of the Brunot Treaty are enforced."

Chipeta was still very uncertain. "I do hope you are right, Lily. But I have learned not to trust the white man. There are too many broken treaties, too many broken promises. And it takes a very strong adversary to fight such a powerful rival. I just don't know how much strength Ouray has, either within himself or within our people."

"What if, Chipeta, you were to try to talk to Meeker? Do you think he would listen to you? Samuel and I will be leaving tomorrow for Avery Hoffman's ranch to look at his herd. It is only about fifty miles from the White River Agency. "

"Oh, no. I could never do that. That would make it seem to my people, and to the whites, that my husband is indeed sick and weak. The only place that my voice counts is within the confines of our home."

Chipeta pulled a bundle of fried bread from a leather bag and they sat in silence as they munched on the bread and drank the rest of the tea. Chipeta tore off a piece and threw it to a couple of chipmunks that had been gathering piñon nuts from beneath a stand of pines. They stopped from their task, divided the treat, sat back on their haunches and filled the pockets of their cheeks with the treat.

"Don't their paws remind you of a baby's tiny fingers?" Lily asked. The chipmunks and squirrels had become like pets to Rose, with one being so bold as to eat nuts right out of the child's hand if she sat still enough.

"Oh, yes," Chipeta said. "All beings on the earth are connected. And all rely on each other to survive. See, already a resourceful ant has latched onto a crumb of the bread that the chipmunks missed and is tugging it back to its people."

They watched the tiny ant struggle to get the crumb, which was twice its size, up to the anthill that was at the top of a small knoll. The tenacity of the creature was inspiring.

"Sometimes I feel like the ant," Chipeta said. "I want badly to provide for my people, but the burden has become so heavy. Sometimes I do not agree with Ouray's decisions, though I know it is the right one."

"What do you mean?" Lily asked.

Chipeta held out her arms, as if trying to embrace the sky. She shut her eyes and breathed deeply. Slowly she put her arms back down and opened her eyes.

"Try it Lily, maybe you will understand."

Lily followed the movements of her friend. Together they sat quietly in the warm afternoon, eyes closed, arms reaching toward the heavens.

After Lily opened her eyes Chipeta asked, "Did you feel it?"

Lily was not sure what she felt. Peace, serenity, but more. It had no name. "It was like I became a part of creation. I could hear bees in the wildflowers."

"Yes." Chipeta said. "It takes practice to be able to mingle with all the Great Spirit has created. When I feel too overburdened, I return to Mother Earth. I let her breath caress my soul. I listen to the grass, the trees, the dirt. The land that feeds my people gives me strength."

Rose stirred, rubbing her eyes with pudgy fists. Her face broke into a wide grin when she saw who was sitting beside her on the blanket.

"Pita!" She snuggled up next to Chipeta, and felt the woman's hand gently brushing the hair out of her face. The child sighed with deep contentment.

"Do you see, Lily? My people respect the land; they respect their mother. But I do not see the whites show any respect at all. They take. And then they take more.

"They tell us to change our way of life—to become like them. But we do not want to be like them. We do not know how to live a life of selfishness and greed."

Again, Chipeta reached out her arms, as if trying to still hold on. "The Great Spirit gave us such a perfect and beautiful world. Why do the whites attempt to play God by changing it?"

11

July 12th, 1879

There were no trees along the road to the Grand River—only sagebrush, cactus of which a few had colorful blooms still clinging to their thick and prickly leaves, rocks and an occasional clump of hardy buffalo grass. Lily and Samuel gave the horses their heads, letting the animals amble their way along the wagon tracks.

Even though the day was sweltering in the lower desert country, Lily enjoyed the feel of Henry's easy gait and the freedom of being on the trail again. There was no washing to worry about, no meals to cook, no "women's work", though she already missed little Rose's ready smile. The thought of her daughter, whom Lily had left in Chipeta's capable hands, left her feeling a bit empty inside but she knew that she and Samuel desperately needed this time together alone.

Samuel must have sensed it as well, having asked Lily to accompany him to check out the heifers he was considering to add to the herd. She could not hide the immense change in herself since the night of the Bear Dance. No longer did she try hard to please him anymore. She was content to drift even farther away. She had become resigned with daydreaming of what she knew could never be in reality, both with Sapiah and with Samuel.

The change in Lily had prompted a change in Samuel as well. In the past several weeks, he had honestly tried harder at their marriage, but he had to wonder if he was too late. It was evident that Lily had lost her passion for him.

Last month Lily had been surprised when Samuel had brought up the idea of going together to check on the cattle every morning, something he usually had Gus do. He tried to speak to her about the ranch, things that needed fixing, things he wanted to build. It was as if he was still trying to settle into the ranching way of life. But Lily could see the ranch did not excite him in the same way the cavalry had. There was no fire in his belly when he spoke of stock prices or feed bills.

Deep down Lily knew her husband sincerely could not change what he was, no matter how determined he was or how stubbornly he tried. Samuel was a soldier. And the strength and toughness that had drawn her to him had also caused her to turn away. Samuel Bodeen needed no one. His hands were rugged, hard, and so were his moods. Not since the day he had broken down in front of her in Pueblo had Lily seen even the slightest crack in the hard shell that encased his heart. Since resigning his commission he had steadily over the past three years lost his playfulness and that teasing twinkle. The only time his steel-gray eyes lit up was when an old cavalry officer stopped by, or if he was called to Denver on the Bureau of Indian Affairs business. Unlike her father, Samuel had not taken to drink, but there was the same far-off look in his eyes, as if he were dreaming, as Lily was lately, of being somewhere else.

Lily knew her way of dealing with Samuel's cold independence was wrong, but she just couldn't help what she was either. Her way of satisfying her passionate soul was to draw into herself and remember the remarkable closeness she had felt with Sapiah. What they had shared was something much different, deeper, and much more spiritual than she had ever felt with Samuel.

Which made the longing for Sapiah's gentleness that much more heartfelt. Lily missed the music. She missed the slim, graceful fingers playing the music. She missed the compassionate brown eyes, the gentle laughter, the quiet voice. She missed the softness of him. She missed someone to count the stars with her. It was all like a fantasy now, a blur in the mist. In the real world, Lily knew Sapiah would never touch her face again. But he would forever touch her soul.

As much as Lily missed Sapiah, she missed her husband as much or more, or at least the man she had fallen in love with. There was still an ember of love that beckoned for a warm breath to bring it back to life. There was a desire that begged to be re-awakened.

When Samuel had asked her to accompany him to the Hoffman Ranch to look at a herd of heifers, Lily felt a small whisper of breath, of anticipation. Maybe he missed her, too. She hoped that maybe they would both be able to adjust to the rugged land, and somehow not let the harshness overtake them.

The road to the Hoffman place was down out of the Shining Mountains and through the desert, to a valley on the other side of the Grand River, a good two days ride to the northeast. Samuel sat tall in the saddle, confident and unbending, undisturbed by the heat, dust and flies. His eyes saw every movement. He glanced at every track in the soft dust. His senses were alive and alert.

"Hold up." Samuel's voice was quiet but firm. He pulled his horse up short and his quick glance advised Lily to do the same.

"What's the matter?" Lily whispered.

"On the horizon, just to the west. They have been steadily gaining on us for the last several miles."

Lily saw nothing but dust. She stared, concentrating. Through the heat waves she faintly saw the blur of several horses and riders. "How many are there?" she asked, trying to swallow a lump of fear that had formed in her throat. Samuel had told her of the risk they would be taking before they left the ranch yesterday. Angry Utes had been banding together, threatening settlers all along the Grand River, stealing horses and killing cattle, in retaliation for Meeker's latest command. Nathan was insisting that Ute braves stop roaming the mountains and stay at the agency to help plow the land. And an even more heinous command—he had disallowed the braves to leave for the summer hunt. Samuel had heard rumors of trouble brewing in the North Park area as well.

"Half dozen, maybe more. You've got your pistol handy?"

Lily patted the holster at her hip. "It's not loaded."

"Take it out and load it but be sure to keep the safety on."

Samuel had taken great care to make sure Lily became proficient using the Colt .45 he had given her when they first moved to the ranch. Every evening after supper they had walked behind the house where he had set up an intricate shooting range. He'd hung bottles from trees, stacked rocks on top of rocks, and hid bits of paper in the brush.

At first she had been uncomfortable with the weight of the gun on her hip and the feel of the weapon recoiling in her hand, but Samuel had been very demanding that she keep it with her at all times and practice using it.

His resolve had paid off. Last year Lily had taken Rose to a hillside west of the house to gather wild strawberries. While Lily concentrated on picking the fruit, Rose practiced her new game, walking. She toddled along for several feet before resuming the more comfortable position of hands and knees. She reached a hole and peeked inside, delighted at the tiny furry bundle that captured her attention.

A large gray mother badger had been hunting for rodents several yards away from the den. When it saw the tiny arm reaching inside the hole, the enraged animal hissed loudly like a rabid cat. Lily looked up just as it flattened its furry body and raced toward the intruder. Without thinking, Lily grabbed the gun from its holster, released the safety and shot the badger just seconds before it would have sunk razor sharp teeth into her baby's leg.

Now the Colt and holster were as much a part of her attire as her hat. She never left the house without them.

Samuel pulled a pair of field glasses from his saddlebag.

"Are they Utes?" Lily asked.

"Yep, and with more paint on 'em than Mattie Silk's entire entourage." He turned and looked at Lily seriously. "I don't know what they are up to, but better safe than sorry. I'd say we best let Henry and Boot Jack stretch their legs a bit. It's about ten miles to the Mills Trading Post on the Grand River. Straight on north. If, for whatever reason, we get separated, or if I tell you to, you hightail it as fast as you can toward the Collbran Ranch. See that draw toward the east?"

Lily looked and nodded her head.

"Head straight toward that draw and follow the creek up about eight miles."

Samuel gave his orders with such bold and steadfast precision that Lily's fear vanished. He was clearly in control, clearly in charge of the situation and she knew she was safe. She wondered if that was how his troops had felt as well when Colonel Samuel Bodeen had stood issuing orders with a firm jaw and calm resolve.

"Check the safety one more time. Had a fella once who shot his own horse. Don't shoot at anything, Lily, unless it shoots at you first. You ready?"

Lily replaced the Colt and nodded at Samuel. His face glowed with power and aliveness. He looked as if he was actually enjoying the situation. Lily felt her own blood pulsating through every cell. She pulled her straw hat down snugly on her head and gritted her teeth.

"Okay."

"Hiyahhh!"

The horses jumped as sharp spurs dug into their sides, as alarmed as if a sudden bolt of lightning had startled them from their drowsy gait.

Galloping through the afternoon heat waves was like riding through a glimpse of hell. Henry's sides heaved and thick white lather quickly formed on his chest and neck. The high country horses were not accustomed to the torrid desert temperatures.

But it was obvious that the Indian ponies were. When Samuel looked back he could see that the Indians had kicked into a hard run as well and were gaining on them. There were still at least seven miles between the hazards in the desert and the safety of the agency. Samuel calculated the risks. Lily's horse was gasping hard, but the look in his eyes was as determined as hers.

Still, she was a woman.

He looked back again. The gap was closing. He had to take the risk.

"Follow me!"

He neck reined Boot Jack to the right, off of the dusty road and down a deep ravine. The drought had left the creek bed dry, but the soil was sandy and the horses' hooves dug deep, making running difficult.

They stayed in the ravine for at least a mile before climbing out and over a steep hillside. The horses' shoes slipped and scraped on a rocky outcropping but both kept their feet. Samuel guided them over several more hills before he found what he was looking for. The creek bed in the next ravine held about a foot of water and Samuel stopped in the middle to let the horses drink.

"Not much," he cautioned Lily. "Just enough to let them wet their whistle."

They rode northeast in the creek for a couple of miles, walking the horses when the water got deeper and the grade steeper. They climbed to the flat table top of a wide mesa covered with spruce and thick aspen. The downed timber slowed the horses gait to a careful walk. Even though the hot July sun had beat down on them in the desert, the darkness of the heavy timber brought a chill to Lily's sweaty body. They came to another creek and followed it for several miles downward off the mesa back to sagebrush and scrub oak.

"Do you know where you're going, Samuel?" Lily asked.

He sniffed the air. "Seems to me supper is that way", he said with a grin while pointing back in a western direction. "We may not have lost them completely, but it will be long enough to get us to the trading post."

They led the horses out of the ravine, through a stand of bushes thick with chokecherries not yet ripe, and then headed back toward a long stand of cottonwoods still on the far horizon. The sun was beginning to find its way down, painting the pale sky with vibrant orange and pink hues.

Between the cooling water, dropping temperature, and the slower pace, the horses soon had their wind back.

"You hungry?" Samuel asked.

"Starving," Lily said with a smile. "Race you there!"

They kicked the horses back into a run and headed toward the sunset.

After a supper of Mrs. Mills' hot biscuits, fresh venison, yampa roots and muddy coffee, Lily walked gingerly to the barn. Samuel had already taken care of the horses and laid out the bedrolls.

Lily's legs and back ached from the rough riding. A prickly heat rash had welted up on her inner thighs. Samuel walked down to the Grand River and brought back a washtub of cool water. He took a blue handkerchief off from around his neck, dipped it in the water, and handed it to Lily.

"You did good out there, Lily. I'm proud of you."

"What do you think they were after, Samuel?"

"Can't say for sure. But with all the ruckus they have been kicking up lately, I wasn't about to stop and find out."

✦ ✦ ✦

Lily wasn't sure what it was that had caused her to be instantly awake. It was as if a mysterious force had slapped her from sleep. She opened her eyes and looked at the sandy-colored beams of sunlight streaming through the cracks of the trader's barn, illuminating the choking dry dust in the air. Barn swallows fluttered in the eaves overhead.

"Sam?"

There was no answer.

Lily rolled over. His bedroll was cold. She quickly pulled on her jeans and boots. As she walked out of the barn she noticed five horses in front of the trader's store. Five Indian ponies.

She ran back to the barn and grabbed her Colt and holster from where she had hung them on a nail the previous evening. She strapped the gun to her belt and quickly checked to see if the horses were still in the stalls. Boot Jack and Henry stood munching new grass hay. She saddled the pair just in case they needed to make a quick getaway.

She walked quietly around to the edge of the barn and listened to the heated voices coming from inside the trading post. She could not make out the words, but the tone of the Indians' voices, particularly Colorow's low growl, made it quite clear that the Indians had not stopped in for biscuits and sugar.

Lily took her gun from its holster, and clicked off the safety. The Colt trembled in her hand as she closely watched the door.

The voices grew louder. Samuel was first to come out of the cabin, followed by Colorow's large lumbering body. Next came Piah and a renegade Ute Lily knew as Antelope. She did not recognize the other three.

Samuel stopped abruptly and turned back to the men.

"I wish I could help, but I can't leave my wife here, and I sure won't send her back to the ranch alone. It's much too dangerous."

Colorow turned to Antelope. "Take woman back to Los Piños."

"No, Colorow," Samuel said firmly.

Samuel stepped back several feet as Colorow drew his knife.

"Mebbeso you are outnumbered. Mebbeso I will make it so the woman is no problem."

The hair stood up on the back of Lily's neck. She carefully aimed the Colt at Colorow's large belly. She took a quick breath and held it, not wanting anything, even her slight breath, to throw off her aim. Colorow was approaching Samuel and was only about a foot away. She was a bit surprised that her hand no longer trembled. Her mind was as sharp as a razor and she felt no fear. She eased the trigger.

A loud yell behind her took her completely by surprise. Suddenly she saw a quick movement coming at her from the side. Before she could respond, the gun had been kicked from her hand. She felt several bones shatter.

Piah grabbed her arm and wrenched it behind her back. She thought he would break it as well. His face broke into a lecherous grin. "Move, white woman."

He led her out into the sunshine.

Samuel was furious. "Let her go!" His voice commanded in a low snap.

"I think no, soldier," Piah said. "She be what you white men say— 'ace in hole'."

He twisted Lily's arm and Samuel saw her wince in pain. But she never cried out.

"What do they want, Samuel?" Lily asked.

He could tell by her flashing amber eyes that she was more mad than scared.

"They want me to go with them to the White River Agency. They think maybe I can talk some sense into Meeker. It seems Meeker has written to Governor Pitkin and asked for troops to come in from Fort Steele."

"Well, has he?" Lily asked.

"I really don't know. I know Captain Dodge and his black soldiers have been roaming all around northwestern Colorado trying to keep the peace."

"And if more troops are called in? What does that mean to the

Utes?" Lily could remember the intense fear in Chipeta's eyes when they spoke of soldiers moving in.

Samuel's silence spoke for him.

"The Ute protect what is ours!" one of the Utes stated forcefully.

Samuel nodded to each chief as he spoke their names, "Chief Jack, Chief Douglas, and Chief Johnson, feel the soldiers will be a direct threat to their people. They will not be imprisoned in the white man's web," Samuel said.

The simmering cauldron was about to reach a boiling point. It was as Chipeta had feared.

"Then go, Samuel," Lily stated firmly. "They need you."

"I won't leave you alone here Lily. It's much too dangerous. "

"Then I will go with you."

"No, Lily. Things could get rough," Samuel said, dismissing her idea.

Lily jerked her arm from Piah's grasp. He was surprised at her sudden burst of strength.

Her eyes glared in fury and her voice became sharp. "When you needed to ease your guilty conscience about leaving me at the ranch alone, you would tell me how tough I am. Last spring you thought nothing of leaving me to brand over one hundred head of calves. When they were sick, I carried them to the house and nursed them back to health in the washtub. I've put up miles of fence, killed coyotes, and fed cows when it's so damn cold my eyes freeze shut."

She strode over to him and looked him straight in the face.

"I was even tough enough to be left alone when heavy with your child. But when it comes to being partners with you, Samuel Bodeen, then I become one of your prissy New York belles that has to be coddled."

Lily glared at Colorow. "Do I look like a damn prissy belle to you?"

The Indian's mouth gaped open, too shocked to speak.

Lily turned and headed toward the barn. The men were still staring at the door when she came out with the horses.

"Well, are you coming or not?"

Lily's hand throbbed in agony but she was determined not to let the men see her pain. They eased their way through a rocky gap, dense with brush. The ride was hard, but Colorow assured them it would cut miles from the route. They camped next to Piceance Creek. Not having enough provisions, Samuel and Lily had to rely on the Utes for their meals, though the Utes had packed very little as well.

Earlier in the day, Chief Johnson had shared leather pouches filled with pemmican: dried elk meat pounded together with dried berries. His eyes were as dark as a piñon nut, but they were kind. For the noon meal, even the gluttonous Colorow had shared jerky and a bundle of biscuits the trader's wife had packed for him.

Piah left the camp and came back a while later with several grouse. He lit a fire and soon the roasting birds made Lily's mouth water.

After eating until they could not force down another bite, the group bedded down, the Indians using only the blankets from their horses. Lily just knew that with her aching limbs, she would never get to sleep. She was surprised to find herself looking up into the bright sun the next morning.

Chief Douglas, whose hair had turned a salty white and face was lined with deep creases, held out the last biscuit to her. "About ten miles to the Old Squaw camp, and another twenty from there. Mebbeso both of us be mighty glad." He rubbed his stomach, and then his backside and smiled.

"Should be there this afternoon," Samuel said, giving her a warm hug before helping her onto Henry's back. "I'm really sorry about all this. You okay?"

"Samuel, Chipeta is my best friend. I can't stand the thought of her, or any of the Utes, in a war. What can you do?"

"I think the fate of the Ute people rests in the hands of one man. Nathan Meeker. I think it's all going to depend on him."

✛ ✛ ✛

As they made their way down the divide and into Powell Park where Meeker had moved the agency, Lily was in awe at the grandeur of the area. Spruce and pine towered on a nearby mountain that Chief Jack called Sleepy Cat. Beyond Sleepy Cat was Pagoda Peak and a range of sweeping flat-topped mountains. It was a country to dream about.

Lily saw no deer or elk and she asked Chief Jack why.

"There is a sacred, deep lake, enfolded in the arms of the high mountains. The animals play there in the summer, raise their young. They are our survival. Our tepees are in need of new skins. We will grow cold when the winter winds begin to blow. Our cooking pots hold only the white man's food. We will starve without the summer hunt. But Meeker says no. We cannot go."

They made their way down the hillside, crisscrossing a creek several times on the way before they reached the valley floor. The trickle of the creek didn't do much to add to the low water level of the White River. Its sandy banks glistened in the sun. The grass was thin from the drought but there was plenty of fragrant blue sage about three feet high, and massive clumps of rabbit bush. A large herd of antelope bounded gracefully away at the intrusion of the riders. The Indian ponies in a pasture on the far side of the riverbank looked curiously at the other horses entering their domain, then put their heads back down to graze.

Samuel explained to Lily that the valley had been named for John Wesley Powell, the famous explorer who traversed the western United States. He had resided with the Utes while exploring the area during the winter of 1868-1869. The original location of the agency had been six miles to the east. Meeker had disassembled the buildings and floated them downstream to the current location, which was warmer. The valley was about three miles wide and seven miles long, with about three thousand acres of open land with rich, sandy loam for growing crops. The water supply for irrigation could come from the creek and the river. The grass utilized as range for the stock was on each side of the valley along the slopes of the mountains that extended for many miles. The mountains surrounded the valley like a bowl, protecting it from harsh winter storms. There was a good-sized vein of coal that ran along a slope a few miles downriver, providing warm fuel for winter fires. Samuel thought that when Meeker saw the valley, his vision of a perfect Utopia must have been made real.

As they entered the agency compound, Lily was impressed at its cleanliness. Meeker had hired an engineer to design the layout of the compound and to survey for the ditches to be dug for irrigation. Indian labor had been used to dig a ditch two and a half miles long to provide water.

Unlike the Los Piños Agency, which had been hastily constructed and the buildings laid out without any special planning, the buildings at the White River Agency had been built to last. The streets had been laid out, starting with the Grand Canal and Arvilla Bridge. Ute Avenue started at Chief Douglas' village on the White River and ran north for a mile, then intersected with Douglas Avenue. Meeker's L-shaped office and home stood at the southeast corner. A large milk house and storage barn were close by. Farther down, there was a sturdy corral to contain the beef cattle that were killed weekly for the Indian rations.

Southward, there was a twelve-bed bunkhouse, a blacksmith shop, a small school and the beginnings of Josie Meeker's new boardinghouse. On either side of Josie's Lane there were vegetable gardens.

"Had to dig a heap bunch of potatoes last year, " Chief Johnson said as they rode by the thriving plants. "Women and children got a half bushel a day for the work."

They rode up to Meeker's house and were greeted by a young woman in her late teens, very pretty, with vivid blue eyes that showed an exuberance for life. She was holding the hands of two barefooted young Ute children with chubby cheeks and wide smiles.

"Pleased to meet you," she said cordially when Samuel made introductions. "And I am Josie Meeker."

Colorow sternly told her to get her father, but his gruffness didn't seem to intimidate Josie at all. Maybe she had come to think of the fierce-looking man as Lily did. After traveling with him for two days, Lily had figured out that his bark was much worse than his bite.

"Father is at the supply house," she said, leading them into the immaculate, but comfortable house. "I will tell him you are here."

She led them to the kitchen where a frail-looking woman was kneading bread dough.

"Mother, we have visitors." Josie made the introductions and then left with the children still in tow.

Arvilla Meeker was a skinny woman with a long peaked nose and thin lips. Her gray hair was pulled back severely in a bun at the base of her neck. Her dress was basic black with no lace or frills. She fluttered around the kitchen like a nervous chicken, sharply stating the available refreshment, which consisted of molasses cake and lukewarm tea.

Mrs. Meeker looked like a woman who had spent her life worrying. Her brow was furrowed with three even creases across her high forehead. Her shoulders were hunched and her eyes looked somber, as if she had recently attended the funeral of a close friend.

Nathan Meeker, on the other hand, strode into his house like a king to his castle. He stood tall and erect, and though his hair was silvery gray, he had remarkably young, almost boyish, good looks. There was an air of confidence about him. His handshake was firm, his gaze direct.

"It is indeed a pleasure, Colonel Bodeen, to finally meet you. Your reputation precedes you. Secretary Schurz speaks most highly of you."

"It is an honor to meet you as well," Bodeen said, hoping he didn't sound as shallow as he felt. The man's intense ego repulsed him.

Meeker, Bodeen, and the chiefs spent the rest of the afternoon discussing the matters at hand.

"Woman's work, ugh!" Chief Douglas stated when Meeker explained the need for the braves to assist with farming.

Samuel carefully watched Meeker's reaction. He had to give the man credit for truly listening to the chiefs complaints over the disagreement concerning plowing the land.

But when the subject turned to the Ute ponies, the atmosphere in the room turned tense. Meeker turned his body away from the chiefs and fidgeted in his chair. Samuel could see that was the real sore spot for both parties. Vocal chords and muscles became taut, lips tight.

"I am paid to show you how to work. I am to teach you to help yourselves so that you can be like the white folks and get rich as they get rich, by work. You spend too much time with the ponies. There are too many and they graze too much land. We need the grass for the cattle and the racetrack for a wheat field." And then Meeker made the most fatal statement of all—"You need to get rid of some of the ponies."

Outraged, Chief Douglas stood up. "Are not all these cattle ours, and all this land to do with as we want?"

Meeker was on the brink of losing his composure. His voice became brittle. "The land belongs to the government, and is for your use, if you use it. If you won't use it and won't work, and if you expect me to weed your gardens for you, white men will come in and by and by you will have nothing. Do you understand?"

Chief Douglas looked at Meeker with contempt. "This valley belongs to the Ute people. The white fathers in Washington signed their names. We will not let you break this treaty as well. Not this time."

Chief Douglas rose from the table. The other Utes did the same. They walked out the door, across the porch, and to the hitching rack. They mounted their horses and rode away in the direction of Douglas' camp without looking back.

Bodeen knew it would be a big mistake to try and stop them.

Nathan walked onto the porch and brushed a few cake crumbs from his vest. "There is just no reasoning with them."

12

Even though Chipeta had been allowed to sit in on important powwows, Samuel had explained the normal Ute traditions to Lily before the meeting with Meeker started. She had graciously agreed to spend the rest of the afternoon with Josie Meeker at the school, realizing the Ute chiefs would have thought it to be disrespectful to them if she stayed.

Josie was a delight. There were only five children at the school, but they drank up the story she read to them like a cool drink of water, so eager were they to learn. Josie said that she was sorely disappointed when the Ute mothers had ceased encouraging their children to attend the school. Of the twenty-five children in Chief Douglas' camp, only four now attended the school, along with May Price, daughter of Flora Ellen Price.

"Last year," Josie said, " when I started the school all the Ute children were eager to learn English. The children would go back to their tepees and teach their parents. But after Father's decree that the braves were to stay and farm instead of hunt, the children's parents would not allow them to come anymore." Josie's disappointment echoed in her voice. It was obvious to Lily that Meeker's daughter had come to care deeply for the Utes, and their way of life. She did not see the situation through the eyes of an immature teenager, but as a mature young woman.

It was clear that someone else saw Josie's beauty that was just beginning to blossom. A young Ute brave, whom Josie had addressed as Persune, had stood in the doorway of the school and listened to her read as well.

After the school session, Persune had asked Josie to accompany him on a ride, pointing to a tethered sleek bay mare next to his muscled pinto gelding. Josie politely refused, stating she would need to help her mother with supper for their guests. Persune had looked sadly disappointed.

That evening Samuel and Lily dined with the Meekers. Once again, Arvilla raced around the kitchen and doted on her husband to a point at which Lily found herself becoming annoyed with the woman and her servile attitude. The only time the old woman ceased her fretting was when Nathan gave a long-winded blessing before the meal. By the time he had finished his sermonizing about praying for the "lost souls of the red heathens," the food had become cold and Samuel had become hot around the collar.

After a scarce supper of beans and cornbread, Josie took Samuel and Lily down to the boardinghouse and showed them to the only finished room. Samuel gave her four bits for the bed. They laid their bedrolls over the cotton ticking to prevent having to pay an additional price for blankets.

"I think the only reason "Father" Meeker didn't charge us for the meal was that he was trying to bribe me into taking his side in this dilemma," Samuel said, taking off his boots the minute Josie left.

As tired as Lily was, she could not get comfortable on the lumpy mattress. The whole place felt wrong, like there was a current of dishonesty seeping through the perfectness of the laid-out streets.

Samuel felt it as well. Both his body and mind tossed and turned, trying to find a comfortable position. But there was none. He feared for the Meekers and for the safety of the Utes. A hot summer wind blew through the yet unchinked logs, and somewhere in the distance a hoot owl called. The walls were tight around his mind. He got up, slipped on his pants and went outside to sit on a pile of lumber in the cool night air.

Lily slipped on her clothes and watched Samuel from the doorway as he puffed on his pipe. The moon illuminated the worried creases in his face. She walked up to him and put her arms around his broad shoulders.

'It's very serious, isn't it," she said, more as a statement of fact than as a question. She found his hand and squeezed it gently.

"Donovan, I love you with all my heart and the last thing I want to do in this world is to lose you. I do hope you understand that." He turned and took her hands in his face. "God, you are so beautiful."

He pulled her close and held her tight, as if afraid she would run if he let go.

She pulled away and looked into his eyes. Yes, there was still love.

"Samuel, if little Rose were headed straight toward a hornets nest, you would move mountains to stop her. I know the battle you are fighting within yourself. I respect the responsibility you feel toward Rose and me and I love you for it. I also know the responsibility you feel toward Ouray, and to all Utes, the cavalry, and even to the United States as well. I can no longer let the duty you feel toward me interfere with these other obligations. It is important to so many. And I can no longer let you dishonor who you are by trying to be something you are not. I understand what you must do and I will support you in it."

She pulled him back close to her and for the first time in months, felt the fire warming their souls.

"It's one hundred sixty miles to Fort Steele. I will understand if you don't want to go. And I am sure by now that you are missing Rose," Samuel said.

"If that is your way of kindly asking about my rash, yes it's still there. But better, thank you. I found an aloe plant along the way and it has soothed the pain. And I am sure that our daughter is having a wonderful time with Chipeta."

Lily hesitated a moment, then said, "Samuel, if you would rather I not go with you. . . "

"Lady, I have left you out of things for too long because of some absurd manly notion that I needed to protect you. Yet you have proved to me, time and time again, that you can hold your own against just about anything. There's nobody I would rather have ride beside me."

That was, by far, the best compliment Samuel Bodeen could ever give, and Lily knew it.

Dawn had not yet broken when Samuel and Lily rode into Douglas' camp. The barking of the dogs brought the old man from his tent.

"You are greatly troubled, friend," Douglas said, as his wife offered up fried bread.

"I spoke long with Meeker," Samuel said. "Yes, his words troubled me. Lily and I will be traveling to Fort Steele to talk with Major Thornburg. From there we will board a train to Denver. I am going to need your help, Chief," Samuel said honestly.

Douglas sat in silence, waiting for the request.

"First, I will need a Ute courier to get a letter to Ouray as soon as possible. It is imperative he meet me in Denver by the twenty-fifth. I would like you, Chief Jack, and Chief Johnson to be there as well. We must stop the situation before it is completely beyond our control."

The chief lit his pipe and offered it to Samuel. "We seem to have the same vision of the future, of what should be, and of what might be. We will be there."

"In the meantime, Douglas, you and the other chiefs must be patient. You must tell your braves to be patient. It won't be easy. I can see that they have been pushed very far already. But it is crucial that you don't do anything, and I mean anything, to upset Meeker."

"I will try. But you must understand, my people are like a horse whose saddle is already too tight. If the white man pulls any more, my people are going to buck."

✢ ✢ ✢

Antelope led Samuel and Lily to Peck's Store on the Bear River, forty miles north of the White River Agency. There they met up with Captain Dodge and his company of black soldiers.

Samuel warned Dodge of the powder keg at the White River Agency. "One small spark is all it's going to take to blow the place clear to 'kingdom come,' taking the Utes and the Meekers as well."

Dodge stated that he and his men would try to stay as close to the agency as possible, without further alarming the Indians.

"The Utes are used to us hanging around by now, and Big Jim, chief of the Yampas up around the Steamboat Springs area, has become a pretty good friend. He'll let me know if there's a storm brewing on the White River. Just hope I can get my regiment there in time to stop a skirmish. We've got so damned much territory to cover, Colonel, that it's a most impossible situation. I just got word that the Indians burned out a man in North Park by the name of J.B. Thompson. Didn't kill anyone, thank God, but we've been ordered to check it out anyway. We'll be mounting up early in the morning. It's a hundred hard miles, and that's if we don't have to go around a forest fire."

Dodge snuffed out the stub of a well-chewed cigar. "Hell, let's be honest. It's just a matter of time."

Joe Rankin, scout for the cavalry, was heading back to Fort Steele after bringing Dodge his latest orders. Rankin said he knew the land as well as he knew his mother's name and agreed to guide Samuel and Lily through a shortcut along the Snake River and over the Medicine Bow Mountain Range to Fort Steele.

The land started out flat, mostly scrub oak and sage and the travel was easy. And even though the terrain through the mountain range was tougher riding, Lily felt more secure in them, and their beauty was worth the extra effort.

Fort Steele was situated on a bend of the North Platte River, sixteen miles east of Rawlins, Wyoming, on the edge of the Red Desert. It stood in a desolate semicircle of red, yellow, and black sand ridges which protected it only slightly from the incessant wind that had begun to blow when they had ridden out of the mountains. It had yet to stop. The terrain was ugly and oppressive.

The fort had been named in the same way that most army outposts were named, as a memorial to some general who had been killed during the fighting of the Civil War. General Frederick Steele had been valorous at Vicksburg and Lily wondered if it was the same man who had led her father in the fighting in which he had lost his leg and his will to live. The fort had been built in the 1860s to protect Union Pacific Railroad crews. Carbon County had been established to accommodate the settlers who had poured off the trains. Fort Steele had become quiet and forgotten by all but a few Washington D.C. delegates from Wyoming. Consequently, when Thornburg arrived in 1878, he had found the post falling to pieces. Biting dust drifted among ramshackle barracks. There was an outdated hospital, the Union Pacific depot, and a sutler store.

They rode through a shantytown on the outskirts of Fort Steele that reminded Lily of the filthy place where she had found Jimmy and his mother living in such abhorrent conditions. Ladies with hollow, sunken eyes watched them warily as they rode through the dusty street. A small child with matted hair came up and asked them for food. Samuel reached in his saddlebag and pulled out a packet of hard candy he had purchased at Peck's Store. He handed it down to the child whose eyes grew wide with excitement.

"You share that now, understand?" Samuel said as the child ran back inside the small shack.

Samuel explained that the hovels were called cribs. "The ladies outside a remote fort like this, and make no mistake, Lily, there are cribs at about every one, are the lowest of the low: harlots who have gotten too old or too used up on opium to make a living at the nicer bawdy houses such as those in Denver or some of the thriving mining towns."

"How can the army allow such debauchery?" Lily asked. "It's a crime."

"And where, Lily, do you think they would be if the fort were to order them out? None of those kids would ever see a decent meal."

"Yes, but Samuel, don't you realize that without the soldiers, there would not be these children? Someone really needs to take responsibility for this disgrace."

Lily was already in a somber mood by the time they rode into the fort, and the dreariness of the place only added to it. They were given the grand tour of the fort, or what there was of it that was worth seeing, by Major Thornburg. Lily noticed that the wives of the officers had tried to make their small rooms presentable. Anything they had brought with them that held some resemblance of grace or elegance was prominently displayed.

Lida Thornburg had planted a slip of Virginia Creeper next to the porch of the commander's quarters. It looked as though the climb halfway up the lattice had been an difficult struggle.

Over a delicious dinner that evening, complete with a fine French wine, Thornburg told Samuel and Lily that when General Crook had offered him the post last year, Crook had said that the fort served no real military purpose, but its proximity to the Medicine Bow Mountains made it a prime place to entertain congressmen and top politicians from Washington who came to the west to hunt for bear, moose and trophy elk and deer. Crook promised Thornburg, who was an excellent hunter and marksman, and extremely bored with his position as paymaster in Omaha, quick advancement to a more prominent post if he would agree to accept the offer as commander of Fort Steele for two years. Thornburg said he realized that the break he had waited for had finally come, and he'd quickly accepted, bringing along his wife Lida and their two small children. There were one hundred sixty soldiers at the fort, twenty-five civilians that included the officers' wives and children, two hundred twenty mules and one hundred fifty horses.

Major Thomas Tipton "Tip" Thornburg was a handsome man in his mid thirties, large figured with curly black hair, gentle black eyes and thick mutton chop sideburns. Lida looked years younger than her husband. She was a small genteel woman, with a head of beautiful blonde hair that fell down her back in a curly cascade, and vivid blue eyes that looked at her husband with sincere devotion. Their son Bobby was seven, talkative like his father, yet well mannered. Daughter Olivia was five, with the same delicate features as her mother and the same shy, sweet demeanor. Two Irish setters sat outside the door. After dinner Samuel and Tip enjoyed brandy and cigars on the porch while Lily and Lida chatted over soapy water in the kitchen.

Samuel and Lily stayed two days at the fort, resting from the past ten days spent mostly in the saddle. Samuel and Tip hunted for sage hens and grouse, accompanied by the very capable hunting dogs, Tom and Bill. They spent the evenings on the porch with several other officers in the regiment, discussing possible solutions to the Ute situation but none could come up with a clear-cut answer.

"What about Dodge and his bunch of blackies? Surely they should be able to keep a few hundred Utes under control." Captain Joe Lawson said. Lawson was a shriveled old-timer of about sixty, with cheeks blazed red from sun and too much bourbon. Samuel had been surprised to see that Joe was stilling wearing the blue. The man had fought more Indians than General Crook. His troop, Company E, numbered forty-nine of the most profane and shabby veterans in the army. All were too young to die, and too old to do anything else. They carried their whiskey in leather flasks on their sides. It seemed that Fort Steele had become something like their retirement home.

"I'm afraid not. There are only forty-three soldiers in Company D, eight of whom drive the supply wagons. They are a young bunch and none have seen any real Indian fighting. Dodge's men have been used basically for escort duty, scouting and border patrol throughout northwest Colorado. They have yet to prove themselves in a real crisis."

"Wouldn't it be best, then, to just have them stay at the White River Agency? Maybe with their presence seen, the Utes won't want to start anything," said Captain Payne.

Payne, Thornburg's sub-commander, was a pale and flabby man, the complete opposite of the major. They were about the same age, but unlike Thornburg who was robust, Payne was in poor physical shape, his health having failed in 1877 during the Chief Joseph campaign. They were opposites in temperament as well. Thornburg tended to try and see the Indians' point of view, while Payne thought of Indian fighting as a tactical problem based on timing, vicinity and firepower. His voice, like his demeanor, was cold and calculating.

"That, sir, is an impossibility. The company has to police over a million acres of some of the roughest country in Colorado. He has to try to keep settlers and squatters on Ute land out, and keep the Indians in. When a hot spot breaks out, as it has recently in North Park with the burning of J.B. Thompson's homestead, Dodge and his men are the only available troop. It takes four days of hard travel to get from North Park to White River.

"Dodge said that he has spent the better part of the last two summers going back and forth every time Meeker 'cried wolf.' Every time Meeker heard a rumor, or got crossways with one of the chiefs, he wired his friend Secretary Schurz in Washington and asked for troops. When Dodge would get his orders to return to White River, he would show up and Meeker would send him packing, not wanting the black soldiers to hang around the agency 'stirring up trouble.' What he really does not want is the army coming along and building a post right smack dab in the middle of his Utopia.

"We can't expect or rely on Company D to be in two places at once, nor can we ask Dodge's to men run to the aid of Meeker every time an Indian refuses to put a shoulder to the plow. There are simply too many other settlers who look to Company D for protection as well. The miners at Hahn's Peak and the homesteaders on the

Bear River in the Steamboat Springs country have had no trouble with the Yampa Utes, but Dodge said that everyone is getting mighty nervous that Colorow and his band of angry renegades will entice them into fighting back against those who mine or settle inside reservation boundaries. If that happens, all of western Colorado will become a shooting gallery."

"What do you propose, Colonel?" Thornburg asked.

"First of all, don't take Meeker too seriously." Samuel took a sip of brandy and puffed on his pipe. "No, on second thought, take him very seriously. The man's ego speaks for him and that is a dangerous thing. He's built himself quite a place, and seems to have forgotten that it doesn't belong to him. Deep down he thinks it does, and will do just about anything to keep it. He is afraid he's going to lose it, and fear causes a man to do pretty bizarre things. Until the Bureau of Indian Affairs can convince President Hayes and Secretary Schurz to remove Meeker altogether and replace him with someone who has a better understanding, and a better tolerance of the Ute people, then the White River is going to be a box of dynamite just waiting for a small spark to set it off. Crook may think this post doesn't have a military position, but it seems to me that your men are the only ones anywhere close if needed. My advise to you, gentlemen, is to keep the rifles clean and oiled, and not just for hunting pheasants," Samuel advised.

The women retired to the small parlor after sharing the chore of supper and dishes, not wanting to brave the dust and wind as the men did, even though at twilight the never-ending howl would dissipate to a slight moan. Lida seemed thrilled to have another woman to talk to. With Tip as commander over the other officers, the wives sometimes were not as willing to speak with her as freely as they did amongst themselves. Finally Lily brought up the shantytown outside the fort.

"I was as appalled as you are when I first came here and tried desperately to get Tip to do something about the situation. He finally agreed and gave each person in the shanties the offer of a free train ticket to anywhere they wanted to go. Some did leave. And after they did, many men at the post grew sullen and agitated. Drinking and fighting increased."

Lida tried to explain to Lily the utter loneliness of the post. "I know it's not much of an excuse, but I do have to say that the women have a way of keeping the men 'occupied,' so to speak. In a strange way, those ladies are the only family some soldiers have. Please understand that we do what we can for the women and children. We ask families and churches back East to send clothes and blankets, which we pass out. Food supplies are taken weekly to the shantytown, and at Christmas every child receives candy and a present."

"It's lonely for you, too, isn't it?" Lily gently asked Lida.

The woman nodded. "Even though we have dances once a month to break up the monotony, there is nothing to keep the wind from blowing. It is next to impossible to keep the quarters clean of dust. It permeates everything. We must cover the butter even as we eat, or it will become gritty in minutes. We are thankful for the train, as it brings fresh rations, and news from home when it stops. On the days that it goes on by, the children and I wave at the people in the cars and make up stories about where they may be going: places with green fields, rose gardens, gentle rains and no wind. Places that have a church with a white steeple, a school with a bell, and a library with books that aren't stained with sweat or tobacco juice."

Lida looked at Lily seriously. "Think hard before agreeing if Samuel ever asks you to go with him to live at an army post. I envy you, Lily. I've never known what it is to have a home of my own, to have a garden that I am sure I will be able to harvest. To have a home I am able to paint whatever color I want. To have furniture I want, not furniture that is durable and easy to move."

Then in a small voice that sounded almost like a plea, she added, "Would you write to me, Lily?"

"Of course."

"One more year. Then we can get on board the train and go somewhere else as well."

The next morning Samuel and Lily boarded the train for Denver. Lily looked out the window to wave at Tip, Lida, and the children standing on the platform. Tip looked cocky and self-assured. Lida looked sad, small, and vulnerable as her hair whipped across her face. Lida pushed it back and the look in her eyes begged Lily to come back and take her away from the wind.

Lily blew her a kiss and then held up one finger, as if to say, "One more year, my friend. Just one more year."

Little did either of them know that it would be much less than that.

July 24th, 1879

13

"It's Rose, right over there! Do you see her?" Both Samuel and Lily were at the door of the train even before it came to a complete stop at the station in Denver.

Lily gathered her daughter up in her arms and gave her a huge hug and kiss. She had never been away from her daughter for over a day, much less two long weeks.

"Chipeta, thank you so much for bringing her." She hugged her friend as well. "Where is Ouray?"

"He sends his best wishes. Unfortunately, the trip was hard on him and he is at the hotel resting."

"Is he ill again?" Samuel asked.

"Yes, and much worse this time. The herbs the medicine woman gives him no longer help at all. I tried to convince him not to come, but he was determined. He said it must be serious for you to ask him to make such a trip on short notice."

"I'm afraid it is. Do you think he is up to meeting with Governor Pitkin tomorrow?"

"I don't know. I tried to get him to see a white doctor when we arrived two days ago, but he refused. Samuel, maybe you could convince him."

"I will tie him up and drag him if I have to. You are at the Markham?"

"Yes."

"After the meeting tomorrow, I'll have a little talk with him." Samuel gave Rose a kiss on her forehead. "I do hope my little sassafras here didn't cause you too much trouble."

"She was pure joy the whole time. Sarah McCluskey offered to keep her after she heard we would be coming to Denver," Chipeta said, smiling at Lily, "but I figured her mother would be anxious to see her."

"If I would have had to wait another week, I think I would have started walking home. Thank you so much, Chipeta. But you must have had your hands full with Ouray being ill along with having to watch over Rose."

Chipeta laughed. "Actually she kept us all entertained. Jack, Johnson, and Douglas met up with us at Glenwood Springs, and we came the rest of the way by train. They have all fallen in love with her."

"So everyone is here?" Samuel asked.

"Yes. I will tell Ouray you are now here as well. I kept the carriage waiting, so I must go. Lily, we would all appreciate it very much if you could sit in at the meeting tomorrow. It seems the other chiefs fell in love with you, too."

Lily gave her friend another hug and promised to be there.

✣ ✣ ✣

Samuel put Rose up on his shoulders and they walked to the boxcar at the rear of the train that housed Henry and Boot Jack. Henry had put up quite a fuss at Fort Steele when they loaded him. When the door was opened, he trotted quickly down the ramp and Lily had to hold tightly to his halter to keep him calm. The horse was clearly agitated at his recent uncomfortable accommodations. Boot Jack, on the other hand, walked out slowly, as if he had just awakened from a long nap. After Samuel saddled his horse, he set Rose on its back and she squealed with glee, hugging the horse's neck.

They rode down to Hank's old livery that was now owned by a gentleman with a thick French accent named Pierre. In the corral was a string of gentle nags that Pierre said he had bought for the "dudes and their ladies" from the Eastern United States and Europe who were flocking to Colorado for extended holidays. He offered Samuel a job as a guide, which Samuel promptly declined.

"Good money," Pierre said. "It be better than skinning the beaver for a living. Besides, mon ami, there be no more pelts in the water. The critters are all gone."

Lily felt a bit uneasy as she walked up the steps to the boarding-house. It had been over two years since she had seen Isabel, but since that first letter Lily had written the night she had stayed at Chipeta's, the two had exchanged letters on a monthly basis in an attempt to re-establish their childhood friendship.

If there had been anything elegant at all about Isabel Hastings Royce, it had been her handwriting. The precise, yet graceful script had amazed Lily when she had received that first letter. And since the first one, Izzie had adorned each new letter with artistic borders of flowers, leaves, and butterflies. Both she and Izzie had been able to put down in words what they could not say face to face.

Several times Lily had wanted to accompany Samuel to Denver when he came on business, but the work at the ranch had not per-mitted them to both be gone at the same time. Someone had to stay and watch over the herd, and up until now, it had always been her. Once again, she was immensely thankful for Gus. Without him, she would have not had the last couple of weeks with Samuel, and prob-ably in the long run, he helped save her marriage.

The sign on the front porch of the boardinghouse was new. It read "Isabel's Boardinghouse." Rose spied a box of kittens on the side of the house and took off running as Samuel rang the bell. The smell of fried chicken greeted them as Isabel opened the door.

"Take them boots off now," Izzie commanded as she turned back to mashing potatoes in the kitchen.

"Are you sure you're not Myrtle?" Samuel asked with a grin before he snatched a biscuit from a linen covered basket.

"Hello, Isabel," Lily said.

"Lily." Isabel glanced at her only for a moment before returning her eyes to the potatoes. "You all be hungry I suppose, after the long ride. Wash up now, before the food gets cold. Everybody knows mashed taters ain't no good cold."

Rose burst through the screen door carrying a fluffy yellow kitten. "Mama, lookie what I found!"

"Honey, you take it back outside this instant."

"Lands sake! That be Rose?" Isabel asked.

"Yes," Lily said, as she tried to take the kitten out of the child's arm. Its tiny claws dug into her dress like a cocklebur. "Rose, you know animals don't belong. . ."

"It be alright, Lily." Isabel said, smiling down at the child.

"Rose, this is my good friend Isabel," Lily said.

Suddenly shy, the child grinned sheepishly.

Isabel bent at the knees, crouching down to meet the child face to face. "Nice to meet you Rose. Are you hungry?"

"Yes'm, a little."

"Maybe your daddy will take you to wash up for supper while me and your Mama get the food on the table."

"Kitty, too?"

"Kitty, too."

Samuel took Rose, leaving Lily and Isabel alone for a few moments.

"She's the spittin' image of her Mama, that's for sure. Just as pretty as a peach."

"Thank you, Isabel."

Isabel gave Lily a handful of silverware and together they set the table.

"I saw the sign on the porch. I didn't realize you purchased the boardinghouse. Good for you," Lily said sincerely.

"Yes. I saved almost all of two years of my pay. Surely didn't have nothing to spend my money on, except an occasional new apron and couple of trips to Illinois to see my papa."

"Grandma's last letter said he is reading again."

"Sure enough. I ain't seen him since last Christmas, and he don't write so good but your grandma writes me about once a week. I tried and tried to get him to come back with me but he wouldn't leave your grandma. So then I tried to get her to come too, but it would take a keg of blasting powder to get her out of that house and on a train. And of course, he and her both swear that neither of them don't need no looking after."

Isabel set down the plates. "Got something I want to show you."

She led Lily to the bedroom and took the rag doll from its place in the middle of the bed, holding it in her arms like a new-born baby.

"Imagine my surprise on Christmas morn when I opened up my present and saw it. I couldn't a been more surprised if Jesus himself would have popped out of the box. But what was even more of a surprise was that you had kept her all them years." She handed the doll to Lily. "Best Christmas I ever did have."

"You gave her a bath," Lily said smiling. "And fixed her up some new hair. She looks wonderful."

"Papa told me how much she meant to you."

Lily gently placed the doll back on the bed and turned to Isabel. "I wanted to tell you. . ." Her voice cracked and she turned away as she felt the guilt of the day long ago wash over her. That horrible, awful day. She hung her head in shame and choked back, yet again, the tears that she had never been allowed to cry.

She felt a soft hand on her shoulder.

"You don't gotta tell me nothing, Lily Belle." The tears welled up in Isabel's eyes as well but she didn't bother to hide them. "It weren't your fault. That's just the way things was back then. You was just the easiest one to blame. God help us all, but that's just the way things was."

Lily turned around as she reached for Isabel's hand. "Do you still have the scar?"

Lily held out her finger and Isabel did the same. Two scars, both in the same spot on the same finger of their right hands, joined once again.

Rose burst into the room and held up her own tiny hands. "See?" Isabel squeezed Lily's hand before letting go and taking the child's.

"Maybe with the Good Lord's help we can teach the children different." Isabel lifted the child into her burly arms and gave her a kiss on the cheek. "You as skinny as you Mama was. Come on, punkin seed, let's go put some meat on them bones."

Samuel was already at the table, knife and fork ready and waiting. "Well, finally. I didn't think you two would ever come out. And just who was it that said something about cold taters?" He smiled at the women and winked just as he had done that first night Lily had seen him at Myrtle's three years ago. Lily felt a burst of joy. It was a blessed miracle to have them both back.

Everyone ate as if the day were a celebration. Samuel asked Isabel how she had come to own the boardinghouse. "Didn't think anyone could serve up a spread like Myrtle did, but you sure proved me wrong."

Isabel explained how she had saved for two years for the down payment, hoping that at some point Myrtle would change her mind about selling. "I knew it would be a might hard for the woman to let the place go," Isabel said, "but I just kept on hopin' and prayin' she'd change her mind. With her and Hank about as happy as two bluebirds in the spring sunshine, and with the livery in Pueblo going great guns like it is, I figured the boardinghouse would be one less thing for her to have to worry about. And even though they were mighty good to me, I just don't want to answer to nobody but me. I guess I'm kind of an independent sort of gal."

She said that once she and Hank finally got Myrtle to agree to sell the house, the bank would not lend her the rest of the money.

"I had me over four hundred dollars saved up. The place was full most every night. Why, even the banker's wife would order my pies and cakes for her fancy dinner parties. But the banker himself said I was too much of a risk. Shoot fire, nobody in this town worked harder than me and he knew it."

"So what did you finally do?" Lily asked.

"Remember I had the place up in Lake City before I come here?"

"Yes."

"Well, I never was much good at turning people away. There was a miner there by the name of Kip Whipple. Nice enough, and a hard worker. I grubstaked him a couple hundred dollars. Shoot, grubstaked a bunch of them poor boys. Well, lo and behold, just two days after the banker turned me down, in walked Kip and handed me ten thousand dollars! Lord almighty, I just about fell over dead from the shock of seeing all that cash. Seems he struck a vein of silver that flowed for almost a year before it finally bottomed out. Even named the mine after me, imagine that. Called it the Little Izzie. Said without me keeping him going that last few months, he'd a turned and hightailed it back to Missouri."

Noticing Samuel's plate was about empty, Isabel passed him the platter of chicken. "You eat up now, and give little Rose there another biscuit. Be sure to put some of that good honey on it." She passed the basket down as well.

"Anyways, imagine the look on that banker's face when Kip and I walked into his bank and closed our accounts. The banker was squawking like a chicken when Kip asked for his money and then stumbled all over himself trying to apologize to me, especially when he saw the wad I pulled out when I asked for a certified check for the money I was going to send to Myrtle."

She giggled like a child. "Course I would have none of it."

"Surely you don't have the rest of the cash stashed in a mattress?" Samuel asked, almost sure she would say yes.

"Lord. No."

Samuel breathed a big sigh of relief.

"Got it buried out back behind the chicken coop."

Samuel set down his fork. "Now, Isabel. . ."

She laughed gaily. "You looked about as bad as that banker did!" She passed him the bowl of mashed potatoes.

"Shoot fire, you think I fell off a turnip wagon? No, Hank had me talk to a man in Pueblo by the name of John Thatcher. Right smart man, he is. He took the rest of the money and put it to some investments. They are doing mighty nice."

"I am truly happy for you, Isabel. But with all that money, why are you still working?" Lily asked.

"Well, girl, just what else am I supposed to do? Don't know nothing else. I ain't the type to sit around and look purty all day, that's a for sure thing. Besides, I like it just fine right where I am. I be sure that the good Lord got a plan for that money, since I don't really got much use for it. I just got to wait until he tells me what to do with it."

The next morning Lily left Rose to "help" Isabel with feeding the chickens while Samuel flagged down a carriage for the meeting at the governor's mansion.

As they drove down the streets of Denver, Lily was impressed by how the town had grown. There was a new air of permanence. Large buildings of stone had replaced the smaller buildings that had been hastily constructed of green lumber. There were well established trees, lawns, and gardens in the sections where immaculate houses now lined the streets.

Governor Pitkin's mansion rivaled even that of Victoria Bannister's.

The Ute chiefs were already seated when Samuel and Lily walked in. They were dressed in their finest buckskins, looking very serious, even if a bit angry.

"They say Meeker is on his way to Denver City," Ouray said to Samuel. Both Lily and Samuel noticed the gray pallor to his face. Pain showed clearly in his eyes.

"How did he find out we were meeting with Pitkin?"

"Don't know. He be here in four days. I be gone in four days," Johnson added.

Pitkin, accompanied by Otto Mears, walked into the room and sat down at the head of the long table. The governor came from a long line of aristocratic Connecticut forebears, graduated with high honors from Wesleyan University, and had practiced law with great success until his health had been broken from consumption. Good friends included intellectuals such as Walt Whitman, who had lost an Interior Department job once for having written *Leaves of Grass.*

Pitkin was a frail, reserved man who had come to Colorado in 1872 to relieve the effects of his disease after having spent two years in sanatoriums in Europe and Florida which had merely brought him closer to death's door.

Having heard about the beauty and healing air of the Colorado mountains, he purchased a horse and determined that he would not die without seeing their beauty. But instead of the four hundred mile trip into the southwest mountains of the San Juans killing him, it cured him. In addition, he made a quick fortune at the Prince Albert Mine.

And there he met Otto Mears. The two became close friends. Otto knew Colorado politics almost as well as he knew his toll roads. Mears assured Pitkin that they shared the same philosophy about life and about Indians. Mears encouraged Pitkin to run for governor in 1878. Pitkin declined, and then later accepted, following the impulse to achieve some sort of legacy despite his physical handicap.

When the article titled "The Utes Must Go" had been printed in the *Denver Tribune,* Pitkin had secretly agreed with every word.

"I thank you for being here, gentleman." Pitkin did not look at the chiefs, but at Samuel. He did not acknowledge Chipeta or Lily. "I have asked Mr. Mears to attend the conference to translate anything I may have to say, just to be sure you understand what I will be telling you."

"It is good to see you again, my friend," Mears said, addressing Ouray. He then nodded to the other chiefs.

Pitkin started the meeting by pulling out a letter from his front pocket. "Nathan Meeker informed me on July fifth that there seems to be an organized effort to destroy the timber in northwestern Colorado." He set down the paper and looked at the chiefs. "Is this a true statement?"

"It is true that there are forest fires in the area, yes." Douglas said.

"And were these set by the red man?"

"If you are asking if the Ute people set the fires, then my honest answer would be that I do not think so. What I do know is there has been no rain for over three moons. The land is thirsty and the thunder and lightning do not release the water from the clouds."

"Meeker also states that you are not willing to farm. Is this true?"

This time it was Ouray who spoke. "Governor Pitkin, when the Brunot Treaty was signed six years ago, there was never a mention that the Utes would be required to farm the land."

"True." Pitkin stated. "But there was a stipulation that the Utes would be required to stay within the boundaries set. Meeker informs me that this is not being met either. He merely thinks that without the Indians farming the land, there will not be enough food to get your people through the winter months."

Ouray paused, forming his thoughts before speaking. "The Brunot Treaty clearly provided for provisions, and for payment of the land which was signed over in good faith. Neither has been met. Once again, if the government would keep its word, then we the Ute people, could keep ours as well. In reference to the hunting ground which the Utes have traveled to, the boundary lines show the people have stayed clearly within their domain."

Pitkin was not impressed. "If you are saying the Ute people expect the United States to provide your people with their every need, while they do nothing but bet on their racehorses, then I am afraid you have seriously misjudged the government. We do not encourage idleness or wanton waste of property. Living off the bounty of the Indian Bureau will only encourage laziness. Nathan Meeker is merely trying to get your people to manage the land allotted to you by setting a good example."

Ouray stood up. "And I, sir, am being assured by your words that you and Nathan Meeker have seriously misjudged the Ute people. We are not beggars. We are not lazy. Long before the white man came, we were a self-sufficient people. We survived, and even thrived, on the bountiful gifts provided to us by Mother Earth. Like the white people, we gathered food from her harvest and prepared enough to last us through the winter months.

"We were also a trusting people. When we give our word, we do not turn away from it. Mr. Mears expects to be paid for his roads, and the government delivers the money. You, Governor Pitkin, expect payment for your services to the people of Colorado. Again, the government delivers. We, the Ute people, are not asking for a handout. In good faith we turned over some of the land to the white man, and in return they were to pay us for the lost hunting ground. We are simply asking for what is owed us so we can remain a self-sufficient people in accordance with our customs and way of life. We do not ask the white people to become like us. And honestly, after seeing the way the white people live their own lives, we do not want to change and become as they are. We simply want to be left alone."

"We both know, Chief Ouray, that is an impossible situation. Change is inevitable. No power on earth will stop progress," Pitkin said.

"That is true, Governor, but I am afraid that the Ute idea of progress is vastly different than that of the white man. I have seen what your idea of progress has done to other tribes. The Sioux, the Nez Perce, the Cheyenne. How many lives have been slaughtered by your progress, Governor? How many children have no father, no home, no food?"

Pitkin's face turned as hard and as cold as granite. "If the children are starving, it is because the leaders of those Indian nations resisted change. They have refused to abide by the treaties which they signed, and have refused to be taught new ways. Nothing stays the same, Chief. The days of being able to roam the mountains no longer remain. There are simply too many people who only wish to share in the beauty that the Utes have known. There is no way to stop them from coming. If your people refuse change as well, if your people refuse to try and get along with the whites, then you too, will be deciding your own fate, not me."

Ouray sat down, knowing there would be no common ground with Pitkin. "I am afraid, sir," he said, "that the beauty the white man sees, and the beauty that the Utes see, are two very different splendors. The white sees riches only in gold and silver. The Ute sees riches in all that Mother Earth provides: the gold in the sunrise to the east, the silver of the clear mountain streams, the bountiful berries in autumn and even the frost on the trees in winter."

Ouray reached for the letter from Meeker and drew a large box on the back. "The white man builds a house of stone, abiding in one place. Once the Utes home was all of the mountains and valleys. That is where we dwelled for centuries." He pointed to the box. "First the white man took a room, then another, and then another until we are left with only a shed." He drew a small box inside the larger one and pointed to it.

"You, sir, cannot take a bear that has roamed free for all his life and put him in a cage, give him a fish or two to eat once a day, and expect him to be tame. Sooner or later he will turn and bite you."

Pitkin looked at his watch and rose from his seat. "If you will excuse me, I do have other matters to attend to today. We will continue this discussion tomorrow morning."

He walked to the door and turned. "But I would like you to think about this before we meet, just remember that if the bear fights too much, sooner or later he will end up as a rug on someone's floor. Good day."

Colorow knocked over his chair as he rose from the table.

Samuel had to keep him from going after Pitkin.

"This is a waste of time," Colorow said angrily. "I say we get a war party together and fight back."

Ouray looked up at him, his face ashen with pain. "No, Colorow. That is exactly what he wants us to do. He was merely poking at the bear with a big stick, trying to get it angry enough to give him a reason for pulling the trigger."

Ouray took Meeker's letter and wadded it into a ball. "Pitkin wants to justify to the American people that we must be either annihilated or be removed. By fighting back, we will be telling him which direction to take."

Ouray looked at the other chiefs. "I understand your anger. I feel it as well, but we cannot let anger make our decisions for us. Samuel, is there anyone in Washington that we can appeal to?"

"Chief Joseph of the Nez Perce tribe is in Washington trying that very thing. His people need rations and blankets to get them through the upcoming winter. I hear the response to his pleas has been favorable."

Ouray knew Joseph well. He was a man of honor, and of wisdom. At first, Joseph had tried to fight back.

After the opening of the Nez Perce land in the Oregon Territory to settlers 1877, his tribe had been ordered to move to a reservation in Idaho, a small piece of land with no buffalo. His tribe rebelled and had tried to escape to Canada. They traveled over 1500 miles through Oregon, Washington, Idaho, and Montana, all the while fighting battles with the pursuing United States Army. Finally, their bullets and arrows, and their strength, had run out.

Ouray had spoken at length with Chief Joseph after his surrender in the Bear Paw Mountains. Ouray remembered the words Joseph had said to the Army on that day:

"I am tired of fighting. Our chiefs are killed. The old men are all dead. It is cold and we have no blankets; the little children are freezing to death. My people, some of them, have run away to the hills and have no blankets, no food. No one knows where they are—perhaps freezing to death. I want to have time to look for my children and see how many of them I can find. Maybe I will find them among the dead. I am tired; my heart is sick and sad. From where the sun stands now I will fight no more forever."

Samuel pulled out a copy of the speech Joseph had recently made to Congress. Copies had been sent to the members of the Bureau of Indian Affairs, in the hopes that they would be able to convince other tribes to try the peaceful approach that Joseph was using.

Samuel read the words aloud to the chiefs:

"There are some things I want to know which no one seems able to explain. I cannot understand why the government sends a man out to fight us, as it did General Miles, and then he breaks his word. Such a government has something wrong about it. I cannot understand why so many chiefs are allowed to talk so many different ways, and promise so many different things. I have seen the Great Father Chief (President Hayes); the next Great Chief (the Secretary of the Interior); the Commissioner Chief, the Law Chief, and many other law chiefs (Congressmen) and they all say they are my friends, and that I shall have justice, but while all their mouths talk right I do not understand why nothing has been done for my people. I have heard talk and talk but nothing is done.

Samuel paused and looked at the Ute chiefs. They nodded in agreement with Joseph's words.

"Good words do not last long unless they amount to something. Words do not pay for my dead people. They do not pay for my country now overrun by white men. They do not protect my father's grave. They do not pay for my horses and cattle. Good words do not give me back my children. Good words will not make good the promise of your War Chief, General Miles. Good words will not give my people a home where they can live in peace and take care of themselves. I am tired of the talk that comes to nothing. It makes my heart sick when I remember all the good words and all the broken promises.

"If the white man wants to live in peace with the Indian, he can live in peace. There need be no trouble. Treat all men alike. Give them the same laws. Give them all an even chance to live and grow. All men were made by the same Great Spirit Chief. They are all brothers. The earth is the mother of all people, and all people should have equal rights upon it. You might as well expect all rivers to run backward as that any man who was born a free man should be contented to be penned up and denied liberty to go where he pleases. If you tie a horse to a stake, do you expect he will grow fat? If you pen an Indian up on a small spot of earth and compel him to stay there, he will not be contented nor will he grow and prosper. I have asked some of the Great White Chiefs where they get the authority to say to the Indian that he shall stay in one place, while he sees white men going where he please. They cannot tell me.

"I only ask of the government to be treated as all other men are treated. If I cannot go to my own home, let me have a home in a country where my people will not die so fast.

"When I think of our condition, my heart is heavy. I see men of my own race treated as outlaws and driven from country to country, or shot down like animals. I know that my race must change. We cannot hold our own with the white men as we are. We only ask an even chance to live as other men live. We ask to be recognized as men. We ask that the same law shall work alike on all men. If an Indian breaks the law, punish him by the law. If a white man breaks the law, punish him also.

"Let me be a free man, free to travel, free to stop, free to work, free to trade where I choose, free to choose my own teacher, free to follow the religion of my fathers, free to talk, think and act for myself – and I will obey every law or submit to the penalty.

"Whenever the white man treats the Indian as they treat each other then we shall have no more wars. We shall all be alike—brothers of one father and mother, with one sky above us and one country around us and one government for us all. Then the Great Spirit

Chief who rules above will smile upon this land and send rain to wash out the bloody spots made by brothers' hands upon the face of the earth. For this time the Indian race is waiting and praying. I hope no more groans of the wounded men and women will ever go to the ear of the Great Spirit Chief above, and that all people may be one people."

The chiefs pondered the words for a long while. Finally Ouray spoke.

"We must support Joseph in appealing to the white fathers for justice for the all Indian people. Samuel, I would like to go to Washington to appeal the Ute cause as well." He looked directly at Colorow. "We cannot take the chance of fighting as Joseph did two years ago. I will not let our people freeze or starve, or to be hunted down like a herd of deer."

Colorow rose and glared at Ouray. "If you want to go to Washington and be lied to again by the White Chiefs, then go ahead. The only reason that Joseph is there is to beg. I will beg to no man. I am no man's slave, nor am I a squaw or a jackass made to walk behind a plow. I am a warrior."

Ouray stood and faced Colorow. "I am warning you, there will be no bloodshed at White River."

"I will fight like a warrior, and I will die like a warrior."

Colorow turned and walked out the door, followed by Johnson and Jack.

Douglas hesitated before following the other chiefs. "We will give you two moons, Ouray. I will see to that. Two moons, but no more."

After the chiefs left, Ouray sat back down and put his head in his hands. "The chiefs think I am a coward. My people think I am a coward. And worst of all," Ouray said sadly, "I feel like a coward. Maybe Colorow is right."

Samuel spoke softly. "It takes more courage to walk away from a fight than to strike. It takes courage to look humiliation in the face and not lose your integrity. Don't question what you are doing,

Ouray. You know as well as I do that if you retaliate against Meeker, or any of the whites who are poking at you with sticks, Pitkin will have every soldier within five hundred miles shooting you down."

Ouray looked at Samuel, the pain in his eyes replaced by rage. "If it was just me, I would welcome the fight. Like Colorow, deep down I am, and will always be, a warrior."

"But this is not just about me." He looked at Chipeta and his eyes softened with wisdom and compassion.

"My place as the Chief is to do what is best for my people and for the women and children that will come after me. If we fight, it will be as it was with the Cheyenne at Sand Creek, the army piercing babies with bayonets and mutilating women. It will be as it was with the Nez Perce, and the Sioux and the Arapahoe. No tribe who has tried to fight back wins. They end up being butchered like cattle, and in the end, they still lose everything."

As he rose again, he stifled the agony he felt inside but his eyes clouded with pain. "I can not let this happen to the Utes. I must go to Washington D.C." He struggled to walk but his legs would not cooperate. He reached for the table to steady himself.

"The only place you are going right now, my friend, is to see a doctor," Samuel said, not as a request but as a command. "You will be no good to anyone if you don't."

Ouray was too weak to argue.

✚ ✚ ✚

Lily went to the boardinghouse and waited anxiously for their return.

Ouray and Chipeta walked in, and then Samuel. He looked at Lily, shaking his head.

Chipeta gave Ouray two teaspoons of medicine from a bottle.

Izzie told Ouray and Chipeta in no uncertain terms that they would stay at the boardinghouse. And neither argued. Neither wanted to be in the fine hotel, surrounded by the riches of the white man.

Samuel helped Ouray up the stairs while Izzie poured tea for the exhausted women.

"I'm truly sorry, Chipeta. Lily told me the meeting didn't go so well," Isabel said kindly.

Chipeta sipped the hot tea, quiet and subdued.

"It ain't easy to be faced with losing what you've known all your life. Lily and I have both been there. And we have both survived." She brushed the hair away from Chipeta's face with a warm touch of comfort.

"I worry about what will happen to the children," Chipeta said.

"It's them that suffer from any kind of war, that's a for sure fact. And it is up to us women to make sure they make it through. It is up to us to be strong. And when we are not strong, we must be there for each other to lean on."

Lily nodded and took Chipeta's hand. Isabel took the other and squeezed hard, as if willing her strength into it. She looked at Rose sleeping soundly in a chair in the corner—so full of childlike innocence to the madness of man.

"We women are the menders, we are the ones that put back together what is torn apart. And whatever happens, we will see to it that the lives of the children will be put back together again," Isabel said matter-of-factly. "Yes, girls, it is surely up to us."

14

September 26, 1879

L ily was pouring jam into jars when she glanced out the window and saw Samuel riding up the road. With the drought, there had not been many raspberries, but she and Chipeta had managed to pick one full milk bucket, which they had split up evenly. Chipeta would not make jam with hers but would dry and pound them into pemmican.

"You just missed Chipeta. Did you get the mail and some more sugar?" Lily asked as Samuel strode into the house.

He dropped the mail on the table.

"Where's the sugar? I need it to make the rest of the jelly," she said as she wiped a wet tea towel around the edge of a jar.

"It's happened Lily."

The tone of his voice made Lily set the towel down and turn around. "Samuel what's wrong?"

"Meeker is dead. He ordered his hired hand, Shad Price, to start plowing up the Utes' racetrack and they went crazy."

"Oh, my God. What about the rest of the family and the hired hands?"

"The men, all ten of them, are dead. The women have been taken as hostages."

Lily sat down in shock.

"And there's more," Samuel said. "Thornburg is dead. The rest of his men are hunkered down in a valley called Milk Creek about six miles north of the White River Agency, trying to fight off the Utes."

"Does Ouray know?"

"Yes. He's sent a courier to tell the White River Utes to let the hostages go and stop fighting the soldiers. Of course he blames himself. Says he should have gone to Washington in August."

"He was in no shape to go. The doctor said. . ."

"White doctor Lily," Samuel interrupted. "Ouray's angry because the treatment the doctor gave him did nothing to help. Said it was a waste of precious time."

Samuel banged the table with his fist, shaking the jars of jam. "Dammit all, Lily. I should have gone."

"You had to finish getting the hay in, and help McCluskey with the oats. And there's nothing you could have done anyway and you know it. Without Ouray, Congress would have agreed to nothing. Pitkin and Mears have President Hayes thinking the Utes have provoked it all. You did everything you could to try and get Meeker replaced."

"Well, the man wanted to be a legend; he damned sure is going to be one now."

✛ ✛ ✛

It had been a day like any other for Arvilla Meeker—the same drudgery of work, bugs, dust, and more work. She had surprised Nathan at the noon meal with a fresh gooseberry cobbler drenched in thick cream.

There had been no warning signal of the doom. Arvilla Meeker had just finished up the noon dinner dishes when she heard the first shots ring out. Several Utes had simply raised their rifles and started firing. At first she thought the Indians had just been showing off their skills, and were probably betting on them as they did everything else. She tried to ignore the noise, scurrying about the kitchen wiping away the dust that, yet again, coated the sideboard with a thin, dull film.

The sound of the gunfire kept up, scratching on her nerves until she threw down her rag and went outside to find Nathan and have him put a stop to the foolishness. It was there she saw Hank Dresser who had been repairing the roof of the storehouse. He yelled something to her which she didn't understand and flapped his arms. There was a pop, and he fell from the roof like a limp rag doll, landing in a crumpled heap on the hard dirt.

Arvilla didn't scream. After all, she had lived this moment in her mind a thousand times. She ran to the school to get Josie, who had been watching the Price children while Flora Ellen hung out clothes on a line.

The women fled to the double-walled adobe milk house. Frank Dresser, shot in the leg, crawled in later and Arvilla dressed his wound. In a voice completely void of any emotion, she told him that his brother Hank was dead. There they hid for five hours, praying that they wouldn't be found.

At dusk, the shooting stopped. Josie opened the door carefully and saw the Utes looting the supply building. Many of the other buildings had been set on fire and smoldered in the paleness of the setting sun.

"We've got to get out of here," Josie said. "It's only a matter of time before they find us. Mother, you must run." She grabbed up May Price while Flora Ellen grabbed Johnny.

They ran as far as the edge of a field of sagebrush before being spotted. Arvilla was shot in the leg, causing a flesh wound to her thigh. Frank Dresser was shot again as well but still managed to escape into the brush.

Persune ran up and grabbed Josie. "I not hurt you. You go with me."

As the women were led back down the streets of the agency, they looked at the desolation around them. The buildings had been looted, and then burned. Plows, wheels, gears and wagons, hay rakes, mowers, washtubs, and hardware had been shot up and smashed. The body of hired hand Arthur Thompson lay on the ground with his gun beside him. Flora Ellen howled like a wounded animal when she saw the body of her husband Shadrach lying in the dust next to a plow. In the doorway of what was left of the storehouse laid the body of William Post. Near Post were the bullet-ridden bodies of Frank Shepard, George Eaton, and Harry Dresser, Frank's brother.

The American flag still waved in the light breeze on the flagpole near the house. Arvilla saw the battered body of her husband a few yards away from it. Blood had long since dried from the bullet hole in his head. Around his neck someone had put a heavy logging chain. It was clear his body had been dragged. A stave from an agency flour barrel had been jammed down his throat, as if an angry Ute had been determined to silence the man forever.

Arvilla looked away from the body, toward what had been their home. It was burned at the far end, but the rest of the house had been left untouched. Chief Douglas shoved her from behind. "Go. Get things. Hurry yup." He motioned at the other women with his rifle.

The women hastily gathered a few belongings. Arvilla grabbed her well-worn leather satchel from under the bed and packed a blanket, a few clothes and a small box of medicine. She found the money she had hidden to purchase a present for her husband, twenty-six dollars in bills and four dollars in silver, stuffed it in a pair of stockings, and tucked the bundle in the bottom of the bag. She grabbed her most precious possession, a tattered copy of *Pilgrim's Progress*. Next she put a clean handkerchief and a packet of needles in the pocket of her apron, and then donned her hat and shawl.

She was amazed at the calmness that came over her as she looked at the bed she had shared for so many years with her beloved. She touched the pillow where last night his head had rested. Even after the past few hours of horror, she felt something of a relief. At least she need not worry anymore about the awful things that might happen. Somehow she had always known it would end up this way.

Arvilla walked back outside where Chief Douglas was waiting for her. She observed that old Douglas was suffering, too. He was tipping up a bottle of whiskey, but he was not drunk. He looked just as bewildered and sad as she felt. She got the distinct impression that the old chief was as stunned by what had happened as she was.

She walked over to where her husband's body lay in the moonlight. She bent to kiss him but noticed the faces of the Utes watching her. She knew they would think it a morbid gesture so instead she said a silent good-bye to her husband, and offered up a prayer that he would now find his perfect Utopia.

The women were led to Douglas' camp. Josie said something in a whisper to Persune and he nodded. She went to Arvilla and did her best to bandage her mother's leg.

Arvilla was instructed to mount an old nag with no saddle or blanket. Feeble in health at age sixty-four, she had to have the assistance of two Utes. As they boosted her up, she was perplexed that she felt no pain from her wound. It was as if her body had become detached from her mind. Persune put a blanket and saddle on a strong filly, helped Josie onto its back, and then set little May Price in front of her. Next Flora Ellen was mounted on a surefooted mare, and Johnny was placed into her arms.

As the caravan ascended up toward Sleepy Cat Mountain, Arvilla said a silent prayer that somehow Frank Dresser would make it to Thornburg's troops at Milk Creek. She felt as numb and cold and dead as her husband, so she prayed the prayer only on behalf of Josie.

The moon was full, illuminating the trail. When they got to a high ridge, Arvilla looked back. Embers from the fires still glowed red hot, the smoke curled up as if waving farewell.

Good riddance, Arvilla thought. She had always detested the place.

✚ ✚ ✚

Samuel quickly threw a few essentials into a saddlebag while Lily saddled Boot Jack.

"Be careful," she said. He kissed her, then Rose.

He mounted his horse then reached down and touched her cheek. "I love you, Donovan."

And then he was gone.

The next morning after a sleepless night, Lily found Gus in the barn and asked him to watch Rose while she went to Chipeta's.

"Did Samuel say it was much too dangerous to be going anywhere right now?" Gus asked, giving her a fatherly stare.

"I'll be fine. I can't let Chipeta go through this alone."

"Then I'll ride along with you."

"No, I can't take Rose."

"Sorry ma'am. I just won't let you go alone. I'll tell Laslo to go along."

Lily shivered at the thought of Laslo anywhere close to her, but she knew there was no arguing with Gus.

As they rode down the road toward Ouray and Chipeta's farm, Lily wondered why the land didn't look any different. It looked as though nothing had changed. But she knew that everything had. She was thankful that at least Laslo had the good sense to remain quiet and not disturb her already disturbed thoughts.

Chipeta broke into frantic tears when she saw Lily. She looked as if she had aged years since just yesterday.

"They have the women, Lily," she said in a pained whimper. "Those poor women. I have to go after them."

"You can't be serious, Chipeta."

"I'm very serious. I would leave right now if I knew where they had been taken. They must not be hurt. They must be brought back."

"Yes," Lily agreed. "Maybe if they bring the women in peacefully, your people will be forgiven."

"Forgiven? Never. What has happened marks the end of our way of life forever." Chipeta spoke this truth as if she had already accepted it.

"But this is not about my people. I can't let the children be hurt. I won't let that happen."

"Children?"

"Yes, they have three women and one of the women has two children."

"Flora Ellen."

"You met the children?"

"Yes, I did."

"Are they as beautiful as Rose?"

Lily couldn't answer. She could only cry along with her friend.

"Let me fix you something to eat," Lily said.

"I'm really not hungry."

Lily started a pot of water to boil. "Then you will at least have some tea. Where is Ouray?"

"He is meeting with Shavano and Sapiah to see if somehow they can get some information as to where Douglas is headed. Not only will they have the cavalry on their tails, they will have Ouray's men as well."

"Is Colorow with Douglas?"

"Strange as it sounds, his name was not mentioned. Only Douglas, Johnson, Persune, Pauvitz, and Antelope."

The water began to boil and Lily poured it into the china teapot, and then added a heaping spoonful of tea leaves.

"What happened? Samuel said something about plowing up a racetrack?"

"That was the final straw. From what little we know, it happened because of Thornburg."

"But he is in Wyoming," Lily said.

"No, it seems Meeker sent an urgent plea to Secretary Schurz around the first of September after he had a scuffle with Johnson. Meeker had told him he would have to get rid of some of his horses. Johnson got mad and threw Meeker over the hitching post. General Merritt ordered Thornburg to White River."

"I am surprised that Thornburg went. Surely it wasn't willingly. Samuel got a letter from him sometime in August. It seems after we met with Pitkin in Denver, Meeker talked with the governor several days later. Not liking what he heard, he headed back to the agency, taking the long way through Cheyenne. At Fort Steele Meeker met personally with Thornburg and stated the same complaints he had told to Pitkin. Thornburg said he had tried to reason with Meeker, just as Samuel had.

"Meeker got blunt and curt, giving Thornburg a lecture. He said that Thornburg only learned all about how to be a good judge of wine and ladies at West Point, and nothing about Indians or agriculture. He said that soldiers were nothing but notorious drunkards who passed the bad habit along to the Indians. Thornburg said he listened to Meeker in polite, but cold fury and as soon as Meeker left, he notified General Merritt and advised that Meeker should be removed immediately."

"How I wish the general would have heeded the advice," Chipeta said, as Lily poured her a cup of tea. "When the White River Utes saw one hundred and fifty soldiers marching into the Milk Creek Valley, Douglas assumed they were coming to drive him out, or even worse, to do the same to his tribe as the soldiers did to the women and children at Sand Creek. He warned Meeker that if the soldiers came across Milk Creek, they would be fired upon."

"And they crossed anyway?"

"Not at first. Meeker told Douglas that only Thornburg and six of his officers would cross and come to the agency to meet with the chiefs. Douglas agreed to this. But for some reason, Thornburg told his troops to move in."

Chipeta took a sip of tea. The cup shook in her hand. "Chief Jack and his warriors were waiting for them. According to what we have been told, it was a white soldier who fired first, having seen one of Jack's men hiding in the brush. Then everyone started firing."

"And it is still going on," Lily said. "Thornburg's men, or those still alive, are pinned down in the Milk River Valley. Samuel is on his way now to try and stop the fighting."

"And Ouray has sent a courier back to tell Jack to stop as well. But you and I both know that though the bullets will cease, the fighting will not."

Chipeta lifted the delicate china teapot and poured the last of the tea in Lily's cup.

"Of all the things that the white people have given me, this is the only thing I have really treasured. It is delicate and beautiful." Chipeta fingered the hand-painted roses on the pot.

"There is a peace when making tea. There is a special feeling when sharing tea with a friend." She handed the pot to Lily.

"Please take it."

Lily looked at her confused.

"I want you to have it, my friend. It will be of no use to me where I will be going."

"Not now, Chipeta. Not yet." Lily handed the teapot back.

"I am not ready to let you go."

✤ ✤ ✤

The white soldiers were on foreign soil. To the Indians it was home. They knew the land as well as they knew the inside of their tepees. It had sustained them for centuries because they had accepted and abided by Mother Earth's rules.

It had clothed and fed them. They had learned even to thrive on her bugs, snakes and toads. They could eat and drink from her plants and when wounded, could make poultices and sedatives from her herbs. Her wind and weather had made their skin as tough as leather, so that only a few clothes were needed both in summer and winter. They could be ready to travel at a moment's notice, taking only a horse and sometimes a blanket on which to ride. For the Indian there was no set time. They ate when hungry, slept when tired, and woke when rested.

All the people native to the land possessed this knowledge of their world. It had been bred into them and was something that only a handful of whites had acquired a hint of after a lifetime of study.

On the other hand, the white soldiers had to haul their environment with them wherever they went and used up a great deal of their strength to guard it. Supply wagons burdened the soldiers. Their food needed cooking and required implements in which to eat it. They needed blankets and tents. For their health they required doctors and drugs.

And finally, the white soldiers biggest downfall was guilt. Deep down, they admired the Indian brave, admired his freedom, his independent spirit, his refusal to be imprisoned in the white man's web.

At least it was that way for Captain Payne. A soldier in his regiment had started firing before the order was given. For what reason, Payne would never know. The boy had been young and scared. Maybe it had been accidental, or maybe it had been fear that had pulled the trigger. And after that first shot, the rest of the men began firing fast and the battle of Milk Creek was on.

Amid the rattle of army Springfields, Thornburg heard the sound of assorted Ute rifles: Winchester repeaters, cheap Ballards, Spencer carbines, and old tip-ups. He saw three Utes fall, and two of Payne's men. He saw mounted Indians crossing Milk Creek and slipping behind the dunes to where the supply wagons were being protected by Lieutenants Paddock and Wolf.

Thornburg yelled for the men to cease firing, but his voice was like a whisper in the autumn wind.

It had been Payne who watched as Thornburg rode out in front, as if his presence could stop the men from firing. He was riding alone in the buffalo grass on the other side of Milk Creek when a slug from a Ute's rifle struck him just above the ear. Payne knew that Thornburg was dead before his long, lithe frame toppled from his horse to the ground.

Private O'Malley could not move the army ambulance. A Ute sharpshooter had killed one of the mules. O'Malley cut the other loose and rode it back to Captain Payne.

"Thornburg is dead. What are your orders, sir?" O'Malley asked, his voice a high-pitched squeak.

Payne was seated on the ground with a painful arm wound. His mount lay dead next to him. By sheer power of will, he got to his feet to cope with his frightening predicament. He was now in charge.

Besides the Ute enemy, Payne was fighting his own thoughts. Like most officers, he had suffered recurrent nightmares of his men being destroyed as Custer's had been. Custer had not known his enemy's tactics, and Payne, as well, had no idea of how to fight against this force that had completely taken them all by surprise.

All afternoon, Payne had watched the Utes genius for concealed and subtle movement. They never attacked head on and avoided foolish bravado. They were fine marksmen, saving their shot for just the right instance. They didn't waste a single slug.

But for all his fears, and even with his painful wound, Payne stood and took command. He ordered the twenty-five supply wagons into a circle and once inside the enclosure he ordered a pit dug for the wounded men. He ordered that mules and horses be lined up in between the gaps of the wagons, and then shot to reinforce the enclosure. The gaps were further reinforced by breadboxes, forage sacks, and rations barrels.

As a stiff breeze blew around the hastily devised fort, Payne saw a new problem rearing its ugly head. The Utes had set fire to the sage and grass around their encampment. Payne sent a soldier outside the compound to start a counter fire. The soldier raced back, his own fire nipping at his heels. The canvas on the wagons soon blazed, and the bullets of the Utes' rifles rained down on the troopers as they beat at the flames. Five more soldiers were killed.

As twilight descended on Milk Creek, an eerie quiet descended as well. Payne desperately hoped the Utes had left and that the battle of Milk Creek was over.

But one huge problem remained. Water.

Payne knew there were enough rations to sustain them for several days, and if need be, they could kill horses and eat their flesh. But neither beast nor man would survive without water. He asked Lieutenant Cherry how many soldiers remained and Cherry reported that out of the original force of one hundred and forty-two, there were ninety-six present and accounted for.

Payne ordered that a water detail be set up, and all remaining soldiers would be required to take a turn at sneaking down to the creek several hundred yards beyond the corral of wagons. It was a very dangerous, but very necessary task.

And finally, at 8:30 p.m., just after dark settled in, Payne took a pen and paper and composed the details of the day, making two copies. He then called for the only men he knew he could ask to do the most necessary task of all, if there was any hope in saving any of the men. It was also the most dangerous.

At 10:30 p.m., Joe Rankin and John Gordon sneaked out of the compound at Milk Creek. Gordon's task was to find Captain Dodge. Rankin's destination was Rawlins, Wyoming.

A great full moon bathed the Milk Creek Valley in light. To the tense soldiers still bottled up in the corral, it was a bad omen. Though the light would illuminate their saviors' path, it would also illuminate their bodies. For over an hour, they listened for the sound of gunfire, which would mean the couriers had been discovered. But there was only silence, and an occasional groan from the pit where the wounded lay.

By five a.m., Rankin had made it past Peck's store on the Bear River. He changed horses at seven a.m. at the Fortification Creek

Depot. He grabbed a biscuit and some jerked meat and ate it on the run.

He changed horses again at Baggs Ranch on the Snake River, and took five minutes to eat a quick lunch.

Joe Rankin rode into Rawlins at two o'clock the following morning. He had traveled one hundred sixty miles on horseback in just over twenty-seven hours.

He woke the clerk at the Western Union office and sent a telegram that would shock the nation.

General Crook and General Sheridan wasted no time in answering Payne's plea for help. At 4:30 a.m., they dispatched Colonel Merritt's troops from Cheyenne, and then an additional two thousand more troops from as far away as Missouri.

By morning, Major Thornburg and the Battle of Milk Creek were as famous as Custer and Little Big Horn. Stories of Payne's helpless plight filled the newspapers. Concerned citizens clamored for information about the fate of the Meekers. Speculation spread as quickly as a wildfire.

Would Merritt's men get to Payne's men in time to prevent another Custer massacre? And where were Captain Dodge and his colored boys?

Dodge was not exactly lost. He just didn't quite know whether he was to be coming or going. That is what he and his men of Company D, Ninth cavalry, had been doing all summer, either coming or going.

As he descended back into the Bear River Valley on Tuesday morning, September thirtieth, he met a flock of terrified settlers. They told him of the Utes ambush of Thornburg and of the battle the day before. Without orders, Captain Dodge decided to head back once more. At noon on Wednesday they met up with John Gordon about one hundred miles from Milk Creek.

Dodge carefully listened to Gordon's account of the battle and the peril still threatening the surviving soldiers. Dodge quickly ordered his men to mount up and they rushed to save their comrades.

Captain Francis Dodge was no conventional army officer. He had been raised a genteel New Englander. After admiring a regiment of black soldiers during the Civil War, he had been shocked to be offered command of them.

For twelve years they had been together, touring the Southwest. His men were as devoted to him as he was to them. And finally, he thought, as he led his horse through dense scrub oak shining bright red in the autumn sun, finally his regiment would be able to show the world their courage and fighting skill. Finally they would get the respect they so deserved.

Just before dawn the next day they descended into the Milk Creek Valley. Dodge and his troops were stunned as they rode past the corpses that lined the ravine, but they showed no fear. The smell of death permeated the air.

They rode into Payne's corral without a shot ever being fired at them. Chief Jack's sentry didn't spot the black soldiers until it was too late.

Dodge quickly took charge after meeting with Payne, whose wound had severely weakened him. The men were in pitiful shape from the effects of bad water, too much sun, lack of sleep, and the awful stench of death that had surrounded them.

Company D, under the steady command of Dodge, staved off the Utes for four more days, until on Sunday, October fifth, Colonel Merritt and the men of the Fifth cavalry from Cheyenne rode in, breaking the siege.

Merritt had brought with him four companies of cavalry, one hundred fifty foot soldiers . . . and a cart full of journalists.

15

Boot Jack was played out after the hard seventy-mile ride to the Grand River. The mount Samuel had traded him for at the Grand River Trading Post had proved to be most unreliable. The mare was old, staggering through the rocks and fighting incessantly to go home. By the time Samuel realized that she was not up to taking the shortcut the trader had mapped out it was too late to turn back and follow the road.

Samuel reined the horse up a steep mountainside, and the horse's hooves slipped. He took two tumbles with her before he was able to break his feet free from the stirrups. He watched as she rolled, end over end, to the bottom of the mountain, landing in a deep ravine.

She was not yet dead when he got to her. But she was beyond putting up any kind of a fight. He loaded a shell in his Colt and put her out of her misery.

His right knee throbbed where it had slammed into a rock during the fall. He unhitched his belt and pulled down his trousers to check for damage. The sharp stem of a branch of rough sagebrush protruded from his thigh and the knee was already beginning to swell. Thankfully he could not feel anything broken. He gritted his teeth, then pulled the stick out of his leg. Blood began to pour from the hole. He washed the wound with water from his canteen, and after taking a couple of long draws of whiskey from his silver flask, he poured the rest into the gaping hole. He took a handkerchief from his pocket, wrapped it tightly around his thigh and then pulled up his pants.

It was still over sixty miles to the White River. He had hoped to be there by tomorrow morning, but without a mount, it would take at least three days through the rugged wilderness.

He untied his supply bags from the saddle and yanked them out from underneath the dead horse. A sharp slab of granite cut a deep slash in the canvas. He unfastened the cinch from under the horse's belly and tried to pull the saddle out as well. A searing pain ran through his knee as he jerked. The saddle would not budge.

The seat was a fine leather, cavalry issued saddle that had taken years for him to break in. It fit him like a glove. There was no damned way he would leave it to the wolves.

He pulled out his knife and gutted the horse as he would gut an elk. He then quartered the animal and was able to remove enough of the horse, piece by piece, until he was able to free the saddle.

He carried the bloody saddle, along with his supply bags and bedroll, up the steep hillside. His leg throbbed and went out from under him. The bedroll slipped away and he had to crawl back down several yards to retrieve it. When Samuel finally got to the top, he tied the saddle up in a large pine at the top of the windy knob, careful to map out the surroundings in his brain so he could come back for the saddle later on his return.

He walked for several miles before he was able to find a sturdy stick with a fork from which to fashion a makeshift crutch. He walked several more miles before the pain became too much for him to continue. Though it was just early in the afternoon, Samuel made camp by a slow-moving stream.

He carefully removed his boot and trousers and looked at the leg. The knee was now swollen to twice its original size and an ugly black bruise traveled from the top of it clear down to the ankle. The kerchief around the thigh dripped in blood. He soaked the leg in the coolness of the stream to try and relieve some of the pain and swelling. He rinsed out the makeshift bandage and hung it on a tree branch to dry.

Just before nightfall he dug out a pit with a sharp rock and attempted to light a fire, wasting several matches in the gusty wind before he was able to light the kindling. He cursed at the heavy gray clouds starting to move in. Having lightened his load by leaving the coffee, pot, and utensils with his saddle, he ate one cold biscuit and a small piece of bacon, knowing he would have to ration his meager supply. He then crawled into the warmth of his bedroll and did his best to try and ignore the emptiness, and the panic he felt deep in his belly. He tried not to remember the horrific sights he'd seen at Bighorn, tried not to wonder if the soldiers at White River were being faced with the same.

But no matter how hard he tried to put the thoughts from his head, they haunted the night like ghosts from the past.

It took him half of the next day to make it back to the road. Several wagons passed, loaded with settlers from the White River country who had hastily packed up and moved out. None would sell him a horse, especially when all he had was twenty dollars and the promise that he would pay them the difference later. He decided to head across country, hoping that there were still folks at a small homestead he and Lily had passed on their trip during the summer.

It took him the rest of the day to get to the place, only to arrive at twilight and find it deserted. The corrals, and the cupboards, were bare. He ate the last of the hardtack, refilled his canteen at a stream nearby, washed out his bandage and laid it out to dry on what had been the kitchen table. He then laid out his bedroll on the floor of the small living room, too tired to light a fire with the few sticks of firewood that had been left.

The next morning his stomach begged for food but there was none to be had. It took all the strength and tenacity he could muster to roll up his blanket and start back the same way he'd come yesterday. He didn't even want to think about the sixty miles ahead after that.

It was actually Colorow that at last gave him a mount.

When Samuel first saw the group of three braves on a far hillside in the morning sun, he expected the worst. If they were the same Utes involved in the Meeker Massacre, they would be on the defensive and ready for a fight. And any white man, especially a white man on foot, would be a target. Samuel felt like a duck with a bum wing.

But instead of approaching, the braves disappeared over the side of the hill. Samuel walked on, the pistol at his side cocked in its holster. The knots in his neck and empty stomach tightened, and every sound made his senses jump in anticipation.

The Utes were waiting for him on the other side of the south fork of the White River. Colorow rode alone across the creek, leading a fine-looking pinto horse. On the horse was Samuel's cavalry saddle. If Bodeen had wondered how long he had been followed, he now knew.

"Good horse. Sturdy. Bad medicine up the river. Many soldiers are coming. Don't let them kill my people like they did the Arapahoe and the Nez Perce," Colorow said as he handed the rawhide reins to Samuel.

"Where are the Meeker women and children?" Samuel asked, mounting the horse.

Colorow pointed at the rugged mountain range that lay east of the river. The rocky crags, granite pillars and dense dark forest looked a formidable fortress. "Hard country, then onto flattop mountain."

"Take me to where they are," Samuel said.

"No. I go home. Don't want no more bad medicine."

"Are the women hurt?" Samuel asked.

Colorow looked at Samuel with a stern expression, but his eyes showed not anger, but panic.

"They are alive. But tell the soldiers that if they exterminate my people, the white children will be the next to die—with their mothers watching."

Colorow jerked his horse back into the river and galloped back across, the water splashing Samuel in the face with an icy slap.

Colonel Wesley Merritt's men were setting up tents to house the wounded when Samuel rode into the edge of the encampment. The sentry eyed him warily and refused to let him pass.

"I'm Colonel Samuel Bodeen. I have an urgent message for Colonel Merritt."

The sentry was a boy who looked no more than sixteen, and he stuttered when he spoke, "Ca. . .Can. . . . Can't let you pass."

Samuel understood the boy's trepidation. He was a far cry from resembling a dignified army officer. His clothes were rank with dried blood, and even worse he was riding an Indian pony.

"Then will you tell Merritt I'm here?"

"Ca . . . Can't leave my post."

The boy signaled to a lieutenant passing by. They walked aside and held a quiet discussion.

After several minutes, Samuel's temper, which rarely surfaced, rose quickly. He was tired, hungry, and his leg throbbed like hell.

Samuel kicked his horse and rode up to the pair. "Excuse me, Lieutenant, but I did say the message was urgent. If Merritt wants to know where the Meeker women are, then you'd better damned sure hurry up and make up your mind!"

The officer pulled his pistol and puffed out his chest. "Maybe you had better get down off that horse and come with me." He commanded the boy to take Samuel's gun.

"Oh, for Christ's sake," Samuel said. He took the gun from his holster and made sure the safety was on before he handed it to the young soldier. As Samuel eased down off the horse, his leg shot white hot sparks of pain when he tried to put weight on it. He bit his lip and tried not to limp as the pair led him to a white canvas tent.

Merritt was sitting behind a drop leaf desk. Samuel found it ironic that while the wounded had not yet been sheltered, Merritt already had all the comforts of home, including a carafe of brandy and two snifters on the desk.

"Colonel Merritt," the lieutenant said with an air of pompous authority, "this man says he has information on the whereabouts of the Meeker women."

Merritt looked up from his desk.

"Yes?"

"You old buzzard, it's me, Bodeen."

"Bodeen? Gawd damn, you're one hell of a mess! Didn't recognize you with that ridiculous cowboy hat." He rose and came around the desk to shake Samuel's hand.

"And even with the awful stench in this camp, I could smell yours before you walked in. Lieutenant, get this man a fresh set of clothes. Are you hungry?"

Samuel nodded. Even that small movement suddenly seemed too much for his body. His limbs felt as if they were filled with heavy lead, and he had to concentrate to keep his wits intact. Exhaustion, along with a steady loss of blood and lack of food had finally overtaken him.

"And bring him a plate of whatever is hot. Sentry, you may return to your post." The lieutenant left in a huff, angry for being taken down to the post of a waiter.

"Young 'cock of the walk,' that one. Surely we weren't so full of ourselves when we were younger."

"You still are," Bodeen said, but the twinkle was gone from his eye.

"You don't look good, Samuel. You get shot in that leg? Want me to send for the doc?" Merritt asked, looking at the blood oozing from the hole in Samuel's pants.

He took a folding chair from the corner and motioned for Bodeen to sit. But before sitting down Samuel stopped the boy and took his gun back. Merritt filled the snifters and handed one to Samuel. The liquid seared like warm fire down through his middle.

Samuel explained the accident with the horse. "Took a stick in the leg and bummed my knee up on a rock, but nothing is broken. With the hard riding the past couple days, the leg would just start to heal and then break open again."

The lieutenant brought in a plate of food and a pile of clothes.

"I could use a clean bandage, if there's any left. I'd hate to bleed all over genuine United States Army-issued duds," Samuel said as he grabbed the plate and wolfed beans and biscuits down like a starved animal.

"Bring Colonel Bodeen a roll of bandage," Merritt commanded the lieutenant, emphasizing the word colonel. "And another plate, but this time add a hefty portion of bacon."

Within minutes the sustenance to Samuel's body began to take effect. The fog in his head began to clear and heightened his senses. "If you will excuse me, Colonel, I'll go wash this stink off and then we can get down to business."

He took the clothes and bandage, walked down to Milk Creek and stripped completely. The water was cold and brisk on his skin. He reached down to the bottom of the stream and scrubbed the dried blood off his body with fine sand. The wound seeped fresh red blood as he walked out of the creek. He wrapped the bandage tightly around his thigh to help stifle the flow. As he pulled an unadorned blue cavalry shirt over his shoulders, the cloth felt good on his skin. The pants were a bit large, and they went on easily over his bandaged leg. The uniform fit. He felt right again for the first time in a long while. The sounds of the camp felt familiar, the feel, and the smell. He realized at that moment just how much he missed it all.

With a sudden surge of energy, he took back command of his body and only limped slightly walking back to Merritt's tent.

Wesley had already refilled the snifters, and a pot of strong hot coffee filled the tent with its tantalizing aroma.

"Ah, now that's more like it. I've smelled better bears than you," Merritt said with an easy smile.

Samuel laughed. "And I've seen better-looking ones than you." Merritt still had the same ruddy face, and gray bushy beard and hair. But then Samuel's demeanor grew serious. "I'm not sure I should be wearing this," he said. "After all, I'm not regular army anymore."

"Do you want to be?" Merritt asked. "I'm sure General Sheridan would be more than willing to get you re-enlisted. We need you right now, Sam."

Samuel didn't know what to say. It felt right. The clothes, the camp . . . all of it. The army was who he was. Without it, he'd felt like a drifter the past three years. But he could never ask Lily and Rose to be put in the position of Lida Thornburg. He knew he couldn't have both. And he knew he was not ready to have to choose.

Merritt read the unsure look in Samuel's eyes. "You don't have to answer now. I know you're extremely tired. But we really need your help to get the Meeker women back. Would you consider a position as my personal advisor until we can get past this crisis? Think of it as returning the favor of saving your sorry hide back in Oklahoma against the Cherokee. You can let me know in the morning." He stood, offering Samuel an out.

Colonel Wesley Merritt had always been a man of honor, of courage, and of incredible skill in devising plans to outwit even the most sly. He took his job seriously, and refused to take unnecessary risks with his men. Instead he relied on careful strategy. He was one of the few men Bodeen respected completely.

Samuel remained in his seat. "You have Ouray's support, he wants you to know that. And he is willing to assist in any way possible to help us get the women back. I have it from a very reliable source that the Utes are passing over onto the Grand Mesa."

"All right then," Merritt said, swigging down the last of his brandy. "Then let's get down to it."

Wesley sat back down and the pair spent the next hours going over a topography map of the White River region provided by Captain Dodge, and devising a complex approach that they hoped would ensure the successful return of the women.

Lily was anxious to get home. The last two miles in the dusky autumn twilight seemed like ten. The wind had picked up, stripping the aspen trees of their golden foliage. The gusts brought in a bank of looming gray clouds and the air turned cold. Several times Laslo tried to make idle conversation, but Lily curtly cut him off like a sharp pair of scissors.

Gus was standing outside the barn talking to David Wood as they rode the horses into the corral. Rose was nowhere to be seen.

"David, I'm so glad to see you!" Lily was thankful for his presence. She knew he would have a sympathetic ear and that was just what she needed—that and a strong cup of coffee and a hot bath.

"I came for the second-year steers, but Gus tells me you haven't been able to get to the high country to gather them up."

"I'm sorry. Samuel must have forgotten, what with all the Indian troubles," Lily said while kneading her tight neck muscles. "I'll make sure that Gus and Laslo get started first thing in the morning." She looked at Gus. "Where's Rose?"

"Hope you don't mind but Sarah was over today looking for you. Asked if she could keep Rose for the night. We both thought you could use a good night's sleep."

Lily sighed with relief, hoping that somehow she would be able to sleep even for a few hours without worrying about Samuel. "Yes, that was fine."

Gus looked up at the sky. "Going to be hard going in the brush if it decides to storm. Course maybe a little snow could be a blessing. Cattle won't want to stay up high if the feed gets covered over."

He excused himself and grabbed the reins of Lily's horse. "Looks like you had a hard day. I'll take care of the horse."

"Thank you, Gus," Lily said gratefully as she noticed that Laslo had already made himself scarce.

"I know the timing is bad. Gus said that Samuel left several days ago," David said as they went to the house and Lily put the water on to boil. "But the miners have been waiting for that beef. Samuel said he would trail them up last week."

"He was called to Fort Lewis a couple weeks ago to settle an argument with the Southern Utes. And now he's gone again to try and make some sense out of what is going on at White River." Lily put coffee in the pot and took some cheese and biscuits from the Hoosier cupboard.

"What about the rest of the herd? How are you going to feed them this winter?" David asked.

"Samuel said he would just have to buy hay this year. He talked to Abe Lufkin over on the Cimarron," Lily said, slicing the cheese and putting it in front of David.

"I tried to buy some from Abe yesterday and he told me he sold his hay to Jess Banks."

"All of it?"

"That was my understanding," David said. "What about McCluskey?"

"He was able to cut enough to get us through to January, but with the drought he was never able to get a third cutting. And the oats barely produced enough to put back for seed next year. Surely there has to be someone else who is willing to sell."

"I don't think so, Lily. I've been scouting the countryside trying to find enough hay to get my mules through the winter. I'm going to have to take twenty strings back to Pueblo and hope that some-how Hank was able to get feed over on the Eastern Slope."

Lily sat down at the table. "What am I going to do? I have no idea how long Samuel is going to be gone. Surely not until the hostages are found. By then it could be too late to do anything. What about the mines? Would they be willing to buy more cattle?"

"That's doubtful. They are cutting crews now, what with winter coming on. But I'll see what I can do." David stood up and took his coat from the hook.

"Surely you're not leaving tonight," Lily said, listening to the wind howl down the stovepipe.

"I'm afraid so. I'm meeting a buyer at the agency who's agreed to purchase twenty mules. It will save me having to feed them at least."

✛ ✛ ✛

Lily poured a cup of coffee, sat down in the chair, and watched the wind whirl the autumn leaves around the picture window. They flashed against the dark glass like speckles of gold, fleeting and gone.

Part of her was worried sick about Samuel and the other part was mad as hell at him. Why hadn't he said something about the hay being sold?

She tried to quash the anger she felt toward her husband as she thought about poor Lida Thornburg now without hers. The woman had tried so hard to make a home in that godforsaken place, tried to be a good, understanding wife, when what she had really wanted was to go home. And now she would. But she would be going alone.

There was a gentle knocking at the door.

"So you changed your mind?" Lily said as she jumped up to answer the door.

Lily stood there with the door open, too shocked to say anything.

She hadn't seen him since the night of the Bear Dance. The cold wind forced her back to reality.

"Sapiah."

"Lily."

He walked in the door, never taking his eyes from hers. Lily felt the heat flush into her cheeks.

"I had to come. You must leave, Lily. You are in great danger here."

"I can't leave. I won't leave. This is my home. The cattle . . ."

"The cattle are gone."

"What do you mean gone?"

"The fences have been cut."

"What? Why?" Lily glared at him. "I thought the Utes were our friends. How could you let them do it?" Lily was past being furious. She was livid. "Samuel is God knows where trying to keep the army from annihilating what is left of your tribe, and here you are stealing our cattle right out from under us!"

"It was not the Ute."

"Right. Sure," she said with venom in her voice. "Just like it wasn't the Utes that killed Thornburg and left Lida a widow and her children with no father. Just like it wasn't the Utes that killed Meeker and took off with those poor women and children. Well maybe the papers were right. Maybe you are just a bunch of bloodthirsty savages!"

Sapiah looked at her with his kind, gentle eyes, never saying a word while listening to her anger rush out like the torrent of a river after a hard deluge of rain.

And after the rain subsided, she sat back down in the chair and put her head in her hands.

He walked over and cupped her face in his hands.

"It was not the Ute. You must believe me."

Lily looked at him and knew he was telling the truth. Sapiah was the most honest person she had ever met.

"I do believe you. I'm sorry, Sapiah."

"Then you believe me when I say that you must go."

"I can't."

"Think of Rose."

"It's her home, too."

"There is no place that is worth risking a child for. No place. For without them there is no future at all."

He took his hands from her face and looked away.

"You are not just talking about Rose, are you?"

"No child. Indian or white. We will have to leave soon as well. I have taken a wife, Lily. She will soon be with child. I cannot risk my children being slaughtered, and that is what will happen if we try to stay. Even Ouray knows this. Our time in the Shining Mountains is over. I am sad for my children."

She touched his cheek, brushing away a lone tear.

He put his hands back to her face. "They deserve to behold the beauty that I have seen." He tenderly kissed her forehead, then her lips. "I will not come again, Lily. I can do little now to protect you and Rose. If you will not leave, then please, be careful."

He stood up and walked to the door. "If you still doubt, remember that Utes have no need for fences, therefore we do not own fence cutters. I will get your cows back but be more careful who you trust. Remember there are white men who are savages, too. And they are much closer than you think."

"Sapiah, wait!"

By the time she had risen and had run to look out the door, he had disappeared into the chilling night wind.

16

Four days later, Merritt's force at Milk Creek was increased to nine hundred with the arrival of Colonel C.C. Gilbert and six companies of the Seventh Infantry from Fort Snelling, Dakota Territory. The incoming men passed the outgoing members of the original Thornburg force who were being escorted with their dead and wounded back to Fort Steele by Captain Dodge's Company D. Dodge was disappointed when, once again, his company of men would be taken out of the true task at hand, and in doing so, would never receive the recognition they so richly deserved.

And four days later, Samuel Bodeen arrived at the home of Ouray. After explaining the plan and getting the approval from the chief, they made a list of thirteen Utes who would be trustworthy enough to set the plan into motion.

Then Bodeen rode to the ranch to spend the rest of the day with Lily and Rose. Somehow he felt like he had some explaining to do. And yet he also felt he shouldn't have to explain anything at all. Besides, he was just too damned tired to talk about it anyway.

The homecoming was as he had expected. Though Lily said she was glad to see him, her eyes were cool, and she clucked her teeth.

Lily was glad. And relieved. But yet she wondered if it were a ghost riding up on the horse. In her mind, her husband had died a hundred times over the past eight days.

"Are you hungry?" she asked, not knowing what else to say.

"A bit. I'll wash up first."

She walked to the bedroom with him to get him clean clothes.

"I'll just take the basin and fill it. Oh, God, Samuel!"

Lily was appalled when he took off his pants. As he removed the blood-soaked bandage, she could see that the wound had festered into an angry redness.

"Samuel, you simply can't go. That leg needs care, and you need rest to let it heal properly." Images of her father hobbling through the house with a crutch and a bottle came tumbling back.

"There's no time for that, Lily. I'll be fine."

She stared at him in disbelief. "I won't let you go," she stated forcefully. "And what about the ranch? Though you may not want to admit it, we've got some pretty serious problems here as well. I've had Henry McCluskey scouring the country for hay, and there is none to be had anywhere. Half the cattle are still missing, as well as King Ferdinand. We've got to get them down off the mountain before winter."

"Are you saying that I can't ride to save three women and two children, but I can ride for a bunch of damned cows?"

Lily set down the basin and walked out the front door, slamming it hard and scaring Rose who was playing with her wooden horses under the kitchen table. Lily heard her begin to cry. Let Samuel handle it, Lily thought. He spent so little time with their child anyway.

As she walked to the far meadow she pictured spunky Josie Meeker and the chubby-cheeked faces of the Price children. What if it were Rose?

She tried to remember the herbs that Pagosa, the medicine woman, had used when Rose had developed an infection from a splinter. The purple coneflowers had ceased blooming after the hard freeze in mid-September. She dug down to the root, hoping it would have the same medicinal value as the flower. She picked a bit of red clover and alfalfa, a few wild rose hips, dug a bit of burdock root and found the seeds of some butcher's broom.

Rose was still playing with her horses under the table when Lily returned. The child looked at the plants and said, "Daddy's sick. I asked him to play with me, but he fell asleep."

Samuel lay flat on the bed, still wearing his shirt and socks. Lily stared at him for several moments. His hair had become streaked with gray, and not just around the edges anymore. The white laugh lines were gone, replaced by deep creases above his brow, as if a world of troubles was pushing down on his brain. Droplets of sweat rolled down into the creases and spread along like oozing worries.

She went to the kitchen and washed the herbs, then put half of them in a pot to boil. Having no bandages on hand, she cut off lengths from her only petticoat. After steeping the herbs, she strained them and saved the liquid in a cup. She took a piece of soft muslin and thickly spread on the herb mixture. She gently pulled back the covers and washed the wound with soapy water. She then applied the poultice and wrapped the strips of petticoat loosely around his thigh. He never even stirred. Samuel slept all afternoon and through the night.

"How long will you be gone?" Lily asked, as Samuel mounted his horse the next morning.

"As long as it takes. I love you, Donovan."

"Be careful," she said. "And don't forget to use the herbs. They are in your saddlebag." But she knew that he wouldn't. Not once did he bring up the problem with the cattle. And neither did she.

As she watched him ride away, she was overtaken by an imminent sense of dread. She wondered which was the bigger fear that gripped her—the fear of losing Samuel, the fear of losing Chipeta and their friendship, or the fear of losing the cattle and her home. She walked back to the house and looked at the lilac bush, grown now as tall as Rose.

And suddenly she knew that the biggest fear was that she was going to lose them all. Or that maybe she already had.

✚ ✚ ✚

Chief Douglas felt a sense of dread as well.

"The soldiers, many, many soldiers, are building a road. They cut down the trees, move the rocks with big horses. They keep coming," the scout said.

Douglas ordered his tribe to move on.

And Ouray, too, felt it. He'd had no choice but to agree to the plan, if there was any hope of preventing complete extermination, especially after Samuel had read him the latest words from Governor Pitkin in a special statement for publication in the *Denver Tribune*. It stated:

> "I think that the conclusion of this affair will end the depredations in Colorado. It will be impossible for the Indians and whites to live in peace hereafter. This attack had no provocation and the whites now understand that they are liable to be attacked in any part of the state where the Indians happen to be in sufficient force. It is my idea that, unless removed by the government, the Indians must necessarily be exterminated."

There was no turning back. Pitkin had the support of the great white chiefs in Washington, and the support of the United States cavalry to enforce it. All Ouray could do now was to be again like the hunted buffalo. All he could do now was to lie down and give in, in the hopes that the young would be excluded from the slaughter.

✠ ✠ ✠

There is a time, a brief moment in a person's life, that is so memorable that the rest seems like merely a dream. That was the way it was for Samuel when he looked down from a rise and saw Douglas' camp. He reined up and stared, spellbound, at the peaceful scene below. Thirty tents glistened on a grassy meadow in the bright autumn morning. Goats and horses grazed nearby. The white-skinned Price boy played alongside the brown Ute children.

The plan had worked. Merritt's troops had pushed Douglas and his tribe out of the rugged White River country to the Grand Mesa and directly into the hands of Samuel and Ouray's braves that accompanied him, including the great mediators Buckskin Charlie and War Chief Shavano.

As he rode into the camp, he saw Josie Meeker emerge from a tent. Samuel was intensely relieved when he saw that she was in good health, her blue eyes smiling in recognition. Tears came to his eyes, which he quickly erased with the back of his hand.

But Douglas was in a sour mood and the conference was stormy. He ordered that the women be confined to their tents. He then stated the hostages would not be released until a message was sent to the white soldiers to turn back, and proof that they did so. After five tense hours, Samuel began to wonder what the true outcome was going to be. Douglas was refusing to cooperate, even after being told of Ouray's demand that the women be released immediately.

Finally Sapiah had heard enough bantering and blame from both sides. He rose and in no uncertain terms stated, "As the official spokesman for Ouray, I tell you these true words—This is Tuesday. If the white women and children are not safely at his farm by Friday, Ouray himself will lead his men in full strength to seize the captives from you. And in doing so, he promises to drive you directly into the waiting guns of Colonel Merritt and his soldiers, all nine hundred of them. How many braves do you have, Douglas, to fight off such an attack? Maybe forty? And what of your own women and children? Are you willing to risk their lives as well?"

Douglas knew he could not fight both the whites and Chief Ouray. Reluctantly, he gave in.

The next morning the women were brought out of the tents. Arvilla Meeker was pale and gaunt. Samuel took her thin hand and told her that he was taking her to Ouray's home, where her son, Ralph, was waiting to take her back to Greeley.

"For myself," she said, "I really don't care anymore. Mr. Meeker is gone, you know, and I have nothing to live for. I am sixty-four years old. An old lady."

As they rode horses down to Whitewater where there was a buckboard waiting to take them to the home of Chief Ouray, Samuel listened as Josie and Flora Price told of their treatment by the Utes. Arvilla had suffered the most at the hands of Douglas' squaws. They had stolen her needles, and threatened to burn her beloved *Pilgrim's Progress*. But later when a baby fell sick and Arvilla had used her medicines to cure it, she was given an extra blanket and even a soft pillow.

Practical Josie said she had passed the time making clothes, in case they were held captive all winter.

Finally, Samuel asked Josie and the other women the question he really didn't want to ask.

"Did the Ute men, um, violate you in any way?"

He knew that the Ute way of claiming a woman was to lay with her. And he had seen the infatuation that Persune had felt for Josie.

All denied being "outraged" as they called it. But Samuel saw by the look in their eyes, that just maybe they weren't telling the real story.

✢ ✢ ✢

On October twenty-fourth, Ralph Meeker sipped tea in Chipeta's home, waiting anxiously for his mother and sister. He was a fashionable man dressed in a high button knicker suit and Ascot scarf, with a slight British accent from living in London. He put on a calm front, but inside he was shattered by the death of his father. To him, Nathan Meeker had been his landmark, a great oak standing as a guidepost for all that was honorable. And he was also saddened in knowing that the marriage to the love of his life, Carmelita Circovitch, would have to be postponed. He could not in all good conscience marry her when he knew he would be required to provide for his mother and sister. He simply could not afford to take care of them all. In his mind he had decided he would ask the government for assistance in getting some sort of retribution from the Utes for his father's murder. And he planned on writing a book in Josie's name, in the hopes of selling the story to interested sympathizers.

When the buckboard finally arrived, Chipeta jumped up and ran outside to greet the women. She cried openly when she saw that the children were safe and happy.

Only later were they to learn the real truth of what had happened to the women. All had been violated, even Arvilla Meeker, by Chief Douglas himself. But that part of the story would never be told in Ralph Meeker's book, to save the women, especially his mother, the embarrassment of having to explain or elaborate on it.

17

Any question that Lily had of whether Samuel would leave her to re-enlist in the army had been buried last October, along with Samuel's leg.

After the women had been brought safely to Ouray and Chipeta's home, Samuel had ridden in a feverish fog back to the Pleasant Valley Ranch. Lily and Gus had found him lying in the dust in the corral when they came down from the north pasture after riding for cattle. He was covered with a light dusting of snow, his face was ashen, and his hands were as cold as ice. His horse was standing beside him, still saddled.

Lily and Gus had been unable to lift Samuel's body, so they dragged it into the barn and covered it with a blanket. Then Gus rode hard to the McCluskeys' for help. It was Mary McCluskey who took charge, instructing Danny to jump on his fastest horse and hurry to find a doctor in the town of Ouray, and for Gus to get the medicine woman, Pagosa.

Lily was relieved when Henry, Sarah, and Mary McCluskey pulled up in their buckboard. Mary warmed rocks on the stove and tucked them around Samuel's cold body, and then waited impatiently for the doctor. When the black buggy pulled into the yard, Henry guided the doctor to the barn. The doctor quickly confirmed what Lily already knew when she had cut away Samuel's pants. A long black strip of gangrene ran from the thigh wound down into the foot.

"If we don't take it off, and I mean right now, he won't make it to tomorrow."

They rolled Samuel's body onto a blanket and carried him inside.

"On the bed for now," the doctor said. "We'll need to sterilize the kitchen table first."

"Have you ever done this before?" Lily asked, her voice trembling in panic.

"I'm afraid so. Spent four years as a sawbones during the war. I came to the West in the hopes of forgetting it."

"But here?" She looked around her home, wishing that they could somehow get him to Denver and a proper hospital.

"Lady, I did surgery in the middle of a swamp filled with every sort of vermin imaginable. Compared to that, this place is immaculate."

They scrubbed the kitchen table with soapy lye water and then laid a clean sheet over it. Henry stoked up the fire, while Sarah took all the pots in the kitchen, filled them with water and set them on the stove. The doctor instructed her to cut a muslin sheet into thick strips and set them in the water to boil. He took instruments from his tattered black leather bag and put them in a pot to be sterilized. Pagosa and Chipeta arrived just as Mary was taking the strips of cotton from the water and was laying them on a rack by the stove to dry.

"Where's Rose?" Chipeta asked.

"In her bed. She fell asleep in my arms on the way back down the mountain," Lily said. "Oh, God, she can't wake up to see this!"

"I'll take care of her," Sarah said reassuringly, and went to the bedroom. She took the still sleeping child out of the house.

It had been a long time since Lily had prayed. But when she saw the men carry her husband in and lay his ashen body on the table, she did it anyway, hoping somehow that God would have the grace to listen.

"Are you squeamish around blood?" The doctor asked Lily.

"I don't really know," she said. Just the thought of what they were about to do made her insides heave.

"I recently completed nursing school. I can assist," Mary said.

"Good," the doctor said. "But Lily, I will need you to administer the ether to keep him under. And I want each of you men on either side to hold him down in case the pain causes him to awaken."

The ether gave Lily an immense headache and made her light-headed. Several times its sickly smell had made her feel the need to run outside, but she stuck with it, doing as the doctor told her. Pagosa chanted and sprinkled Samuel's body several times with a foul-smelling herb she produced from her medicine bag. And then the doctor took the saw from the boiling water. Lily looked away, and concentrated her eyes on the snow falling outside the window. Winter had come early this year.

She listened to the calm voices of Mary and the doctor as they performed the surgery. How queer, Lily thought, that it was Mary assisting in saving Samuel's life. It had been Samuel who had mentioned in a letter to Victoria that the young woman had an intense desire to be a nurse, just as she had been. Within two months Mary had received an acceptance letter from the New York Institute of Nursing, and a receipt for full payment of the tuition. Also enclosed had been funds for the trip East, and an invitation from Victoria to stay at Bannister Manor while completing her studies.

Yes, it was odd how lives become intertwined. Was it coincidence, Lily asked herself, or did some power weave them together for a higher purpose?

When it was over, Lily quietly left the house and went out behind the cottonwood tree. She wrenched violently.

"It will be okay, my friend," Chipeta said, holding Lily's head until there was nothing left in her stomach.

"He will never forgive me for this." Lily clutched Chipeta's hand as she watched Henry carrying the leg and a shovel to the far hill-side.

"He will. He is a good man and he loves you deeply. It is not your fault. You did it to save his life."

"But what if he ends up like my father? It was the same leg." Lily then told Chipeta about the anger and humiliation her father had felt, and the irreplaceable sense of loss that he was never able to overcome.

"But do you not see? It was not the same leg because it was not the same man," Chipeta said.

"But it is the same loss," Lily said.

✛ ✛ ✛

It had been two months, and still Samuel had not left his bed, even to see Victoria.

"I am so thankful you are here," Lily said honestly when she picked Victoria up from the stage five days before Christmas. She desperately hoped that Samuel's sister would be able to do what she could not, to somehow lift the dark depression from the bedroom now occupied solely by Samuel. He was like a wounded animal, striking out at anyone who came near him.

He would not let Lily anywhere close. He did not allow her to change the bandages, and even refused to let her or Rose sit on the bed beside him. He demanded only two things from his wife—that the room stay dark and that the glass remain full.

He had looked away when his sister walked into the room and refused to even try the wheelchair or crutches she had brought. There was no talking him into it.

"Please, Samuel," Lily said on Christmas morning. "It's Christmas, don't ruin it for Rose. Won't you at least try to come out and have dinner with us? Gus shot a beautiful goose, and there's your favorite apple stuffing. And Ouray, Chipeta, and David Wood will be here in an hour."

"Just bring me a plate." He turned away and looked at the wall. "I have nothing to celebrate."

Victoria left the next day, after trying unsuccessfully to convince Lily to move Samuel to New York.

"I would drag him there myself if I thought it would help. But you know as well as I do that he won't leave that bed," Lily said.

After she returned from taking Victoria to the stage, Samuel asked her if she had brought the whiskey.

"I didn't buy any."

"Dammit, I told you before you left to stop by Jake's Tavern and pick me up a couple of bottles. I ask you to do one thing, but you can't even do that!" Samuel yelled.

"Then I guess you'll just have to go and get it yourself."

"What the hell am I supposed to do? Get up and walk to town?"

"I guess if you want it badly enough, that is just what you will have to do."

He sat up in bed and threw the empty glass across the room. The sound of the glass shattering had also broken the promise Lily had made to herself.

She was suddenly very calm. She had made a silent vow to stick with it until he got better. But it was clear that until the self-pity was somehow vanquished, Samuel Bodeen would remain a cripple in his own mind. She had watched her mother go through the same thing, and she was not about to let Rose lead the same life that she had, to listen to the constant abuse, day after day.

"And from now on, you will have to clean up your own messes as well. I am your wife, not your nursemaid." She took the leather valise from under the bed and went to the dresser.

"You're leaving me?" He was shocked.

"No, I am leaving this house. You, Samuel, left me a long time ago."

"Go then! Go back to your Indian buck, that's what you've wanted all along anyway. I couldn't serve you well enough when I had two legs, I damned sure can't satisfy you now."

Lily stopped packing and turned around.

"What are you talking about?"

"Cut the innocent act, Little Miss Purity. I knew all along about your thing with Buckskin Charlie. Or, should I say Sapiah. Sounds a bit more romantic to you, doesn't it?"

"Samuel, I . . ."

"Don't bother denying it. Laslo told me all about it the day I left for White River. I had to ride with that red son of a bitch, hell, trust him, when all along I knew he had been keeping your bed warm when I was gone."

"It wasn't that way at all. I won't deny that I love him. I do. But as a friend. A very dear friend." There was much more to intimacy with a person than just sexual desires. But a man like Samuel would never understand it.

"Is that why Laslo saw him kissing you? Some friend. By the way, you never did tell me what happened to Laslo. What did you do, send him packing so he wouldn't tell your little secret? All you ever did was tell me that he was, how did you put it? Oh, yes, you said he was 'Gone'."

"He's dead," Lily said quietly.

"You killed him? Jumped up Jesus, I never dreamed you would take it that far to keep your sordid secret! My God, Lily, was your secret worth taking a man's life to keep it?" The veins in Samuel's neck pulsed and his face was bright red in anger. Lily thought that if Samuel could walk, he would have risen out of the bed and slammed her against the wall, he was that livid.

"I didn't kill him. Gus did."

"What the hell are you saying?"

"King Ferdinand is dead. I didn't tell you because you were already faced with so much. But enough. It's time you knew the truth. It was Laslo who cut the fences. Sapiah had warned Gus about him, so Gus starting checking up on Laslo and following him. Gus came up on Laslo in the south pasture just as he was putting a Ute arrow through Freddie's heart."

"But why?"

"He told Gus that his parents had been killed by the Arapahoe on the eastern plains. He figured he would fuel the fire to get the Utes out of Colorado once and for all. When Gus refused to go along with his scheme Laslo tried to kill him, but it seems that Laslo was a pretty poor shot. Gus, on the other hand, is an excellent marksman. We buried Laslo right beside Ferdinand's body."

"Why didn't you go to the law?"

"Gus made the decision not to, and I agreed with him. It was just after the massacre. Could you imagine what would have happened to Ouray and Chipeta if the papers had sunk their teeth into the story? No one would have believed for a second that it wasn't the Utes who cut the fences or killed the bull, and you know it. It would have been just one more thing for Pitkin to have his bought and paid for reporters use against Utes. With fear already rampant among settlers, it would have made the Meeker Massacre look like a Sunday school picnic, only it would have been the Utes slaughtered. And every rancher in Colorado would have been in on it."

She resumed packing. "If you don't believe me, just ask Gus. But don't ask him to buy you any more whiskey because he won't do it either."

She buckled the valise.

"I love you with all my heart, Samuel Bodeen. And because I do, I can't bear to see you blame me day after day for the loss of your leg, instead of thank me for saving your life. And I can't watch you, or let Rose watch you slowly kill yourself. I watched one man I dearly love do that, and I watched my mother die a bit every day along with him. I simply won't do it again."

She turned to go. "And just for your information, if you care about this place at all, there's enough hay to make it 'til March. We were only able to find half the cattle during the fall roundup. If you decide to pray, ask for an early spring as well."

"Lily, don't go. I need you. This ranch needs you. I can't do it alone," Samuel said.

"Yes, you can. I did it."

She looked into his pleading eyes, and for a moment, but only a moment, she thought about changing her mind.

"You know, Samuel Bodeen, I wonder if you ever really let yourself need anybody at all. But that was one of the things I first loved about you. When I first saw you on the train, I thought that you were the only man I'd ever met who could do anything he set his mind to do. And, my love, I still believe that with all my heart. You don't need me, Samuel. You don't need anyone."

As he heard the door shut, he said quietly, "But I do."

He watched Lily put Rose in the buggy. As she drove away, he wondered if there was any way that a one-legged scoundrel like himself could ever win her back.

✤ ✤ ✤

The Ute Peace Commission was unique. Some called it the knothole commission. The hearings that had been held for the past two months at the Los Piños Agency were boring, confused, and futile.

When faced with the reality that they were defenseless against being moved out of the Shining Mountains, the Utes would start to brawl and there was nothing that Ouray could say or do to stop them. And deep down inside, there was the warrior in him that wanted to fight right alongside them.

Ouray was constantly threatened with assassination attempts for being a part of the white commission. Many of his people no longer believed in him. Chipeta saw her husband's body continue to deteriorate, just like the future of her people. And she saw her friends, Lily and Samuel, crumbling as well.

After Lily left, Chipeta urged Ouray to go and try and talk some sense into Samuel. But Ouray said that it was something that Samuel first needed to ponder for a few days.

"He needs to realize that to wallow in the mud of self-pity and drink will never get him anywhere. He needs a few days to dry out and think—and do—for himself. Only until he can feel kindred to the man that he has been left with will he let others back in as well." And the wise chief was right. When he went to see Samuel days later, he was ready to talk, and more importantly, ready to listen.

When Samuel awakened the morning after Lily had left, the house was freezing. There had been no one there to keep the fire going. And, he was terribly hungry.

He looked at the crutches still against the wall. He tried to get out of bed, but his muscles were weak from lack of use. And being weak made him angry enough to fall out of bed and crawl over to the crutches. But it was no use. Try as he might, he could not stand. And having to crawl like a baby made him that much angrier.

By the time he had crawled to the kitchen and lit a fire in the stove, he was too exhausted to eat.

When Gus came in with a bucket of morning milk from the cow, he found Samuel sitting on the floor crying. Samuel quickly turned his head and wiped his face on his sleeve.

"Dammit, Gus. First I have to crawl like a baby, and now I'm sniveling like one," Samuel said apologetically.

Gus pretended to ignore the remark. "Thought I would rustle me up some eggs while I'm here. Want some?"

He helped Samuel to the table and together they ate runny eggs and drank weak coffee. Gus slugged down the last drop from his cup and put his dishes in the pan.

"Well, gotta git. The cows will be bawling, too, if I don't get out there and feed them." He winked at Samuel.

"Before you leave, would you mind filling the wood box? I used the last of the kindling this morning," Samuel said.

"Don't got time. With it just me now, it'll be all I can do to get them cows fed before lunch. I'm sure you'll manage just fine, even with you being an invalid and all."

Samuel was furious. "Hey, you get paid to do what I tell you to do!" But if Gus heard the remark, he ignored it. He was out the door before Samuel could finish his sentence. "And I'm not an invalid. Do you hear me?"

Samuel resolved right then and there that as soon as he was able, he would fire that ungrateful Gus Crenshaw and find someone who would treat him with a little more respect. He crawled back to the bedroom and grabbed the crutch. It was pure, white-hot fury that willed him up on the crutch and to the front door to grab his coat.

But it wasn't Gus Crenshaw, it was Henry McCluskey that took the brunt of Samuel's pent-up anger.

It had taken Samuel all morning to fill the wood box. And to top it off, the coffee had boiled over on the stove and made a hell of a mess, not to mention quite a stink. By the time he finished cleaning it up and had brewed a new pot, he was dog tired, and feeling pretty surly.

Henry walked in and helped himself to a cup from the shelf.

"Just stopped by to tell you that with Lily leaving and all, I've made a deal with Abe Lufkin to sell the hay and grain to him."

"What are you talking about?" Samuel said suspiciously.

"Well, with you being laid up and all, and no one to run the ranch, I just figured you wouldn't be needing the hay anymore. Of course, I'll try and pay you when I can for the land. Wouldn't want to cheat a man like you."

"And just what is that supposed to mean?"

Henry looked at the stump on Samuel's left leg.

"Now just a minute here, McCluskey, I may have lost my leg, but I sure as hell didn't lose my mind. We made a deal. I've always held up to my end of the bargain, and I expect you to do the same. Don't try to swindle me, do you understand?"

"Well, sure. I just thought . . ."

Samuel banged the table with his fist. "You just thought you'd take advantage of me. I can assure you that will not happen. I am as capable of running this ranch as Lily. And don't you forget that for a minute. Is that clear?"

"Well, all right then," Henry said as he grabbed his jacket from the hook by the door. "But if I see that things aren't working out here, you have to know that I will do what I can to keep my place going."

Samuel took Henry's cup and threw it against the door, then cursed himself for having yet another mess to clean up.

As Henry went to the barn to get his horse, he gave Gus a wink and a nod.

The next day Samuel's body ached and his stump throbbed like someone had hit it with a hammer. A big part of him wanted to stay in bed and pull up the covers. But his stomach thought otherwise, and he would be damned if he would ask Gus to cook for him. They had been the worst eggs he'd ever eaten.

He rolled from the bed and grabbed his crutches. He went to the kitchen and from the window he saw that David Wood and Gus talking by the barn. He grabbed his coat and went out to see what was going on.

"Good morning, Samuel," David Wood said is his routine cordial voice. "I stopped by to ask Gus what you were planning to do with the rest of the cattle."

"Why didn't you come to me?"

"Well, I just thought . . ."

"Get this straight, Wood," Samuel said, his voice seething in vehemence. "Gus is merely the hired hand around this place. Any business done goes through me!"

Samuel Bodeen hobbled back to the house, more determined than ever to prove to all of them that he may have lost a small piece of his body, but he was not a crippled derelict to be pitied. He was still a man, and by God, they were all going to know it when he was through with them.

✠ ✠ ✠

When Ouray arrived four days later, he was astounded at the change in Bodeen. Samuel was mucking out the barn, his cheeks bright red with color. And Samuel was surprised at Ouray as well. He looked haggard, tired, and old. And Samuel noticed that Ouray had given up white men's dress, in favor of full buckskin and beads. It was not a good sign.

Samuel grabbed his crutch and invited Ouray to the house for a cup of coffee. He put a plate of biscuits on the table.

"They're a bit scorched on the bottom, but eatable if you use enough raspberry jam."

"You're looking well my friend," Ouray said as he declined the biscuits.

"Stomach still got you down?" Samuel asked.

"Don't tell Chipeta, but I don't know how much longer I can hang on."

Samuel set down his cup. "Now, it can't be that bad."

"You are my friend. Don't make me pretend with you as well. And how are you really, Bodeen?"

"Getting by. But it is frustrating as hell. What about the Commission? Have they come to any conclusions?"

"Without you, the talks go round and round like a top. Then everyone gets mad. And now they have produced the testimony of the women who say they were violated. They put together a list of twelve Utes, and commanded me to turn them into the Commission, who will send them to trial for unspecified crimes, before an unspecified court, at an unspecified date and time. I, in turn, informed the commission that there was no possible way I can honor such a request. They are looking for scapegoats. Even the young Price woman admitted that all the Indians looked alike to her. I also told the Commission that there was no way that any of the Utes could get a fair trial in Colorado."

Ouray paused and sipped on the coffee.

"I have requested a meeting with Secretary Schurz in Washington."

Samuel nodded in agreement. "And did he meet that request?"

"He did. We leave in four days. I need you to be there, Samuel."

"I can't." Samuel didn't hesitate in answering the request.

"You can't or you won't?"

"You don't understand what you are asking," Samuel said. He was safe here, with no one to stare at him.

"I understand well, my friend. But I am asking you anyway."

"I'm sorry, Ouray."

"And so am I."

✛ ✛ ✛

That evening as Samuel lay alone, yet again, he swore he could see Lily. He could smell her scent, but he could not quite touch her. The words she had said to him the morning she had left him echoed in his mind. He tried to ignore her voice.

She whispered it to him softly again during the night: "When I first saw you on the train, I thought that you were the only man I'd ever met who could do anything he set his mind to do. And, my love, I still believe that with all my heart."

Now it was up to him to prove her right. And it was also up to him to prove to her that though she had been right about one thing, she had been mistaken about another—he needed her. God, how he needed her—not as a nursemaid, but as a lover, as a friend, and as a wife.

He hugged her pillow to him and prayed for the strength to become the man that would get her back. To become Samuel Bodeen again.

He couldn't do it alone. And for the first time in his life, he didn't want to.

January 5, 1880

18

When Lily had arrived in Denver just after Christmas, she had been surprised when she had walked into Izzie's boardinghouse. No longer was it filled with adults needing a bed and a meal. It was filled with children who had needed a home.

But what was even more shocking was walking through the kitchen door to see Victoria in an apron washing dishes.

"What are you doing here?" Lily asked.

"And I might ask the same of you," Victoria said. "Here, let me take Rose and put her to bed." She took the sleeping child from Lily's arms.

"It was a hard trip for her," Lily said.

"And you as well. You look worn-out."

When Victoria returned to the kitchen, Lily told her the reason she had left. Lily expected Samuel's sister to be angry. But she was just the opposite. Victoria understood completely.

"I left Oliver once, just after he was injured. Of course we weren't married then, but I still had felt a deep obligation to him. It was one of the hardest things I ever had to do, walking out that door."

"I feel like I've abandoned Samuel just when he needs me most," Lily said.

"Only puppies and children can be abandoned, Lily. Samuel is neither, though I have to say he sure acted like one at Christmas. It took all the strength I could muster not to drag him out of that bed and give him a swift kick in the shorts."

"But what are you doing here, Victoria?" Lily asked.

Victoria explained that when she came to Denver after Christmas, she spent a few days with Molly Brown, a Denver socialite, she had met at a soiree in New York.

"Molly and her husband became millionaires almost overnight after their mine in Leadville hit pay dirt. Or should I say gold."

Isabel came into the kitchen, gave Lily a confused look, and put the teakettle on the stove.

"Molly spoke highly of Isabel's cooking, and I remember you talking about how wonderful Isabel is as a person. My own cook retired after Oliver died. Molly and I came to the boardinghouse so I could recruit Izzie into coming East with me. Of course, she would have none of that."

She smiled at Isabel. "Molly and I were impressed with what Izzie was doing for the children."

Izzie explained how she'd fried up a bunch of donuts for a lady who never came and picked them up. Rather than let them go to waste, she took them down to the shantytown as a treat for the children.

As Lily sat and listened to Izzie's story, she had the notion that the donuts had never been ordered by anyone at all and that Izzie had made the donuts because of her big heart.

"And there was little Judy Martin," Izzie said, "standing in the back of a crowd of children. Looked just like a little abandoned kitten in a snowstorm. Her toes were sticking out of what was left of her shoes. She was wearing a thin coat that wouldn't have kept a bird warm, and scared to death, poor little thing. Well, I asked her where her mama was and she said she didn't know. One of the other kids said that her mama was up at one of the brothels. Had been gone for over a week. Made my heart weep, it did. I left word with the children that if the mama came back, she could pick up her child at my place."

"Well, it seems that Molly and I had walked into a bit of a crisis," Victoria said. "One of the other children had put a bean in Judy's ear and it was stuck tight. Molly and I offered to take the child to the hospital to have it removed, as there were five children waiting anxiously for a chocolate cake to come out of the oven.

"I was appalled at the horrible conditions of the hospital and encouraged Molly to set up a fundraiser. But Molly is, what would you say, a bit unfinished. She asked me to stay in Denver to assist her. And I agreed. Besides, I have the sheriff searching for Judy's mother, and my lawyer back East drawing up the necessary paperwork for when they finally do."

"Paperwork?" Lily's tired mind was having a hard time following what Victoria was trying to say.

"I intend to adopt Judy. She is a delightful child. I will be leaving in the morning for New York to get my affairs in order so I can move to Denver. It seems I am needed much more here: you and Samuel and little Rose, the hospital, the Children's Home. Besides, that drafty house is just too big for one person."

"You're selling the house? The Children's Home?" It was all too much for Lily to take in so suddenly. And Victoria, her eyes sparkling with excitement, was talking much too fast.

"No, I will be donating Bannister Manor to a group of missionaries to be used as a children's home. And when I return, Molly and I are going to pool our resources and build one in Denver as well. Isabel has graciously agreed to run it."

✛ ✛ ✛

The children crowded around the kitchen sink and Lily ran a cloth over their hands and faces.

"Chicken and dumplings? Oh, boy, my favorite!" Little Judy Martin grinned widely as she took her place at the long table.

Lily laughed. Victoria was right. Judy was a delight. Every night the child said the same thing. It seemed that everything Izzie put before her was her favorite. But it seemed to be that way for all the children that Izzie had taken in.

Now, at least twenty times a day there would be a faint knock on the back door. It seemed that once Izzie took Judy's hand and guided her back to the boardinghouse for a hot meal and a thick coat, word had gotten around the children in the shantytown that Izzie's was a warm house when the wind was cold. And there was always a warm bowl of soup and a warm heart waiting for them. Most didn't stay, for one reason or another. Many had odd jobs, and odd families to care for. But there were now five that lived at the boardinghouse including Judy. The sheriff had brought the newest young boarder. The boy's father was in jail for stabbing a shopkeeper after he had been caught stealing a Christmas turkey.

Lily spent her days teaching the children to read while Izzie cooked and cleaned and knitted red mittens.

"Most everything in those kids' lives is dull," she'd said while picking up the bright-colored yarn, "seems to me they need something cheery as well as warm."

There was little time for Lily to think about Samuel during the day, but he was all she could think about after the lights went out and guilt spread over her like a cold, wet blanket. But guilt had not been enough of a reason to stay, and was not enough of a reason to go back.

She had worried about how Rose would adjust to such a drastic change in lifestyle. The child had been shy at first, having gone from being alone at the ranch to a house full of children. She didn't like sharing her mother either, but within just a few days she was playing well with the other children and no longer seemed to mind when another child would climb into Lily's lap alongside her.

Lily had just finished up the supper dishes when there was another knock at the door. Izzie was upstairs giving yet another bath. Lily dried her hands and hung the tea towel on a rack above the sink.

She opened the door, expecting to see another child. But instead she came face to face with Samuel.

He held the old bowler hat in his hands that she had worn on the train when she came to Denver. That day had seemed so long ago, but seeing the hat again made it feel like yesterday.

"You forgot your hat, Donovan."

"Samuel."

He then gave her the exact same speech he had given back then, telling her that "Big Chief Ouray" and his lovely wife Chipeta were expecting her for dinner.

"Ouray and Chipeta are in Denver?"

"Are you going to leave me standing here out in the cold, or can I come in?"

She opened the door and watched as he clumsily maneuvered himself with a cane. In shock, Lily noticed that there were two feet, and both feet had boots on them.

"Your leg. How . . .?"

"I grew it back," he said with a wink.

"It's not funny, Samuel," she said seriously. "Is this some kind of a joke?"

"No. Actually, Sapiah made me a new one and a cane to match. Brought them by about a week ago. Said it wasn't much different than carving a flute. Chipeta lined the top of my new leg with a soft rabbit fur and Ouray made the straps out of tanned deerskin. I'm not quite used to this new setup yet, can't bend a wooden leg. But it will get me to Washington okay."

"Washington?"

"If you would cut me a slab of that cherry pie on the table, I'll tell you all about it. But first, is Rosebud around? My God, I've missed that little sassafras."

"Daddy!" Rose was thrilled when she saw the surprise her mother had told her was waiting for her in the kitchen. She noticed nothing different about her father, having never actually seen him without his leg. Rose told him all about her new friends, and about getting to see a real live elephant that had come to town with the circus. They shared not just one, but two pieces of pie.

When Izzie walked in the kitchen she had just one thing to say. "Well, it's about time you showed up. I've baked pies every day since Lily's been here. Come on sunshine, it's your turn for the tub and way past your bedtime already. 'Sides, I bet your mama and daddy want to talk."

"Oh, do I have to?" Rose whined, looking at her father.

"Tell you what. Tomorrow you can go show me that elephant."

"I get to go see the circus again?"

"You bet you do."

"Will you be here when I wake up?"

Samuel looked at Lily.

"I'm sure your father has already taken a room at the hotel where Ouray and Chipeta are staying," Lily said firmly.

"Pita's here? Think she would want to see the elephant, too?"

"I'll be sure to ask her," Samuel said.

After Izzie and Rose had gone upstairs, Samuel said quietly, "I didn't mean to put you on the spot."

"It's all right. You do have a room, don't you?"

"Actually, no. I guess I was hoping that I would have one here."

Lily sat in silence.

"Guess not. Maybe I should go. But would you do me just one thing?"

"What is it, Samuel?" Lily asked warily.

"Would you go see the elephant with me?"

After Samuel left, Izzie came downstairs. Lily was still sitting at the kitchen table. Izzie put the teakettle on to boil, then split the last piece of pie and put it on two plates.

"No thank you," Lily said, pushing the pie away.

"Eat up. It will do you good," Izzie said. "You know I'm no expert on marriage. Shoot fire, never even came close to it. But it seems to me that marriage is a lot like cherry pie."

Lily looked at her quizzically.

"Yep, the secret to a really good piece of pie is the sugar. Oh sure, you have to start out with good ingredients—plump, juicy cherries that are ripe for the picking. You know, the kind that is sour alone, but with the right amount of sugar, they make a right nice pie. Yes ma'am, not enough sugar, and the pie is too sour. Kind of makes your mouth pucker and you get an awful look on your face. Too sweet, mind you, will do the same thing. Then it takes like that awful medicine my mama gave me when I had the croup. Nope, it's got to be just the right amount."

"And what does that have to do with marriage?" Lily asked.

"Well, you got to have good ingredients to begin with. And then you got to have a bit of the sour in a marriage for flavor. And you got to have enough of the sweet to make the sour not make you get that awful look on your face, the kind you have right now."

"Just what are you trying to say, Izzie?" Lily knew there had to be point, but she was not up to a ridiculous guessing game.

"I guess I'm trying to say that you're sour."

"Thanks a lot."

"No, what I mean is you're sour on marriage. Am I right?"

"Don't kid yourself Izzie, marriage is really not all hearts and flowers and cherry pie."

"And thank the Good Lord for that. Why, you would be sick to your stomach if it were. What I'm saying is I think you need a little bit of sugar. And so does Samuel."

"Don't you think I tried that? I did everything I could to help him, and yet he proved to me once again that he doesn't need me at all. The man who walked in here tonight was not the same man I left just two weeks ago. Before I left, he wouldn't even get out of bed. He was drunk, he was surly, and he was mean."

"Yes, but he knew that you were helping him, not out of love, but out of guilt and pity. And a man like Samuel Bodeen don't cotton to that."

"I did not!"

"What did you feel when he came in here tonight? It wasn't love. It was relief. I saw it; for sure that's what I saw. And you know why?

Cause if that was what you felt, it went a long way to easing your conscience. You can't tell me that you don't feel just a bit better about leaving, now can you?"

Lily knew she was right. That is exactly what she had felt, especially when she saw the twinkle in his eye again.

"I don't think it was Samuel that blamed you for making the decision to remove the leg, as much as I think you've been blaming yourself, for whatever else you may or may not have done. But I'm here to tell you, it's not your fault, child. Things just happen."

"But don't you see, he just proved what I've always known. He doesn't need me at all."

"You're wrong about that. He's just afraid to show you."

"But why?"

"Cause if he needs someone, he thinks somehow it makes him less of a man. And he don't feel like much of a man anyway right now. When was the last time you sprinkled a little sugar his way and really meant it?"

"You mean . . .?"

"Oh, for crying in the daisies, you know exactly what I'm talking about. You know, I've always wanted what you have—a man to love, and a man to love me back. And here you are, with the whole pie, cherries and all, right in front of you. And yet you won't even try to take a bite out of it. Don't throw it away, girl, just because there may be a pit or two."

Lily looked at the ridiculous hat still setting on the table and remembered the words Lu Simpson had said on the train, something about God had sent her to the West for a reason. Once she had been certain that it had been Samuel Bodeen. Was it still?

✛ ✛ ✛

Chipeta giggled like a child when she saw the large, gray gentle beast with two tails. Even the serious Ouray had to smile. And after it was over, they all had to admit that it had been more fun watching the wonder in the children's eyes than watching the circus itself.

That night after everyone had gone to bed, Samuel and Lily sat in the parlor of the boardinghouse in silence.

Finally Samuel pulled something out of his pocket. "I have something for you, Lily."

He handed her an envelope and she noticed that his hands were trembling when he passed it to her. She looked inside. It was a ticket to Washington.

"Do it for Chipeta. I'm afraid this is going to be a very difficult trip for her. Ouray is sick and the treaty negotiations are sure to make him worse."

She fingered the ticket carefully.

"Oh, hell. What am I saying? Lily, do it for me." His lips quivered. "Watching Ouray sign that treaty and knowing what the outcome is going to be . . . I've decided it's time to see my father. What I'm saying is I don't think I can do this without you. I need you, Lily. And you were right. Not as a nursemaid, but as a friend, as a wife, and as a lover."

She led him upstairs. And then she took a big piece of the pie and relished every bite.

19

January 20, 1880
New York City

I know you think of me as a despicable old bastard. Well, Boy, you ain't a bit far from the God's honest truth. So if you're here to tell me that, then don't pussyfoot around and just get on with it."

Samuel stared at the pale shell of a human being that he had once called his pa. The man's hair was a dull yellow, matching the color of his teeth, or what was left of them. It curled down around his shoulders in a lifeless mop. Deep cobalt veins, like the coarse of a slow-moving stream, flowed under the translucent skin that looked as thin and dry and fragile as a piece of old parchment. But his eyes were steely blue, piercing and sharp.

The man sat straight up and slid his legs over the side of the bed. He reached down and tried to put on his slippers, but his hands shook uncontrollably. "Sons a bitches," he cursed under his breath. Samuel leaned down and slid the slippers on his father's feet.

"Your sister told me about the leg. Makes you wonder about God's wisdom a bit, now don't it? Seems to me he gave us all two of everything he thought we needed, just in case we was to lose one of them. Two eyes, two ears, two arms, two legs. Hell, he even gave women two breasts, in case one was to get plugged up or something. But I find it brilliant on the part of 'the man upstairs' that he only gave us one mouth. I sure have known plenty of folk who could get into enough trouble with the one they had, me being one of them. Could you imagine what the world would be like if he'd given us two?" He gave Samuel a sardonic and sly grin. "Course, I do have to wonder why he only gave us just one heart. It seems to be the thing we could use the most, beings how it's the one thing that seems to get broke the most."

Tyrone Bodeen pointed to a wheelchair parked in the corner.

"I know I don't got the right to ask you for a damned thing, but if you could wheel that chair over here by the bed, we can go outside and have a real talk, man to man like."

Samuel helped Tyrone into the chair and covered his bowed, scrawny legs with a blanket. He steered the chair to the door using the wheelchair for support.

The air was frigid but the old man didn't seem to mind. He pointed the way to a spot of sun by a bed of withered flowers. "Right there would be just dandy. God dammit to hell, I hate being cooped up in that place. Damned if I don't know if I'm smelling someone else's piss or my own. But then I guess it don't matter much—it all smells the same anyway."

So many times Samuel had rehearsed in his mind what he would say to his father. And now no words would come. It wasn't going as he had expected at all. He expected to be angry, but it seemed instead it was all almost amusing, sitting outside in the middle of winter, talking about piss.

They watched people hurrying along on the street outside the fence, both waiting for the other to start the conversation in a sort of draw or dare game. Finally the old man spoke.

"Yes, it's true I was a real son of a bitch as a father. Guess I didn't know any different. My father was a son of a bitch, too. We were both born with what my mama called wandering feet. Couldn't seem to make them stay in one place very long."

He lifted a shaky hand and pointed his finger at the street. "Like them folks I guess. Always seemed in a hurry to get nowhere fast. Hated schooling, what a damned waste of time that was. Guess the only time I got nowhere slow was those God-awful long days I spent behind that damned plow. Day after day, up and back, up and back. And all I had to show for it was a pile of rocks and enough seed to do it all again the next year. Don't know much about religion, but if there is a hell, that would be it."

Samuel thought about the last few years on the ranch. Cutting the hay, up and back.

"Then came the war. Made enough when I enlisted to take good care of your ma and you young'uns. Well, enough to get by. It was freedom, pure and simple, walking away from that plow. And that, my boy, is probably the closest feeling to heaven that I'll ever get." The old man paused for a long while, the winter breeze whipping at his hair.

"Then someone showed me a way to do better than to just get by. Yeah, maybe it was wrong. But they said the war was to free the slaves. Well, I can tell you this—you don't have to be a blackie to be a slave. Being a sharecropper was a form of slavery, too. White slavery. Besides, I didn't much like what I saw them cocky southern overseers doing to the darkies. . . Chained like animals, they was. I figured they wanted their freedom as much as I wanted mine, and had as much right to it as I did."

The old man reached out and picked a dead flower from the bed. "What convinced me, though, was one night I was laying in my bedroll looking up at the stars. I pictured your mama putting flowers in a mason jar. See, your mama loved pretty things. All summer long she would pick wildflowers and put them in a mason jar on the kitchen table. She did everything she could to that shack to make it pretty. Dyed flour sacks with indigo and made curtains for the oilcloth on the windows. Woman's stuff like that."

He gently picked the dead blossom and held it in his hand. "God rest her soul. Victoria looks so much like her it makes my eyes water when she walks in my room. She likes pretty things, too."

He plucked the dried-out petals off the flower and let them fall to the ground. "I bought her a pretty vase once. Crystal, it was. Made rainbows on the walls when the morning sun hit it. But she gave it to the doc when you were down with the scarlet fever. She didn't say as much but I knew it broke her heart. And if it didn't break hers, it sure as hell broke mine. After the war I looked for another one. Found one just like it, too. But of course by then it was too late."

He broke the stem in half and threw each half back into the flower bed. He put his hands to the wheels and turned the chair around. "It's getting cold. Don't you have some place you need to be?"

The piercing eyes had turned a faded gray by the time Samuel had helped him back into bed.

"Don't expect any apology from me, Son, cause you ain't gonna get one. I can't help the way I was. And if I could have changed anything, I wouldn't have. Made peace with what I was, what I did. Can't ask anyone else to do the same. You'll just have to make up your own mind with it.

"All we can do in this life is try and do the best we can—not caving in to what others think is best. But I can tell you this, do what's right for you. Cause if you live your life trying to please others, the only one you're really going to end up pleasing is the devil himself. I'm living proof of that. If you are ever going to make a difference in this godforsaken world, you can only do it by being who and what you are.

"Follow your gut. If you came here wanting fatherly advice, well, that's about it in a nutshell. And if you don't want it, then just hurl it to the squirrels. Now get the hell outta here and let me take a nap."

Victoria and Lily were anxiously waiting in the carriage.

"Did the old man really bring a crystal vase when he came back, or was he putting me on?"

"I still have it," Victoria said.

"Good."

✤ ✤ ✤

January 25, 1880
Washington D.C.

Chipeta looked around the conference table at the faces of the white men in their fine clothes, the men who were deciding her fate, and the fate of her people. They were smug, even smiling. One with fleshy, overblown cheeks and puffy pink hands wrote lofty strokes on an alabaster-colored piece of paper, just as she had seen the white man write their words three times before, signing each treaty with a flourish. These men were men of importance, of wealth. . .and of deception. She guessed that like the other treaties, this one would be broken within months.

As Ouray, Samuel, and the white chiefs discussed the details, Chipeta glanced out the window at a large brick church on the corner of the busy street below. The magnificent stained glass windows gleamed like a rainbow in the sun.

She thought about the missionaries who had told her people about the white men's God they called Jesus, this God who was revered even still. The white man had built beautiful houses for their God, but Chipeta could see children begging on the streets in front of the building, cold and hungry.

The story made no sense to her. This Jesus God had tried to bring peace to the white man's world. Instead, he had been brought to the enemy by a man who had called him friend, even kissing the cheeks of his God to reveal his identity. And then they had killed him.

The white man betrayed their God, just as these white men betrayed her husband and her people with more empty promises. And like the children on the streets, her people were cold and starving.

Ouray had called these men friend. He had shared his fire with them, shared his dreams with them, and would have laid down his own life for each of them. He had sincerely believed that they were men of honor, men of their word, when all along they were merely scavengers just waiting for the first blood to be shed, waiting to go in for the kill.

And of all the men at the table, she had thought of Otto Mears as a friend, a trusted ally. But now she saw nothing but the greed on his face. The friendship had been as false and full of lies as the previous treaties. Otto spoke of the fear that the white people had for the Utes.

Ouray asked Mears, "And in our fifteen years of friendship, Otto, did I ever give you cause to fear me, or cause you to question my word to you?"

Otto did not answer.

In frustration Ouray asked," What are you more fearful of, Otto? The Indian, or the thought of losing the opportunity to become rich off the land which you, yourself, signed over to the Ute in the Brunot Treaty of 1873? Only back then you did not know the streams of silver that were hidden beneath the Shining Mountains. And now that you know, you push to go against your word to me."

Again, Otto said nothing and Chipeta saw the deep hurt in her husband's eyes.

As the conference continued, it was clear to Chipeta that the Ute people were like a doe trying to protect her offspring from a pack of hungry wolves. The white wolves nipped at a heel here, and tore a bit of flesh there, while the doe tried to fight back until finally she had no more strength. And once the pack had tasted blood, there was no way for the doe to defend her fawn against all the gnawing teeth.

As much as her heart ached for her people, it cried out in silent agony when she saw the sheer sadness on Ouray's face as his requests were denied time and time again.

Chipeta had watched his body weaken over the past months as it was broken down from the betrayal of those he had called his friends. Their lies had finally been revealed by the stark and bitter truth. The breaking of Ouray's faith in them had broken his spirit. Once such a powerful warrior, now Ouray was a man who had lost the will to even get out of bed in the morning and look at the sunrise. The pain of betrayal caused him to suffer much more than the pain his body felt from the sickness.

Chipeta wondered how they should have, or if they could have, handled it differently, if anything could have changed the course of the future of their people.

They had let themselves be intimidated by the big guns and the powerful chiefs in Washington. They had cowered in the presence of the enemy like a hunted animal, and had not chosen to stand tall and self-confident as the hunter. Yet, the Indian chiefs who had tried to fight back, like Joseph of the Nez Perce, had watched their people shot down like dogs. That had been Ouray's biggest fear. And it was that fear which had become the whites' most powerful ally.

On the outside, the white men had been full of kind words, presents and pats on the back as friends, making promises with sincerity and handshakes. But on the inside they had been full of lies, greed, and deceit. In the past, they showed no guilt, no regret in breaching previous words as they signed their name to each new pact and treaty.

Here they sat, yet again, making more promises and telling more lies, self-important and self-satisfied.

But the fault had not been just with the whites. Chipeta knew that. The Utes had been a willing target, wearing their gifts of medals and shiny beads and standing in the sunshine facing the whites with waves of welcome. They had treated these gift givers as brothers, sharing the food in their pots, and sharing their peace pipes and their honesty. But trust and truth did not mean the same thing to the white man as it meant to the Ute. The people had walked willingly into their web of greed and fraud, not once, but three times.

Chipeta looked at the pictures of the white faces in the gilded frames that covered the walls, looking as serious and as conceited as the men sitting at the table. She looked at the flag in the corner and then down at the rug with its grotesque gray patterns. And she looked down at her dress, an uncomfortable white woman's dress that bound her around the middle like a tight fist. She longed for the feel of soft doeskin against her body.

She longed to be home, not in her white man's house, but in her tipi made from her own two hands. She longed for its simplicity, its warmth wrapping around her like a warm wool blanket. She longed to be in her mountains, feeling the snowflakes falling on her cheeks, smelling the fresh scent of pine and aspen, instead of the heavy grime of the city. She needed pure air, pure thoughts.

The horror of this civilized attack against the destiny of her people made her want to scream. Scream like a warrior at this enemy. Chipeta wished she were a man, someone with the will and the power to fight back against the injustice. Someone with a less gentle spirit.

She had not condoned the taking of the Meeker women and children, but neither did she condone this robbing of her people, the white men turning them into beggars, the children's stomachs groaning with hunger because their parents were not allowed to feed them as the Ute children had been fed for hundreds of years. Instead, mothers and fathers stood at the white man's table humiliating themselves, begging for a piece of bread to be thrown their way.

Chipeta listened as the white men bargained with Ouray about how many sacks of flour were to be rationed per person. The last supply of flour had been full of weevils and the thought of it made her ill.

No longer could she sit and watch the fate of the children written down on a piece of paper by the greasy, fat-faced white man, like he was filling out an order for cattle to be bought and butchered.

Chipeta quietly excused herself from the meeting and hurried down the long hall to find a lavatory.

✠ ✠ ✠

The next morning Chipeta asked Lily to accompany her to the conference. It was just too painful to sit through it all again alone.

And Lily, too, was appalled at the lack of support for Ouray and his people, even from her own husband. Several times she herself wanted to speak, but he had warned her before the start of the meeting that it would disgrace the chiefs if she spoke. She felt it more of a disgrace that she did not.

The long morning went into late afternoon. More and more demands were made on Ouray, and less and less given back. And finally Sapiah rose from his chair and in his quiet, gentle manner, asked to speak. The commissioner took his pocket watch from his vest pocket and let out an impatient breath. Not waiting for an answer Sapiah said:

"The Ute people have always been a quiet, peaceful people. For generations we lived in the shadow of the Shining Mountains. We hurt no one. We lived at peace, with ourselves and with our neighbors. We worked for our food, not by cutting the Mother Earth and planting crops, but by graciously and thankfully harvesting the bounty she bestowed upon the people. She gave us the animals, the plants, the water, the clean, pure air and the life-giving water. She gave us everything we needed to survive and to thrive. She gave us shelter, food, medicine, and clothing. She gave us coolness in summer and warmth in winter.

"The Ute was at one with the Mother Earth. Her breath caressed our souls. Her land gave us strength, and in return, we respected her.

"I do not see the white man show any respect at all, not just for the Mother Earth but for all living things. They take, and then they take more. They hurt her and she bleeds from the wounds, and then she scars.

"The white man maims the animals with traps and snares, leaving them to suffer for days. The fox has to chew off his own foot to try and escape starvation. The white man killed all the buffalo on the plains, taking only the choice parts, and leaving the rest to rot in the summer sun. And when the buffalo were no more, they took the beaver. And now they take the elk and deer.

"This angers me.

"And yet you sit here today and tell me I must become like the white man. I don't want to be rich as they do; I just want to be free. I do not want to be like them. I would rather not live at all than to live as a selfish and greedy man. I do not want to be like a spoiled child, demanding more and more from Mother Earth, and show her no respect for the gifts she gives.

"You call us lazy because we don't spend all day toiling behind a plow, cutting up the earth. We don't want rations and handouts from the whites, as you seem to think we do. What we want instead is to spend our days gathering fruit and nuts and roots, as we have done for hundreds of years. We don't want your cattle, but to accept the gifts of the animals that Mother Earth has provided: the elk, the deer, the fish and the birds.

"The Great Spirit gave us a perfect and beautiful world that we were willing to share with the white. But now you want it all. I know this truth—even when you have it, you will not be satisfied. You will demand more, and keep trying to change it.

"Sadly, even if I could become like the white man, to somehow adopt his selfish ways, I would still, deep inside, be Ute. And I would be Ute on the outside as well. My skin would still be the color of the white man's copper penny. I would still be condemned in the eyes of the white man. I would still be labeled as a savage and a heathen, though I am neither.

"And I would lose the land anyway. No matter which way I face, all I see is the soldier's sword.

"My heart breaks with each treaty. And with each broken promise, it crumbles a bit more. I am afraid that when this conference is over, I will have no heart left—that it will have been broken down as rocks are broken down into sand, and there will be no way to put it back together again. I will have no heart to feel love for my wife and children, the Mother Earth and the Great Spirits that have guided us.

"I must go home before that happens. I cannot stay any longer and listen to your promises, for I can see in your eyes what I have seen times before, that they will never be kept.

"I can't let your words torture my soul anymore."

Then Sapiah reached inside his buckskin shirt and pulled out a small flute.

The song he played was as angry as the thunder during a summer storm. It was as sweet as the ripe berries in autumn and as bitter as the chokecherry. And finally, it was as lamenting as the sad song of the mourning dove.

And when he was through playing, he set the flute down gently in the middle of the large table and walked out the large double doors of the big stone building.

And one by one the rest of the thirteen Utes at the table followed: Chief Ouray, War Chief Shavano, Severo, Galota, Ignacio, Woretsiz, Sowerick, Wass, Alhandra, Ojo Blanco, Tap-uch, Captain Jack, Johnson, and Henry Jim. And finally, Chipeta.

Lily looked at Samuel with pleading eyes but he shook his head. She remained seated for a few moments, then got up quietly, walked out and shut the door.

Samuel knew he would never be forgiven for staying—not by the Ute warriors, not by Ouray or Chipeta, and not by the one person he loved most in his life.

But he also knew that if he walked out the door, the Utes would have no defense left at all. Through secret contacts with the army, he had been told of the plan to exterminate the Utes if a satisfactory treaty could not be met and abided by.

Walking away could not stop this enemy, the great white enemy of greed. If the Utes turned away, they would be devoured. If they faced the whites head on, the forces of the whole United States Army would be waiting.

This enemy would have to be fought silently. Careful planning, cunning and even a bit of deceit would be the ammunition. Samuel would have to fight this enemy using the same ammunition they had used against the Indian nations for the past fifty years.

For the Utes, as it had been for all the other Indian nations, this enemy was too strong, too powerful. Even the great and powerful Ouray would not have been able to conquer this enemy. And now that he was sick, the enemy was sure to eat him alive.

The Indian did not know how to defend themselves against dishonesty and broken promises, for those concepts were as foreign to the Indian as many of their ways were to the white.

There was no way for the Ute to win this war, but Samuel was going to make sure that they would not die from it—even if it meant taking the chance of losing everything in life that he had ever held dear. He, like the Ute, would lose his land. And he would lose the respect of the army, the respect of his friends. He would lose his precious wife just when he had been so close to getting her back and making things right again. His daughter would despise him for years as he had despised his father.

For what he was about to do, he would lose the best friend he ever had. The ultimate betrayal would kill him. But in another time and another life, he hoped the Great Warrior, Ouray the Arrow, would realize that it was the only way to save the Ute from complete annihilation. It was the only way that Samuel could assure his friend that the Ute people would go on.

The words of his father spoke to him once more. "All we can do in this life is try and do the best we can. If you are ever going to make a difference in this godforsaken world, you can only do it by being who you are and following your gut."

He just prayed that he had the strength to pull it off.

20

People on the busy street stopped and stared at the Ute entourage standing in front of the large gray building. Fearful mothers clutched their curious children and guided them around the group.

The Utes started walking back to the Tremont House, where the owner, F.P. Hill, had reserved a floor of rooms for them at a dollar-fifty per head per Ute per day, which included meals. Magnanimously, Hill had thrown in free use of the bathroom at the end of the hall.

Ouray did not follow.

"Ouray, aren't you coming? Chipeta asked. "Would you like me to flag down a carriage?"

"I will wait here for Bodeen," he said.

Lily looked to see not anger on the chief's face, but concern. Sapiah offered to stay and wait with him.

"No, please, go back and have a nice meal. I would rather wait and speak to Samuel alone."

Chipeta was uncomfortable leaving Ouray standing on the street, but did as he requested. He waited in front of the building for over two hours. He tried to think, but the constant din of the city noise kept interrupting his already troubled thoughts. He had to crawl deep inside of himself to escape.

By the time that Samuel finally emerged from the building, the sun was beginning to set.

"You look tired, my friend," Ouray said.

"As do you," Samuel answered.

"We need to speak, away from the others. I wish there was a quiet place to go, but there seems to be no such place in the city. How do people think with all this noise?"

They walked several blocks before finding a dimly-lit café. They sat down at a table in the back. A tired looking waitress eyed Ouray suspiciously, spoke only to Samuel, and then glared back at Ouray. Instead of treating the chief as the great leader of a nation, she treated him worse than she would have treated a vagrant from the street.

"You want to eat, too?" she asked coldly.

"Just some broth, please," Ouray said kindly.

She left in a snit, but not before wiping off the table with a dirty rag where Ouray had touched his hand. Ouray did not seem to notice, or if he did, he did not acknowledge it.

"I do not fault your decision to stay at the conference, Samuel. I am glad that you did."

"Then you understand?"

"Without your presence to keep Mears and the others in check, there would have been no one to speak for the Ute. But I do hope you understand why I chose to leave. Sapiah spoke, both through his words and his music, what I feel in my heart as well.

"I am finding it more difficult every day to sit through the meetings, to hold my tongue and not loosen the anger that eats away inside me. For six weeks now, I have heard nothing but empty promises and orders, which the Utes must follow. Not once during these meetings have I felt that we walked together on common ground. And the more the members of the Commission speak, the more I do not believe their words, and neither do the other Utes.

"War Chief Shavano is an old man, he wants to fight. And my heart is the same as his."

"You can't do that Ouray," Samuel said firmly. "If a single one of your people raises any kind of weapon to a white, then there will be no more Utes. You must think of the children. You must think of their future."

Ouray sat quietly as the woman brought the food. She set Samuel's plate in front of him, and set Ouray's bowl of broth at the end of the table. Ouray pulled it to him and sipped the broth. It was cold and full of salt. He pushed it away.

"But if I sign the treaty as it stands, what kind of future will I be signing for the children? If I sign, they will lose their freedom. They will be confined in a cage of desolate and barren land, dependent on the white man for everything."

"The government has assured you that they will be provided for," Samuel said.

"Do you really believe them? Would you want that for your own children, your own precious Rose?"

"Ouray, you have no other choice if you want them to have any future at all. It is up to you. If you go ahead with Shavano and give the order to fight back, I can guarantee there will be no future for your people at all. If you try to fight their fire with your own fire, there will nothing left of the Utes but ashes. There are those in the army anxiously waiting to start that fire, and Pitkin is just as anxious to give the order to do so. That would be the easiest, and the cheapest way out for them. The only thing they would owe the Utes then is a burial."

"They won't hear what I have to say. I have been patient in listening to them, but they don't even try to hear my words."

"And they won't. The loudest words you can speak are words of silence. If you persist in peace, the government knows that they will have to some day pay for, and honor that request. The future comes but one day at a time. They can tell your people where to live, but they can't tell them how or what to think. They can't take away either your history, or your heritage."

"It seems to me," Ouray said, "that the more uncertain and uncivilized a man is, the more he thinks he knows what is better for another. I have sat there, day after day, putting up with their bad manners and self-serving attitudes. They think themselves better than the Utes. But I have never met one man so much better than another that he is given the right to tell others how to live."

"And that will be the real test of your courage as a warrior, to choose peace over fighting and not to give into the pushing and shoving and goading of you or your people into making that one last fatal mistake. In demanding a peaceful settlement, we both know what the final outcome will be. But at least there will be one."

Ouray thought for a long while before he spoke. Finally he said, "Before I sign anything, I want to speak to the Great White Father and Secretary Schurz first."

"I will arrange it," Samuel said.

Later, President Rutherford B. Hayes would tell reporters that Ouray was the most intelligent man with whom he had ever conversed.

"And I request one more thing of you, my friend, but I ask you not to speak either to Lily or Chipeta of it."

"Whatever you want," Samuel said.

"I want you to take me to a doctor."

But the doctor just confirmed what the Chief already knew.

Two days later, Chipeta and Sapiah accompanied Lily to the train station. Samuel had not chosen to see her off, but to attend the meeting between Schurz and Ouray. In Lily's eyes, it had been for the best. Their conversations since the day she had walked out of the conference had been formal and cold. He had not touched her, nor had she wanted him to.

"Thank you for being here," Sapiah said sincerely, softly touching her hand.

"Please understand, it's been six weeks since I've seen Rose. I just can't impose on Izzie any longer to take care of her."

Lily hugged Chipeta and they both wept.

"Give her a big kiss for me," Chipeta said, her eyes kind with understanding. "Oh, how I wished I were going with you!"

"Soon, my friend, very soon," Lily said gently.

Lily found a seat and looked out the window at her friend, standing alone on the platform surrounded by strangers in this foreign place. Chipeta was dressed in a silk dress and fashionable hat. A reporter flashed a camera in her face. The bright bulb made her jump back in terror.

The Washington papers had made Chipeta into a heroine, saying it was she that had braved the ire of the Ute savages and rescued the women. The stories had sold a great number of papers, but the fluffed up stories tore at Chipeta's heart.

"Why are they telling these lies about me?" she had asked Lily. "Why don't they just let me alone?" Sapiah tried to shield Chipeta from the reporter, but soon there was yet another.

Lily wanted to jump off the train and rescue her friend, as she had once wanted so badly to rescue Izzie. But now, as back then, she could only watch silently as she waved good-bye.

✤ ✤ ✤

Ouray and Schurz quietly worked to draw up a more amiable treaty, without the assistance from the House Committee on Indian Affairs. The agreement would move the White River Utes to the Uintah Reservation in Utah, would move the Southern Utes thirty miles west from their land near Pagosa Springs and cut their acreage by one-third. The Uncompahgre would move sixty miles north of the Shining Mountains to the Grand River-Gunnison River junction, but they too, would remain in Colorado.

The final treaty was deemed to be one of the most remarkable documents in the whole history of American Indian policy. It reflected revolutionary thinking by Schurz and Ouray regarding the peaceful co-habitation of the Utes and the whites. The agreement was designed to destroy the anachronistic tribal setup. Each reservation would be owned by individual bands instead of the whole Ute tribe, making each band responsible for their own land. Every Ute male would be allotted a homestead-sized farm, similar to Ouray's.

Most of the Ute delegation approved of the Schurz-Ouray agreement, which included a provision to pay annuities to the ten relatives of the white men killed at the White River Agency. It also allotted $100,000 to the Ute tribe to be used to help relocate the people and give them the funds needed to make a start in farming the land.

But Congress refused to ratify the agreement until the twelve Utes said to be involved in the massacre were surrendered for trial.

Sowerick and Jack journeyed back to Colorado and found three of the accused men: Chief Douglas, a Uintah Ute named Thomas, and the boy Tim Johnson. They were taken to Fort Leavenworth for trial. Tim, a young teen, cried so piteously that Sowerick could not stand to leave him there. He made the boy a part of the Ute delegation and brought him to the Hotel Tremont. The Uintah, Thomas, escaped.

Old Chief Douglas, with his wispy gray whiskers, said he might as well be the goat, and agreed to serve the time for all the Utes involved.

And finally the agreement was signed on March sixth. But for the agreement to become official, three-fourths of all the Ute men would have to sign it.

It was time for Ouray and Chipeta to go home. But Ouray knew that even after he arrived back at the farm located in the valley of the Shining Mountains he loved so much, it would only be a matter of time before he was to leave for good.

✠ ✠ ✠

It was snowing hard when Samuel rode into the Pleasant Valley Ranch. Seeing the small calves standing beside their mothers in the blinding cold tugged at his heart.

But the weather was just as cold inside the house. Lily barely looked up from the desk where she had a stack of papers in front of her.

"How is Chipeta?"

All the way back on the quiet train ride, Samuel had hoped and dreamed for a different homecoming. He imagined Lily falling into his arms and then kissing his sadness away.

"She's tired, but doing fine, I think. I saw the calves when I rode up. Is everything okay here?"

"Fine. There's hot coffee on the stove."

He poured himself a cup and sat down in the dark leather chair beside the desk. He noticed that one of the papers on the desk was a bill from the feed store. The big red handwriting on it read Final Notice.

"Do we have the money to pay that?" He took a sip of the coffee and it burned his mouth.

"No. And I received notice yesterday that the mercantile is cutting off our line of credit. Last week we lost twenty calves during a storm. And now it is snowing again and the hay is almost gone. I honestly don't know what we are going to do."

"I've taken care of that," Samuel said.

"I am not asking Victoria for additional money," Lily said bluntly.

"We won't have to."

He pulled out a bank draft in the amount of three thousand dollars. "This should get us through for awhile."

Lily stared at the draft. "Where did you get this?"

"From the House Committee on Indian Affairs."

"They actually paid you this much for your services at the conference?"

"Not exactly. They want to lease eighty acres to set up temporary quarters for Colonel McKenzie's troops from Fort Garland. The south pasture will be perfect. It's flat ground and there is plenty of water. They will be scouting for an area to build a temporary fort to keep the peace this summer. They should be here some time in May. They also agreed to buy as many cattle as we are willing to sell."

Lily turned slowly and looked him squarely in the eyes.

"And you agreed?"

"Yes, I did."

"Does Ouray know about this?"

"I haven't told him yet."

"You rode back two thousand miles with him and didn't bother to tell him?"

"The time wasn't right. It's our way to hold onto the ranch, Lily."

"You would actually sell out the Utes to keep this place?"

"I did it for you and Rose."

"The hell you did. Well, then, you can just give it back. I'd rather lose this land than to be part of shoving Ouray and Chipeta off theirs so Mears and his cronies can make their millions."

She threw the draft back in his face.

"Samuel Bodeen, I thought I knew you. But now I realize that I never really knew you at all." She walked to the bedroom and shut the door.

The next morning Samuel rode back into town and deposited most of the draft and took the rest in cash. Then he went around to all the businesses in town and paid off his debts. He was going to lose his dream, but he would be damned if he would let Lily lose hers.

He then rode to Ouray's farm. Chipeta came outside to greet him. "How is he?"

He's been asleep since we got back yesterday. But I'm sure he will want to see you."

"No, don't wake him," Samuel said. "I know how tired he is." And how sick, Samuel thought to himself. "I'll talk to him later."

✤ ✤ ✤

Ironically, the first soldiers arrived the same day the first lilacs came into bloom. It was a warm day in May. Lily and Chipeta had taken Rose up on the hillside behind the house to look for spring flowers to accompany the lilacs on the kitchen table. She saw the dust from over the rise and had thought that the south pasture was on fire. And then she saw the blue uniforms coming down the road like a line of colored ants.

There were at least fifty of them in line behind the United States flag.

Chipeta jumped. "I must go and warn Ouray!"

"It's okay," Lily said.

"You knew they were coming?"

"Samuel assured me that they are here only to protect both the whites, and the Utes. It is only temporary, Chipeta."

But as Chipeta watched the riders behind the flag, sitting tall and confident in their saddles, she did not feel a sense of security at all. She felt a heavy, black cloud of impending doom settle over the valley.

Ouray and Samuel were watching Gus break a young colt when they heard the beats of the many horse's hooves shaking the ground. Ouray nodded his head in agreement when Samuel told him why the soldiers had come.

"Maybe their presence here will keep Colorow and his followers from starting something. And maybe it will convince more of the braves to sign the agreement."

Once again, Samuel was astounded at Ouray's perception and his ability to see both sides of the situation.

"So you still haven't been able to get the necessary signatures?"

"My people do not wish to leave. They are hoping that the streams of silver in the mines will dry up and the white men will go away. And then they can go back to the way things used to be."

"How many soldiers are there?"

"About fifty now. They will be setting up temporary quarters about three miles north of the Los Piños Agency. In July, there will be over two hundred. They will stay through the summer, patrolling the area, and then go back to Fort Garland in the fall."

"Are you sure this is only temporary?"

"Yes," Samuel said. But he could not look his friend in the eyes when he said it.

"Then I will trust you on this, and tell my people the soldiers presence is nothing to be alarmed about."

On the way back to the farm, Chipeta asked Ouray why Samuel had not told them earlier about the soldiers. He had no answer for her. He had been wondering that himself.

There had been no one more relieved to see the soldiers than Sarah McCluskey. The next morning she stopped by the Pleasant Valley Ranch on the way to sell eggs to eager miners in Ouray for a dollar apiece. She also sold butter and bread, and her apple pies were grabbed up for ten dollars each.

"I know you and Chipeta are friends," she said carefully as she sipped a cup of tea, "but aren't you sometimes fearful of them?"

"You mean of the Ute people? Not at all. They are good people. Just afraid."

"Yes, but even good people are sometimes forced to do bad things out of fear and desperation."

Lily wondered if Sarah had been talking about the Utes, or about Lily. Sarah had made it very clear that she had thought it selfish of Lily to leave Samuel last winter when he was going through such a bad time after losing his leg.

Sarah McCluskey was a good Christian woman. She was a devoted mother and dutiful wife, something that Lily could only dream of being. Sarah's house was spotless and she stayed up after the others had gone to bed to keep it that way. During the day she worked tirelessly alongside Henry, never complaining. She was instrumental in establishing a Methodist Church service on Sundays in the back of the Ouray Mercantile. Sarah was the type of woman who always had mending or knitting needles in her hands when she finally sat down. And she was the type of woman who would never be caught dead in the pair of dirty dungarees that Lily was wearing. She and Lily were as different as fire and ice.

"I considered telling Hank and Myrtle not to bring Jimmy this summer, but knowing the soldiers are close by. . . Lily, do you honestly believe it is safe?"

"If I didn't think so, Sarah, do you think I would keep Rose here?"

Sarah was much too polite to answer but Lily could see the answer in Sarah's condemning eyes. She had been appalled when Lily had left Rose with "that darkie" to spend six weeks in Washington with "the savages." And besides, Henry was the type of man who never would have asked her to do that.

✚ ✚ ✚

The rest of McKenzie's troops arrived on a hot day in July when once again, the rain clouds teased the dry land, and then showed it no mercy. The dust the horses kicked up made it look like the land was on fire.

The Utes grumbled as they watched the wagon loads of supplies go by the Los Piños Agency. The soldiers brought an immense amount of food and ammunition. And they didn't just bring tents. They brought green lumber and nails.

The morning after the arrival of the regiment, Samuel slipped out of bed, tied on his wooden leg and slipped on his pants. Then he went to the barn and retrieved a tattered leather valise from the tack room. He took off his canvas jeans and put on his blue trousers with the yellow stripe down the side. And as he had done for so many years in the past, he pulled on the double-buttoned shirt, and then polished the buttons and the insignia on the collar with his handkerchief. He strapped on his holster and donned the Cossack-style cavalry hat. He saddled the best horse on the ranch with his United States Army issued saddle and led it to the house, tying him to the hitching post out front.

Then he went inside to wake Lily.

She looked beautiful, asleep in the still of morning. Her auburn hair, now long, lay spread out on the pillow, and the sun just beginning to stream through the windows made its golden specks dance with color.

She stirred when he sat down on the bed beside her. She stretched like a cat, and then looked at him. When she saw the uniform, she didn't seem surprised at all.

"I'm sorry, Lily. I've tried. God knows how I've tried. But I can't change who I am, no matter how much you think I can."

"Nor can I," she said softly. "I guess we both knew this day would come."

"There's a bank draft on the desk. Do with it what you want."

She didn't ask him where it came from. She didn't want to know.

"Lily, no matter what you may have thought of me these past few months, or what you will hear in the future, try to understand that I am doing this for a reason. If you don't trust me now, remember back to a time that you did. I'm doing what I have to do. There will be days when you, and a great number of others, will question that."

He reached down and let a lock of hair run through his hand. "But never question my love for you. I have loved you since the first minute I set my eyes on you. That has never changed. Nor will it."

"Where have you been assigned?"

"Fort Uncompahgre. They will begin building the post today."

"So it will be permanent?"

"Yes. But I will not ask you to live there. You have grown deep roots here, and it is where I want Rose to grow up. I won't ask you to go through what Lida Thornburg went through. I want to know that you and Rose have a home if. . ."

"Thank you for that," she said sincerely.

The pain in his eyes was replaced by firm resolution. "But I want you to promise me something. If a courier comes, day or night, and tells you to leave, don't question him. Just do it. If things go bad and there is even a remote chance that you or Rose could be in any danger, I will send word. Do as you are instructed. There is a wooden box in the tack room packed with supplies: canned food, utensils, matches, bedding, and the like. I have already directed Gus to stay close to the ranch. Just ring the dinner bell if you have received word from me. And whatever you do, I don't want you riding in the mountains.

"But the cattle. . ."

"I hired two men yesterday. They are old, but reliable. They will be here this afternoon."

He was, once again, the Bodeen she used to know, organized, direct, and giving orders with self-assured simplicity.

"Are you expecting trouble?"

"Lily, I can honestly say I don't know what to expect. It's just better to be prepared, that's all. To have a well thought-out strategy. I'll try to stop by when I can to check on you and Rose, but if you need anything at all, just send Gus and I'll be here. Promise me that."

"I promise."

He gently touched her cheek. "And there is one other thing I would like you to do before I leave." He pulled her to him. "Kiss me. Kiss me like you really mean it."

She kissed him, hard and long and deep. She allowed herself to feel his touch. She drank in the scent of him and caressed his hair, and his eyes. She let her hands glide down over his broad shoulders. She allowed her lips to feel his on hers, soft and supple and smooth. But she would not allow herself to feel anymore until it was all over. If she was going to lose him, whether it be to his mistress the army, or to the higher spirits, she was going to make it easier for herself than it had been for Lida Thornburg. She would fill her life with other things, so that when he did leave, she would not feel so empty inside.

Then Colonel Samuel Bodeen, renowned army officer who looked so handsome and right in his uniform, and the father her bright and precious child, walked out the door with saddlebags in one hand and cane in the other. And Lily felt herself being sucked into a great hole, as dense and black as a long moonless night.

And at that moment she knew what Arvilla Meeker had meant when she said she was just relieved that it was finally over, so she would wake up not to nightmares, but to peace. The wondering and the worrying and the wanting had begun.

And as he left, Lily knew he had forgotten something. He had left that curtain of mysterious secrecy that had always seemed to surround him like a shroud. She knew that Samuel Bodeen would never let her completely inside of it.

She was either going to have to accept him as he was, or let go and turn him loose. He could only give so much. And now she would have all the time in the world to decide whether it was enough.

She just prayed that it would be her decision to make, and that fate would not end up making it for her.

21

hief Ouray clung to life with magnificent tenacity, determined not to go home until the Ute agreement was ratified. But through the sad, hot summer of 1880, his people refused to sign the treaty until Otto Mears stood outside the Los Piños Agency with a large wad of dollar bills in his hand. He gave each Ute male two bills to sign their names or their Xs to the piece of paper. None of them could read. The agency soon ran out of candy. But Mears, ever prepared, went to his horse and reached in the saddlebag for more.

By the first of August, Mears had secured the number of signatures needed to send the treaty to Washington to be ratified by Congress. The commissioners left with the agreement on August fourth.

On August fifteenth, Ouray sat on his horse on the hillside above the Uncompahgre army encampment. He watched Colonel Samuel Bodeen as he commanded a garrison of two hundred soldiers. The fort was being built, not out of temporary tents, but with hammers and nails. It was the ultimate betrayal by the one man he had trusted most. And that was the ultimate defeat.

Ouray rode back to the farm and told Chipeta and Sapiah, "I'm ready to go home."

Chipeta answered quietly, "My love, you are home."

"No, not here on the white man's soil, in the white man's house. I want to go home to Ignacio where my father is."

"My friend, you are too ill to ride," Sapiah said. "Let me hitch the buckboard."

"No, that was the white man's, too. I will ride my own pony."

They packed a little food and several blankets, and then started on the journey to Ignacio, two hundred and thirty miles over the Shining Mountains. They did not take the wagon route, made by the white man to take miners seeking their fortunes, but instead rode through the granite heart of the mountains. They rode out of the green valley and through the splendid peaks, some still topped with snow, even in August. Their ponies slid and tumbled their way through deep ravines, across windy ridges and alpine meadows alive with wildflowers.

Ouray did not complain, though it was obvious he was in great pain. Nor did he ask to stop to rest. It was as if the once great warrior drew strength and peace from the mountains. They rode for three days and three nights, reaching Ignacio on August eighteenth. He then slept for two straight days.

On the twenty-first, he called for a powwow with the Southern Ute leaders and asked them not to resist the treaty, knowing that had been their intention.

On August twenty-third, he tried valiantly to attend the day's council. But he could not be moved from his tent due to the pain. He dismissed the white doctor attending him and called for the medicine men. They began their howling and lamentations at once.

Chief Ouray, the Arrow, died of Bright's disease the next morning, August twenty-fourth, 1880. He was forty-seven years old. Chipeta, Sapiah, and a few other close friends, wrapped his body in a blanket made from the wool of Chipeta's sheep, and woven by Ute hands, tied the body to the back of his favorite horse, took it to a secret ravine and placed it under a huge rock. They then killed the horse for the chief to ride in the next world.

✚ ✚ ✚

After the death of Ouray, Chipeta returned home and gave away all the gifts that the white men had bestowed up them. She gave away the forks and spoons, the lace curtains, the lamps, the beds. She burned the clothes.

She wrapped the teapot in a blanket and rode to the Pleasant Valley Ranch.

When Lily came out to meet her, Chipeta handed her the bundle.

"Come in, please," Lily said, not bothering to wipe away the tears that flowed freely down her cheeks.

"Perhaps another day. But not today. Please do not come anymore. I need time alone to grieve . . . and to forgive." Chipeta turned her horse around and rode away.

✛ ✛ ✛

Within two months after President Garfield took the oath of office as president of the United States in 1881, the treaty that Ouray and Schurz had so carefully drawn up was already being amended. The reduced commission of Otto Mears and a selected handful of dignitaries and businessmen, decided that the Gunnison-Grand River area that had been allotted to the Utes was "deficient in farmlands." They decided instead, that the Ouray's band of Uncompahgre Utes would be moved to a tract of land in the Bitter Creek Valley of Utah.

The change was ratified by the Commission in June of 1881. It was never ordered to be ratified by the Ute.

In early August, financed with $100,000 from the Commission, Mears went to Utah and had an army of contractors from Salt Lake City bring supplies and build the new Uncompahgre Indian Agency.

On August twenty-third, the Commission ordered McKenzie's troops to escort the Indians out of Colorado to the reservation at Bitter Creek, Utah, 350 miles away—land that even the most hearty Mormons had refused to live on.

On August twenty-fourth, the first anniversary of Ouray's death, Lily packed the teapot carefully in the same blanket, and rode to Chipeta's house. It was bare and vacant.

She walked to a tepee located nearby. Chipeta was sitting on a wool rug beading a small pair of moccasins. The pattern was a beautiful, ornate rose, with beads of bright reds and pinks.

The inside of the tepee was simple and neat, quiet and cool under the shade of the large cottonwood tree several yards to the west.

For the past year, Lily had honored Chipeta's wish. But she could not let their friendship end in bitterness. She pulled out the teapot and carefully unwrapped it.

"Have tea with me, my friend. Please."

Chipeta slowly stood up, and with the graciousness of the queen that she was, she made tea, serving it in brightly painted hollowed out gourds.

"You're right. You can hear the birds sing in here," Lily said.

And together, they sat and listened to their song. Finally, Chipeta tied the last bead and handed the tiny shoes to Lily.

"For Rose to remember me."

✛ ✛ ✛

On August thirty-first, the Los Piños Indian Agency was sold to one of the thousands of white settlers waiting to grab the old reservation land.

On September first, General McKenzie and his troops began moving the Uncompahgre Ute tribe. There were 1,458 men, women and children, 8000 ponies, 10,000 sheep and goats, travois and tepees, and three weeks worth of rations provided by the government.

Lily rode beside Chipeta, neither of them speaking. There were no words left to say. It had been the same with Isabel, but this time, Lily was determined not to let her friend ride to her new home alone. Samuel knew better than to try and stop her. He rode with his well-armed regiment.

On September third, the Ute exodus passed the Uncompahgre-Gunnison junction in the Grand Valley that was to have been the home granted to them in the treaty set up by Ouray and Secretary Schurz.

Bodeen rode up a hillside for a better vantage point. He watched Colorow closely. The angry Ute and fifty braves hung back and loaded their rifles.

Samuel signaled to General McKenzie. The general looked through his field glasses to see the Utes turn their horses, painted brightly with war paint, and come galloping back in one last mad, futile attempt at an attack.

The general shouted the order and seconds later, the mesa flamed. Cannons boomed and rifles shouted out in fire. Soldiers by the hundreds plunged down toward the valley.

Colorow reined up his horse in bewilderment, overwhelmed by the quick and powerful display of the United States Army. He sorrowfully hung his head, and in a gesture of utter hopelessness, turned his pony around and rode toward Bitter Creek.

As per Colonel Bodeen's specific instructions beforehand, the bullets had never been shot directly at the Ute people. The only minor injury was to a young brave whose horse had bolted and bucked from the cannon fire.

Chipeta looked up at a lone rider still on the hill. She and Lily turned their horses and rode up the rise to Bodeen. Tears flowed down his face as he watched the tribe moving slowly toward Bitter Creek. And for the first time in his life he didn't try to stop them.

"Thank you, my friend," Chipeta said, looking at Bodeen with soft, velvet eyes. "We have all been given much . . . and lost much. Please, teach your people to love the land and nurture the gift given to them. Teach them to feel the freedom of warm sun on their skin, the soft breeze touching their faces. Teach them to listen to the music of the elk and to look for the glory in a hillside alive with wild-flowers. For those are the true gifts. Tell them to stop searching for treasure. Show them that it is already there before their unseeing eyes. Do this, Samuel, for me. And do this with the grace of knowing that you have already been forgiven."

She turned to Lily. "My friend, I must continue on this journey alone now. Someday we will meet again, in a better place and at a better time. But until then, may the Great Spirit be with you both." Chipeta turned her horse and headed back down the slope toward the western horizon.

Colonel Bodeen looked hard at Lily, then at the regiment waiting for him below.

"It is done. May God have mercy on their souls." He looked softly at Lily. "And on ours as well." He waited, searching for the answer to the unasked question.

Lily looked down at Sapiah, riding tall and proud in the saddle. "Go in peace, my friend," she whispered softly. Sapiah turned, looked back, and then touched his hands to his lips, as if capturing the words. He then nodded and rode onward.

Lily turned her horse, and together, she and Samuel rode back toward the Shining Mountains waiting on the horizon.

EPILOGUE

The removal of the Ute Indian Nation in 1881 signified the end to the presence of all the Native Americans who once occupied Colorado, with the exception of the small strip of barren land occupied by the Southern Utes in the southwestern corner of the state. The rest had been swept away: the Arapahoe, Cheyenne, Kiowa, Comanche, Jicarilla Apache and Ute. They were all gone.

Even as the Utes were leaving, settlers, miners, and speculators moved in, although Congress did not declare the Ute Reservation to be public land until June 28, 1882.

With the help of Otto Mears, the railroad quickly moved in as well. The Gunnison-Grand River juncture, which Mears had proclaimed did not have enough farmland to accommodate the Ute tribe, filled up with over 1,000 residents by the end of 1882. The town of Grand Junction was established and the area is well-known today for its massive orchards and wineries.

Chief Douglas, sixty years old, was never formally charged with any crime. The Commission felt that an accusation of rape would have been too embarrassing for Arvilla Meeker. He served 348 days in the Fort Leavenworth Prison. After his release, he developed a deep suspicion of all people, and drank heavily. In 1885, he became threatening and was shot by a member of his own band.

Arvilla Meeker became very ill and lived for a time in Greeley. Her health improved after Nathan's body was moved from White River to the Linn Grove Cemetery in Greeley. She later moved to White Plains, New York, with her son Ralph. She died of senility in 1905.

Josie Meeker moved to Washington D.C. in 1881, and became the private secretary to new Interior Department Secretary, Henry

Teller, for the salary of seventeen dollars a week. She also received ten dollars a week in the annuity set by the treaty. She sent five dollars a week to Arvilla, and spent two more dollars a week on the black children in her Lincoln Mission Sunday school class.

On December 21, 1882, Josie woke feeling tired and did not go to work. She was still ill on Christmas and her brother Ralph summoned a doctor. She died on December twenty-ninth of pneumonia. She was buried in Greeley next to her father.

Lida Thornburg never remarried. She passed the years raising her children in Washington D.C. and Oakland, Maryland.

Mattie Silks opened her brothel and soon became the undisputed queen of the "red light district" on Holladay Street, known as the wickedest thoroughfare in the West. Her "boardinghouse" was widely known for its beautiful ladies and elegant décor. Mattie died in 1929 at the age of 83. Although it was estimated that almost two million dollars had passed through her hands during her illustrious "career," she left barely enough for her burial. Her funeral was quiet, with no songs or flowers and very few to grieve for her.

Ann Eliza Young continued her fight against polygamy, speaking to Congress with dignity and strength. In 1882, they passed a bill banning polygamy in the territories, but it wasn't until 1890 and federal agents were ordered into Utah that the Mormon Church relinquished the practice of celestial marriage. In 1883, Ann Eliza married her third husband. They separated in 1892 and a year later she divorced him for infidelity.

Captain Dodge left his command of the black regiment to become an army paymaster. In 1904, he was commissioned as paymaster general.

Scout Joe Rankin spent the 1880s in Wyoming, and when Benjamin Harrison became president, he named Rankin as the United States marshal for Wyoming.

War Chief Shavano, also a medicine man, was killed in 1886 after prescribing the wrong medicine for a sick child.

Sapiah, known as Buckskin Charlie, abided with Ouray's deathbed request and succeeded his friend as chief of the Utes. He stayed with the Southern Ute tribe in Colorado, where he became an excellent farmer and an outstanding leader of his people. He died in 1936 at age 96. He was buried next to Chief Ouray in Ignacio. His son, Antonio Buck, took his father's place as chief of the Ute nation.

Colorow refused to stay in Bitter Creek and came back to Colorado to hunt. Some settlers found him amusing, while others didn't, especially the ranch wives who found it annoying when he would walk into their kitchens and demand biscuits.

In 1887, Colorow and members of his band were accused of stealing horses while hunting at the White River. A posse of seventy-two deputies was sent to round them up. The fifty men, women and children in his band retreated up the White River Divide. Jim Kendall, newly-appointed sheriff of the White River territory, tried to make a name for himself by attempting to banish the Utes from Colorado for good. He trumped up the charges and sent for the army. One thousand soldiers were called in, only to find Chipeta and other squaws picking berries. The Utes were escorted back to Utah.

The "Colorow War," as it was later called, cost Colorado taxpayers over $80,000, and it solved nothing. The Utes kept coming back for years to hunt above White River. Colorow died on December 11, 1888. The biscuit-beggar would frighten the white women no more.

David Wood made good on his dream. His passenger and freight wagon service was the biggest ever to operate in Colorado. When a newcomer once asked him how long he had lived in the mountains, he answered, "Madam, I hauled these mountains in here!"

On Christmas Day, 1884, David married the beautiful Mary Dill, a talented and vivacious pianist. But tragedy struck, and Mary died during childbirth. David's newborn son died a week later. In 1888, David met the enchanting Fannie Parker. They married and had eleven children, with seven making it to adulthood. In 1893, the crash in silver prices brought an end to David's once thriving business. He did a little prospecting, and then began managing mines for others. He died in 1944 at the age of 92.

Otto Mears bought Chipeta's farm for six hundred dollars. She gave the money away. He later sold the house and it burned down. The new owners rebuilt the house, but it burned yet again. It was never rebuilt.

Mears started building a railroad to the mines near Silverton even before the Utes were escorted out of the valley beneath the Shining Mountains, known today as the San Juan Mountains. Mears became known as the "Pathfinder of the San Juans" and built a huge empire, which later included an elaborate railroad system known as the "Rainbow Route." He introduced the reaper and grain machine to Colorado farmers and was instrumental in the building of the State Capitol in Denver, complete with a dome plated with Colorado gold. Today, there is a stained glass window with the image of Mears in the Capitol building. There is also one of Ouray.

Mears left Colorado in the late 1890s and moved back East where he helped form the Mack Motor Company, later famous for producing the sturdy Mack truck.

Ironically, it was the introduction of the automobile that became the savior for the Ute nation. Once again, the land given to the Ute by the United States government held secret treasures underneath the ground.

On the surface, the reservation at Bitter Creek is barren and desolate. But inside the Mother Earth lies millions of gallons of gas and petroleum reserves, providing the financial resources needed for the Ute nation to grow and prosper. Chipeta's great-nephew, Roland McCook, is a tribal leader in the movement to help the Ute to use the resources to best serve the people.

The colorful Ute heritage is kept alive by dancing. Each September, a three-day dance and powwow is held at the Old Ute council tree in Delta, Colorado, in the Uncompahgre valley that the Utes once called "Kannega"—home.

Chipeta spent the next forty years at Bitter Creek tending to her sheep and goats, and a number of children she adopted. She made beautiful cradleboards, enhancing them with colorful beadwork, and then gave them away.

The government had promised to provide Chipeta with a home similar to what she'd had in Colorado. But it was yet another promise that was not kept. The two-room shack was never finished. She chose instead, to live as her people lived, in a simple tiepee.

She sent one of Ouray's brightly-beaded buckskin shirts to Charles Schurz, and thanked him for the friendship he had with Ouray. As was the Ute way, she demanded that no gift be sent in return.

She came back to Colorado from time to time to visit friends and bathe in the healing hot springs located in the town named after Ouray. She became a heroine, with her gracious, forgiving attitude, and her kind acts toward others. She was often asked to be the guest of honor at parades and festivals.

In her later years, Chipeta became blind from cataracts. She had surgery at St. Mary's Hospital in Grand Junction. But it did not help. Rope guides were set up around her tipi to enable her to do simple chores. And still she beaded, the colorful beads distributed in bowls to assist her in making the intricate and beautiful designs.

Chipeta died at Bitter Creek on August 16, 1924. She was eighty-one. She was buried in the Ute style, her body placed in a gulch where her exposed bones were found six months later. Through the initiative of the many who respected her, her body was brought back and placed in a mausoleum just one mile from where she and Ouray had made their home. Over 5,000 people attended a memorial service in her honor.

Today, the Ute Indian Museum is just south of her grave. It is filled with artifacts from the dazzling, yet bitter time in Colorado history when two diverse and different worlds collided.

We
Are the spirits of the earth.
We are the mothers who nurture the future.
We are the mothers who feed it, and
set it on the right path when
it goes astray.
It is now up to us to
Honor the Fragile Treaties
made from without
and made from within.
For good words
do not last long
until they amount
to something.